# SYMBOLS OF TRADE

# SYMBOLS OF TRADE

*Roman and Pseudo-Roman Objects found in India*

S. SURESH

MANOHAR
2004

First published 2004

© S. Suresh, 2004

ISBN 81-7304-552-6

*Published by*
Ajay Kumar Jain for
Manohar Publishers & Distributors
4753/23, Ansari Road, Daryaganj
New Delhi 110 002

*Typeset by*
Ajay Art
Delhi 110 085

*Printed at*
Lordson Publishers Pvt. Ltd.
Delhi 110 007

# Contents

# Illustrations

FIGURE

PHOTOGRAPHIC CREDITS

Andhra Pradesh State Department of Archaeology: Plate nos. 5, 6, 7, 8, 13

Tamilnadu State Department of Archaeology: Plate nos. 9, 10, 11, 12

Government Museum, Madras: Plate nos. 3, 4, 16

Government Museum, Pudukkottai: Plate nos. 1, 2

Kalaimagal Kalvi Nilayam Museum, Erode: Plate no. 14

Prof. I. Mahadevan, Madras: Plate no. 15

# Abbreviations

AI:      Ancient India
*AJA*:   *American Journal of Archaeology*
AE:      Copper (coin)
AR:      Silver (coin)
AV:      Gold (coin)
E:       Find from archaeological excavation—stratified find
H:       Hoard find
*IAR*:   *Indian Archaeology—A Review*
IIRNS:   Indian Institute of Research in Numismatic Studies, Nashik
IOC:     India Office Collection
*JNSI*:  *Journal of the Numismatic Society of India*
*JRAS*:  *Journal of the Royal Asiatic Society*
NBP:     Northern Black Polished Pottery
*NC*:    *Numismatic Chronicle*
PMC:     Punch Marked Coin
RCP:     Russet Coated Painted Pottery
RPW:     Red Polished Ware
S:       Stray find; Surface find
*SSIC*:  *Studies in South Indian Coins*
TPQ:     Terminus Post Quem

# Preface

THE PAGES THAT follow partially include my doctoral thesis on Roman antiquities found in India, as a full-time student of the Jawaharlal Nehru University, New Delhi from 1987 to 1991.

Upon completion of my doctorate, numerous friends and professors have been constantly goading me to publish my thesis as a book. Converting this voluminous thesis, crammed with statistical jargon and bibliographic citations, into a reader-friendly publication, proved more challenging and time consuming than producing the thesis itself! While the basic structure and format of the thesis has been retained here, unlike the thesis, the book presents the subject in the form of an interesting narrative or discussion.

The publication of this book provides me an opportunity to gratefully acknowledge all those who helped and encouraged me when I was writing this thesis and later when it was revised for publication.

First, I offer my respects to my dear mother Mrs Saraswathi Sethuraman who sacrificed all her joys and comforts to ensure my academic success. She was a pillar of strength for me while I was preparing my thesis. She was so thorough with the contents of my thesis that friends would often remark that she too deserved a doctorate in the subject! It was her desire to see the thesis in print. Unfortunately, she did not live to see her dream come true.

I would like to place on record my gratitude to my supervisor, Prof. R. Champalakshmi. I have immensely benefited from the several fruitful discussions, many of them spanning several hours, which I had with her, during the course of my research. She often went out of the way to help me by procuring relevant publications from abroad for my study.

I had numerous opportunities to discuss the various problems pertaining to my research with a galaxy of eminent scholars such as the late Mr K.R. Srinivasan, the late Dr Vimala Begley, Prof. F.R. Allchin, Dr David MacDowall, Professors B.N. Mukherjee, Romila Thapar and

I. Mahadevan, Drs C.R. Whittaker, O. Bopearachchi, and O. Guillaume, Prof. B.D.Chattopadhyaya, Prof. S.F. Ratnagar, Mr R. Krishnamurthy, Dr I.K. Sarma, Mr N. Kasinathan, Miss R. Vanaja, Prof. Y. Subbarayalu, the late Prof. C. Krishnamurthy, Professors S. Gurumurthy, P. Shanmugam and Prema Kasturi and Dr K. Rajan. I am grateful to all of them. I would like to make a special mention of Dr Bopearachchi from whom I learnt a lot about Roman archaeology and numismatics, mainly when we travelled together to many ancient sites of south India.

Several museums, both in India and abroad, granted me access to their collections and archives. Notable among these are the Government Museum, Madras; the Government Museum, Pudukkottai; the Kalaimagal Kalvi Nilayam Museum, Erode; the Tamil University Museum, Tanjavur; the Tamilnadu State Archaeology Department Museums at Coimbatore and Karur; the State Archaeological Museum, Hyderabad; the National Museum, New Delhi; Bharat Kala Bhavan, Varanasi; the British Museum, London; the Fitzwilliam Museum, Cambridge; the Ashmolean Museum, Oxford and the University Museum, Manchester. I am grateful to the authorities of all these museums, specially Mr R. Mohammad of the Government Museum, Pudukkottai; Dr Rita Sharma of the National Museum, New Delhi; Dr Savita Sharma of Bharat Kala Bhavan, Varanasi; and Drs Richard Blurton, Robert Knox, A. Burnett and Joe Cribb of the British Museum, London.

A. Sitaraman of Tanjavur, Vidwan I. Ramaswami of Boluvampatti and several others allowed me to examine and photograph their private collections of coins and medals. I owe special thanks to all of them.

The Institute of Archaeology of the Archaeological Survey of India, the University Grants Commission and the Indian Council of Historical Research provided financial support during the different stages of my research. The INLAKS Foundation awarded me a special travel grant that enabled me to visit the museums in the UK. I am grateful to all these organizations.

Thanks are also due to Mrs Rukmini Sampath and Miss P. Sugandhi for their assistance in computerizing the final manuscript of this book.

Finally, any opinions and comments about the book are welcome from the readers.

S. SURESH

# 1

# Prologue

INTEREST IN THE study of Roman coin finds in India dates back to the early nineteenth century. The presence of these coins in remote areas of India appeared strange and unusual to the nineteenth century scholars because such finds, that too in large numbers, had never been recorded earlier. Hence, the attention of early scholars was confined to simply reporting these finds. No attempt was made to analyse the historical significance of the coins. Thus, most of the early published accounts are descriptive notices of the finds. These notices, scattered in various obscure journals and museum reports, have often been authored by individuals possessing little or no knowledge of the subject. Further, these notices are too brief and do not furnish details such as the state of wear and weight of each of the coins in any particular find. The value of these notices, however, lies in the fact that often they constitute the sole evidence, published or otherwise, for many of the early finds. The writings of H.H. Wilson (1832), J. Prinsep (1832, 1834), Walter Elliot (1844, 1856-7), G. Bidie (1874), Capt. Waterhouse (1879), Henry Little (1883) and Edgar Thurston (1888, 1889, 1891,1894) fall under this category.[1]

The nineteenth century authors did not identify many of the features unique to the Roman coins found in India. Such features include the presence of imitations among the finds and the countermarking of a few of the coins with minute symbols. The significance of the slash marks on the Roman coins in India was, for the first time, analysed in detail by G.F. Hill (1898) in his famous article on the aurei find from Pudukkottai in Tamilnadu which, till date, is the largest slashed aurei hoard in the country.

The utilization of Roman numismatic finds in India for the study of the pattern of Indo-Roman trade was first attempted by Bishop Caldwell (1851). Basing his observations on a study of the large Kottayam (Kerala) hoard, he made a pioneering attempt to trace the route adopted by the Romans to reach the Malabar ports. He also hinted at the use of Roman coins as 'money' by the ancient Indians. It was, however, Robert Sewell (1904) who systematically classified all the Roman coins found in India, known to him, emperor-wise and concluded that Indo-Roman trade began under Augustus (27 BC–AD14), reached its zenith under Nero (AD 54–68), and then began to slowly decline until the time of Caracalla (AD198–217) and then almost entirely ceased but was revived somewhat in the fourth-fifth centuries AD. Many of the later scholars including E.H. Warmington (1928, 1974), T.G. Aravamuthan (1942), Mortimer Wheeler (1951, 1954), P.L. Gupta (1965), Paula Turner (1989) and Peter Berghaus (1991) have accepted most of Sewell's observations in the light of additional evidences. David W. MacDowall (1990, 1991, 1996), however, differs from the other scholars by asserting that Indo-Roman trade reached its peak after Nero and that all the Roman Republican and Julio-Claudian coin finds in India were exported from Rome after AD 70.

A noteworthy observation is that several of the writings of the nineteenth and the early twentieth centuries are based solely on numismatic data, to the virtual exclusion of all other evidence including literary sources. A few of the early scholars did, however, make use of the references in the classical literature in their works but ironically, they have not fully utilized numismatic evidence. Credit goes to Warmington (1928) for attempting to correlate numismatic data with the evidence in the classical accounts, mainly the *Periplus*. Most of the subsequent scholars, both in India and Europe, have relied heavily on Warmington's monumental work.

Following Warmington, the *Periplus* has been the focus of numerous studies and much research has also been done by classicists on Rome's interest in trade with India and the effect of the trade on Rome's economy. Such studies including Raschke's (1978) mainly identify the place-names in the *Periplus* and the cargoes loaded and unloaded at different locations. Many of these studies have, albeit to a limited extent, made use of the available archaeological evidence. Issues relating to navigation directly from the Red Sea to the coast of India, and the technology of shipbuilding have also been researched (Casson, 1986, 1991; V. Rajamanickam, 1988).

Studies on the Indian literary and epigraphical sources pertaining to Indo-Roman links are comparatively few. The references to the *yavanas* (Romans?) in the ancient Tamil poems, incorporated in the Sangam texts, have been studied by Meile (1940-1), Zvelebil (1956, 1973) and Champakalakshmi (1990).

Mortimer Wheeler's famous excavation (1945) at Arikamedu on the south-eastern coast of India provided, for the first time, archaeological confirmation for the export of a variety of Roman objects other than coins to India. Following this excavation, scores of sites in southern, western and to a limited extent, even in eastern India, have revealed Roman and/or pseudo-Roman pottery. These sites are often referred as 'Roman sites' or 'Indo-Roman sites' by Indian archaeologists, and the Roman and pseudo-Roman ceramics at these sites are mostly dated on the basis of the chronology of Arikamedu. Detailed studies of such ceramic finds from Arikamedu have been done by V. Begley (1983, 1986, 1988, 1991), H. Comfort (1991) and E.L. Will (1991). These studies throw fresh light on the nature of Indo-Roman trade specially with regard to the varieties of edible products stored in the various types of ceramics at Arikamedu. Such studies, if undertaken for similar ceramic finds at other sites as well, would yield extremely useful information.

Studies on the minor Roman antiquities such as bronze vessels, gold jewels and glassware found in India are limited and are largely descriptive accounts of specific finds.

Several general studies pertaining to ancient Indian trade and economy refer to Indo-Roman links and the Roman antiquities found in India. The writings of B. Srivastava (1964) fall under this category.

During the last 25 years, there has been a spate of M.Phil. and Ph.D. theses on the trade and commerce of early historical Tamilakam.[2] These research studies refer to the Roman finds in the Kerala-Tamilnadu region. Unfortunately, most of them have failed to make effective use of anthropological concepts and integrative frameworks within which changes in the nature of trade can be analysed. Also, the authors of these works did not personally examine any of the artifactual materials but merely relied on the published descriptions of the objects. Hence, these studies offer nothing new by way of interpretation or even information. Even some of K.V. Raman's papers, published between 1987 and 1993, merely enumerate the archaeological discoveries published earlier.[3]

Regional and local histories, attempted by a few south Indian scholars in recent years, sometimes refer to the Roman finds in that particular region of the country. A case in point is V. Ramamurthy's *History of Kongu* (1986) which deals with many of the Roman finds in the Coimbatore region of Tamilnadu. These studies discuss trade as an isolated and static phenomenon and not as part of the ever-changing socio-economic processes.

Roman coins found in India have hardly received attention in any general study on Roman economy and trade. There are, however, two notable exceptions to this—one is Sture Bolin's work (1958) on the role of the denarius in the Roman economy and the other is C. Rodewald's study (1976) on the monetary policy of Tiberius. Both these scholars have relied on Wheeler's work for the data pertaining to India. Both, Roman ceramics and minor Roman antiquities found in India, have rarely been discussed in any general work on Rome's economy, history or archaeology. One reason for this is that the exports from India to the West were mainly perishable commodities such as animals and birds, textiles, various kinds of woods and spices. Thus, there is a marked paucity of concrete material evidence for the trade in the Mediterranean region. Hence, scholars, unaware of the discoveries in India, may tend to underestimate the volume of Indo-Roman trade.

The latest writings on the subject include numerous papers on the new discoveries in Rome, Africa and India. For example, the discovery of a papyrus from Vienna which documents the shipment of nard, ivory and textiles from Muziris (Kerala) to Alexandria (Africa) forms the subject matter of a series of important papers by H. Harrauer and P.J. Sijpesteijn (1985) and Casson (1986, 2001). Again, as Indian scholars are largely unfamiliar with authentic Roman objects, some of their recent reports and articles on such antiquities including coins, are factually incorrect.[4]

At this juncture, it may be pointed out that in recent years not only Indian students and scholars, but also coin collectors have evinced an increasing interest in the study of Roman coins found in India. This is largely due to the efforts of European scholars like Peter Berghaus who have delivered lectures on the subject in various museums and universities throughout the country. They have also provided encouragement, support and guidance for the documentation of these coins. These efforts have led to the publication of a series of useful catalogues and mono-graphs such as those of V.V. Krishna Sastry (1992), T. Sathyamurthy (1992) and R. Krishnamurthy (1994). Another descriptive monograph-cum-catalogue (Suresh, 1992b) on Roman antiquities in Tamilnadu was brought out for a unique exhibition on the same theme, jointly organized by the Government Museum, Madras, and the C.P. Ramaswami Aiyar Institute of Indological Research, Madras. This assignment provided a rare opportunity to personally examine and photograph all the relevant materials in the rich but not easily accessible collection of the Madras Museum. Being an exhibition publication, a limited number of copies were released and the work remains unknown to many scholars outside south India.

This historiographical survey reveals that so far, no attempt has been made to provide a systematic, exhaustive and integrated collation of all the Roman and pseudo-Roman antiquities—coins, ceramics, jewels, glassware, etc.—found in India. One of the objectives of the present study is, therefore, to undertake such a survey which may be expected to throw fresh light on the nature of Indo-Roman contacts.

The distribution pattern, chronology and the historical significance of each category of finds have been detailed in the chapters that follow. The main purpose of this exercise has been to investigate and analyse the reasons for the significant differences as well as 'overlaps' in the distribution and chronology of the different types of objects. Roman coins which constitute the bulk of the finds have been discussed in greater detail. Problems pertaining to the circulation of Roman coins as 'money' in various regions of ancient India, the significance of imitation coins and the use of some Roman coins as jewellery by ancient Indians have been analysed.

The Byzantine finds—mainly coins of the late fifth and the early sixth centuries AD—recovered from a few sites of south India, have also been included in the present study. Although finds of such a late date are numerically very few, they are definite indicators of the continuation of Indo-Mediterranean contacts in the early medieval period.

Throughout this volume, the word 'Roman' has often been used to include the 'early Byzantine' as well. Again, for the purposes of this study, 'Roman trader' or 'Roman merchant' denotes not only traders from Rome, but also their Egyptian, Arabian and other representatives who brought Roman objects to India. The name 'India' has often been used to denote not only the present Republic of India, but also the entire Indian subcontinent, viz., Afghanistan, Pakistan, India and Bangladesh. It may be noted that modern political boundaries have hardly any relevance to studies focusing on a very early period of Indian history.

At this stage, it should be pointed out that in the case of cities and districts whose names have recently been changed, their older names have been used as they are better known. For example, the names of the two major Indian cities Bombay and Madras have recently been changed to Mumbai and Chennai, respectively. But this book retains their earlier names, viz., Bombay and Madras. Also, diacritical marks have not been used for wellknown as well as modern names of places and persons, as also in the maps.

The scope and purpose of this study necessitates the use of varied source materials. Archaeological data forms the backbone of this study. Tracing the history of trade on the basis of archaeology is a complicated process beset with several problems. Till date, archaeological excavations in south India have largely focused on recovering antiquities rather than on collecting information about such phenomena as settlement patterns and trade or other matters relevant to the economic and social basis of political organization. Also, many of the important excavations remain unpublished or have been only partially published. Even in the case of those excavations which have been fully published, the 'quantitative' and 'relational' information provided in the reports is seldom detailed enough to permit the application of the kind of sophisticated analysis now almost 'standard' in archaeological studies in the West.

Wherever possible, antiquities in the collections of the various museums and with private collectors have been physically examined. Several museums granted access to their archives and records. Interesting information was obtained about many little known, unpublished and recent finds through correspondence and personal discussions with museum curators, coin collectors and field archaeologists. A number of new sites and objects were discovered during the course of the field explorations in Kerala, Tamilnadu and coastal Andhra.

An examination of the various objects in the museums revealed a lack of correspondence between the objects available for study and the archival records/published catalogues/monographs of the collections in those museums. For example, many of the coins and jewels which, as per published accounts, have been acquired by the Government Museum, Madras, are not traceable in the museum. Similarly, the entire Pudukkottai hoard of 501 aurei was initially sent to the British Museum, London, for examination. To date, only about 20 coins from the hoard are available in that museum. The fate of the rest of the hoard is not known. It is plausible that some of the worn aurei with no find-spot assigned to them, in the collection of the Madras Museum, may be from the Pudukkottai hoard although there are no records to confirm this. Recently, two coins—one belonging to Claudius (AD 41-54) and the other, a broken aureus of Nero—at the Government Museum, Pudukkottai, were examined. Although the history of these two coins is not known, on the basis of the coin types and the worn condition of the issues, it may be presumed that they belong to the Pudukkottai hoard (Plates 1 and 2).

The value of 'intact' coin hoards for the purposes of historical research, especially for the study of the widely varying state of wear and weight of the various coins constituting the hoard, was not recognized in Asia till the mid-twentieth century. Hence, whenever a large hoard was acquired by a museum, all the common coin types as also worn and damaged specimens of the hoard were either sold or gifted to other museums, without any proper records of the coins thus disposed off. For instance, in 1913, the Madras Museum acquired the entire Kathanganni (Tamilnadu) hoard of 233 denarii but subsequently, many of the coins from the hoard were gifted to various museums in India and the U.K.; 2 coins from this hoard are in the Fitzwilliam Museum, Cambridge, and 2 other coins have been traced in the collection of the British Museum, London. Similarly, the Indian Museum, Calcutta, acquired 8 aurei from the large Kottayam hoard but these are now lost.

A similar problem pertains to the distribution of antiquities recovered from a single archaeological excavation, between two or more institutions, again with no record either of the precise stratigraphic position of many of the objects or of the number of objects acquired by each of the institutions. In such circumstances, it becomes difficult for the researcher to investigate the relative stratigraphic sequence of the different objects recovered from a single excavation. To mention but one instance, the objects recovered from each of the excavations at Arikamedu have been distributed among a number of museums and other institutions mainly in India and Europe.[5]

In addition to archaeological sources, information on Indo-Roman trade is available from several Graeco-Roman works, chief among them being the *Naturalis Historia* of Pliny the Elder (AD 77), the *Periplus Maris Erythraei* of an anonymous author (AD 80-9?) and the *Geography* of Claudius Ptolemy (mid-second century AD). Of all these works, the most important and unique is the *Periplus*. Written in Greek, it is primarily a guide for sailor-merchants operating in the Indian Ocean. It appears to have been authored by a person who travelled from the ports of the Red Sea to the western coast of India, most probably in the second half of the first century AD. There is, however, no unanimity amongst scholars on the exact date of the work. Among other things, the *Periplus* throws light on the routes from the Red Sea to the western coast of the Indian subcontinent.

Apart from these major classical works, the *Tabula Peutingeriana*

PLATE 1. SLASHED CLAUDIUS AUREUS FROM
PUDUKKOTTAI HOARD (TAMILNADU): OBVERSE AND REVERSE

PLATE 2. NERO AUREUS (SLASHED AND BROKEN) FROM
PUDUKKOTTAI HOARD (TAMILNADU):
OBVERSE AND REVERSE

(fourth century AD?) records a saddle-roofed temple for Augustus near Muziris (Kerala) but no trace of the same exists to date. It is plausible that the said temple may have been dedicated to the Hindu sage, Agastya.

The classical accounts are significant not only because they provide valuable data on the Indo-Roman trading network and the ports, marts, exports and imports of India, but also because they are datable. Thus, a comparative study of the information provided in these texts may reveal a clear picture of the gradual development of the trade between south India and the Mediterranean region.

The Tamil Sangam works constitute another source for the study of Indo-Roman links. The use of this remarkable corpus of poems for historical research is, however, a hazardous exercise mainly because the poems were composed and compiled at different times spanning over 600 years. The poems were composed by individuals of varied backgrounds—princes, chieftains, merchants, potters, peasants, Brahmins, Jains and Buddhists. Moreover, being bardic literature eulogizing kings and chieftains, its concern with aspects of economic and cultural life is incidental. Nevertheless, it does provide some insights into several little known features of ancient trade.

The Sangam works refer to all foreign traders—Greek, Roman, West Asian and others—as *yavanas*. But the reference to the *yavanas* bringing wine (*Puranānūru* 56, 17-20) and gold (*Ahanānūru* 149, 7-11) to the Tamil country undoubtedly indicates that the *yavanas* were largely Romans because wine and gold were the chief commodities exported from Rome to India. There are ten references, each under different contexts, to the *yavanas* in the entire gamut of Sangam literature.

It may be recalled that the term *yavana* first appears in the Behistun inscription of Darius I (519 BC). The term is frequently mentioned in ancient Sanskrit and Pāli literature as well. Initially, the term was used to denote the Ionian Greeks who were the first foreigners to establish contact with India.[6] The Sangam literature clearly indicates that the majority of the *yavanas* were initially traders and with the passage of time, some of them entered other professions.

The chronology of the various Sangam works has been a subject of considerable controversy, with each scholar suggesting his own chronological scheme and basing his interpretations on his scheme. Most authorities now agree, on the basis of internal evidence and linguistic styles, that the majority of the poems can be attributed to a period from the first century BC to the third century AD. The controversies regarding the date of the works are beyond the scope of this study. Yet, the date of some of the poems referring to the *yavanas* is very crucial, specially in the light of the latest archaeological evidences which indicate that Tamiḷakam's commercial contacts with the Hellenistic world began in the second century BC or even earlier.

A few of the early Tamil Brāhmī inscriptions found on rocks, potsherds, coins, seals and jewels have also been utilized for the present study. Many of these inscriptions are short and fragmentary and, despite the admirable pioneering work of I. Mahadevan, unintelligible. Yet, their potential as sources of historical data is fairly attractive in terms of their distribution pattern and the names of persons and professions furnished by them. Several Tamil Brāhmī lithic records document the gifts to Jain monks by various groups, such as salt merchants, textile traders, iron mongers, stone masons, goldsmiths, lapidaries, kings and nobles some of whom would certainly have been *yavanas*. It is, however, a bit strange that the term *yavana* is not mentioned in any of these inscriptions. In this context, it may be noted that the cave epigraphs of the Western Deccan categorically mention donations by *yavanas* to religious establishments.

The three major chapters of this volume deal with the coin finds, ceramics and other antiquities, respectively. This is followed by conclusions derived from the study. Maps, charts and photographs of objects have been included wherever appropriate.

The list of Roman coins in India (Appendix I) is an improvement over all the lists published earlier and has been updated till 2002. The lists of the rouletted ware and amphora finds in India (Appendices II and III) are the first ever comprehensive lists of these objects. Lists of the other pseudo-Roman and Roman objects have not been furnished because such objects are not very large in number and they have all been clearly mentioned/discussed in the respective chapters.

This volume will be of immense academic interest, more for the problems that it raises than for the new interpretations and conclusions that it has to offer.

## NOTES

1. Bibliographies of Roman coin finds in India have appeared earlier in a series of publications and have not been repeated here. For a good bibliography of the nineteenth and early twentieth centuries writings, see P.J. Turner, *Roman Coins from India,* London, 1989, pp. 144-52. For a bibliography of the finds from Tamilnadu-Pondicherry, see S. Suresh, *Roman Antiquities in Tamilnadu,* Madras, 1992b, pp. 88-94.

2. A few of these works are P. Arasu, 'Ancient Ceramic Industry from Kanchipuram Excavations', unpublished M.Phil. dissertation, University of Madras, 1979; R. Jayasurya, 'The Trading Community in Early Tamil Society up to 900 A.D.', unpublished M.Phil. dissertation, University of Madras, 1980; P.V. Radhakrishnan, 'Korkai and its Environs', unpublished M.Phil. dissertation, University of Madras, 1987; S. Ramadass, 'Sirupānāṟṟupadai—A Historical Study', unpublished M.Phil. dissertation, University of Madras, 1984; R. Santhakumar, 'Roman Coins in Tamilnadu', unpublished M.Phil. dissertation, University of Madras, 1985; I. Usha, 'Trade and Mercantile Community during the Sangam Period', unpublished M.Phil. dissertation, University of Madras, 1985.

3. K.V. Raman, 'Archaeological Excavations in Kanchipuram', *Tamil Civilization* vol. V, nos. 1 and 2, 1987, pp. 61-72; idem, 'Roman Contacts with Tamilnadu (South-eastern India): Recent Findings', paper presented at the international seminar on *India and the Roman World between the 1st and 4th Centuries A.D.,* Madras, 1990; idem, 'Further Evidence of Roman Trade from Coastal Sites in Tamilnadu', in *Rome and India: The Ancient Sea Trade,* ed. V. Begley and Richard Daniel De Puma, Madison, 1991, pp. 125-33; idem, 'Roman Coins from Tamilnadu', *SSIC,* vol. II, 1992, pp. 19-34.

4. In K.V. Raman 1992 (supra n. 3), pp. 19-34, a coin of Diocletian has been wrongly identified as an issue of Hadrian (?) (Plate II, no. 17). In I.K. Sarma, 'Roman Coins from Andhra Pradesh: Their Contexts, Chronology and Cultural Significance', *SSIC,* vol. II, 1992, pp. 35-50, an aureus of Claudius has been assigned to Constantine the Great (Plate III, no. 1). Again, in V.V. Krishna Sastry, *Roman Gold Coins—Recent Discoveries in Andhra Pradesh,* Hyderabad, 1992, most of the coin legends have been incorrectly read.

5. I have examined the finds from Arikamedu in the collections of the Government Museum, Pondicherry; the Government Museum, Madras; the Archaeological Survey of India, New Delhi; Musée Guimet, Paris and the British Museum, London. Some materials from the excavations at the site by the French are reported to have been sent to the French Museum at Hanoi.

6. For more details on references to *yavanas* in Indian literature and inscriptions, see P. Meile 'Les yavanas dans l'Inde tamoule', *Journal asiatique,* 232, 1940-1, pp. 85-123; H.P. Ray, 'The Yavana Presence in Ancient India', *Journal of the Economic and Social History of the Orient,* 31, 1988, pp. 311-25; idem, 'The Yavana Presence in India', in *Athens, Aden, Arikamedu—Essays on the Interrelations between India, Arabia and the Eastern Mediterranean,* ed. Marie-Francoise Boussac and Jean-Francois Salles, New Delhi, 1995, pp. 75-95; K. Zvelebil, 'The Yavanas in Old Tamil Literature', in *Charisteria Orientalia,* Prague, 1956, pp. 401-9; idem, *The Smile of Murugan,* Leiden, 1973, pp. 35, 42-3.

# 2

# Coins

ROMAN COINS found in India belong to the period between the Republican (second-first centuries BC) and the Byzantine (fifth century AD) (Map 1). For purposes of the present study, coins up to the period of Constantine I (AD 307-37) have been classified as 'early Roman' and the issues of all the later rulers as 'late Roman'. This division has been made because there is a marked difference in the distribution pattern and other features such as the occurrence of imitations between these two 'classes' of Roman coins in India.

## EARLY ROMAN COINS

Finds of early Roman coins abound in the Indian subcontinent—there are nearly 170 recorded finds spread over around 130 sites (Appendix I). Two major areas of concentration of the finds are the Coimbatore region in Tamilnadu and the Krishna valley in Andhra Pradesh. The adjoining Karnataka-Kerala regions have yielded a moderate number of finds. However, there is a paucity of such numismatic finds on the west coast, specially in the Maharashtra-Gujarat region. The finds from central, north-western, northern and eastern India are also scarce. Further, each of the finds from the latter regions contain very few coins, compared to the large hoards in the south.

A majority of the finds occur as hoards, usually in a spherical earthenware pot called a *lota*. The Kottayam (Kerala) hoard is the only one which was not found in an earthen vessel. Most coins of this hoard, one of the largest among the Roman coin finds in India, are reported to have been simply buried in the soil. Some of the coins of this hoard are also supposed to have been buried in bags(?) which may have been destroyed. A few issues of the hoard were found inside a brass (bronze?) vessel.

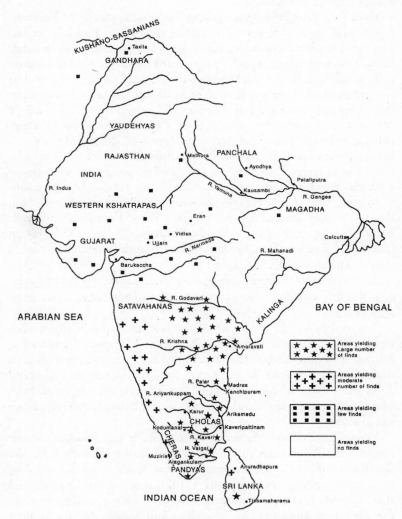

MAP 1: DISTRIBUTION PATTERN OF ROMAN COIN FINDS
IN THE INDIAN SUBCONTINENT

Surface finds of single Roman coins are often reported from south India. Chavadipalaiyam and Coimbatore have yielded Roman issues within megalithic graves.

Finds from Ahin Posh, Manikyala and some other sites in the Pakistan-Afghanistan region are part of ritualistic deposits in Buddhist *stupas.* The use of Roman coins as ritual offerings is comparatively rare in south India. However, recent reports have revealed that a few sites in Andhra such as Bavikonda and Totlakonda have yielded Roman coins within the precincts of Buddhist monuments. Roman coins have also been found beneath the foundations of an old Hindu temple at Nellore (Andhra) and within the precincts of a Hindu temple at Saidapet (Madras). Many published accounts, however, do not distinguish between coins found within the compound of a monastery or temple, viz., coins intended for future use, and those purposely deposited below a temple or within a *stupa,* as a gift to the shrine, never to be used again.

Roman coins from archaeological excavations are not very common, the noteworthy specimens are those from Karur (Tamilnadu); Dhulikatta, Kondapur, Nagarjunakonda, Peddabankur and Yellesvaram (Andhra); Chandravalli and Vadagaon Madhavapur (Karnataka); Nevasa (Maharashtra) and Taxila (Pakistan).

At this juncture, it should also be noted that the precise circumstances of a number of other Roman coin finds in India have never been recorded.

The earliest coins, the issues of the Roman Republic, have been reported from Karur, Krishnagiri, Kallakinar and Tiruppur (Tamilnadu); Eyyal and Nedumkandam (Kerala); Laccadives (or Lakśadvipa islands); Ajaigadh (Madhya Pradesh) and Kohat, Pakli and Manikyala (Pakistan). Some more finds of the Republican denarii have been reported from Maharashtra, south India and Sri Lanka, but full details about these are not available.[1]

Several scholars like Mortimer Wheeler, Bolin and Raschke did not consider the Republican coin finds in India to be of much historical significance. There is a widespread but erroneous belief that most of these coins are from *stupa* deposits. Until recently, it was also assumed that Indo-Mediterranean contacts were not firmly established before the period of Augustus (27 BC-AD 14) and hence, the few Roman Republican denarii in India would have reached this country at a much later date. Many of the wellknown Republican coin hoards in India contain evidence of a *terminus post quem* (TPQ) in the late first or second centuries AD and hence, David MacDowall has argued that the export of these Republican issues to India took place after Trajan's (AD 98-117) currency reform of AD 107.[2] The reduction in the purity of the silver denarius envisaged by this reform, in accordance with Gresham's Law, accelerated the disappearance of the denarii (with a higher content of silver) of the Republican and the early imperial (pre-64 AD) period from circulation in the Roman empire. Western traders could, according to MacDowall, reap huge profits by bringing the older and purer denarii to India precisely at this point of time because Indians were concerned not with the nominal value of these coins prevalent in Rome but only with the purity and weight of the coins.

On the basis of a series of recent discoveries and studies, it can be argued that commercial links between India and the West began long before the time of Augustus and that some of the Republican coins reached India shortly after they were minted. In fact, the recent discoveries of single unworn specimens of the Republican denarii in such places as Ajaigadh, Krishnagiri and Tiruppur clearly indicate that these coins were not in circulation for long before being lost or buried. Although the TPQ of the Nedumkandam hoard is not known, the mint condition of the Augustan denarii in the hoard shows that the date of burial of the hoard could, at the latest, be a few years after the reign of Augustus and in all likelihood, some of the Republican coins of the hoard should have reached India in the pre-Augustus period. Also, the discovery of Republican coins at Kallakinar and Tiruppur in the heart of the Coimbatore region, famous for its early imperial (first century AD) Roman coin finds, suggests a pre-Julio-Claudian phase of trade in this region.

The not very widely known recent antiquarian finds from Karur, an important early historical site of Tamilnadu, also provide valuable clues for maritime trade prior to the time of Augustus. The site has yielded, besides a few ill-recorded Roman Republican coins, Seleucid, Phoenician and Greek coins of the third-second centuries BC.[3] A Greek copper coin dated 300 BC is also reported from Hassan in Karnataka.[4] Several Greek silver coins of the Hellenistic period have also been reported from Sri Lanka.[5]

The most clinching evidence for the Roman Republican trade with south India is provided by a recent reassessment of the varied ceramics excavated from Arikamedu near Pondicherry.[6] It has now been established that the site was first occupied in the middle of the third century BC while its contacts with the Mediterranean region began by the late second century BC. The recent archaeological excavations at

Arikamedu and a few other sites including Alagankulam (Tamilnadu) confirm this revised chronology of the trade.[7]

In the initial years of the trade, the circumnavigation of Cape Comorin was considered dangerous and some of the Western traders reached the Coromandel coast from the Malabar coast through the famous Palghat pass. Similarly, on some occasions, merchandise from south-east India would have been sent by land to the Malabar ports for onward transmission to the Mediterranean by the sea route.

Contrary to popular misconception, sea trade reached its peak not during the age of Augustus but during the reign of his successor Tiberius (AD 14-37). The gold and silver issues of no other Roman ruler occur in such large numbers in every part of India, as those of Tiberius. Hoards exclusively containing the issues of Augustus or with a TPQ of Augustus are almost unknown in India. Stray finds of single coins have, however, revealed issues of this ruler; it is not possible to determine the date when these 'single' specimens were exported to India. Some of them may have been part of an unreported hoard. The Mambalam and Pennar hoards (Tamilnadu) consist of a denarius of Augustus along with silver punch marked coins, the date and other details of which remain unknown. One of the hoards from Vellalur (near Coimbatore), discovered in 1931, comprised 121 coins of which 118 are of Augustus; if the remaining 3 coins are also of the same ruler, the find would be the only 'Augustan hoard' in India. One of the denarii hoards from Karur was described as 'mainly Augustan' implying that there were other issues as well in the find. The published coins from the Nedumkandam hoard are all of the Roman Republic and Augustus, but it should be noted that details about the majority of the coins in the hoard are not known; some of the latter coins may be of Tiberius. Also, although all the 10 coins from the Uthamapuram (Tamilnadu) hoard have been tentatively assigned to Augustus, 4 of these coins are broken and corroded beyond identification. As such, there is no clear evidence that the denarii or even the aurei of Augustus were buried in India during his reign. On the other hand, many of the Julio-Claudian finds south of the Vindhyas, specially in the Coimbatore region, have a TPQ of Tiberius. All the coins of the Vellalur aurei hoard, unearthed in 1939, are of Tiberius. Further, in any hoard containing coins of Tiberius and other Roman rulers, Tiberian coins usually outnumber those of all other rulers including Augustus. In fact, the majority of the stratified finds of Roman coins in India are of Tiberius. It is thus clear that many of the Augustan and Tiberian coin finds which together constitute over 50 per cent of the early Roman coins in India, were brought to this country at a time when Tiberian money was in common circulation in the Roman empire—most likely, during or within a few years after the reign of Tiberius. Further evidence of this is the comparative paucity of the issues of Gaius or Caligula (AD 37-41), Claudius (AD 41-54) and other later rulers in India. Only around 35 coins of Gaius, 300 of Claudius and 200 of Nero (AD 54-68) have been recorded; coins of the later emperors are even less whereas over 2,500 issues of Tiberius have been discovered in India. If it is argued that the Augustan and Tiberian coin finds could have reached India during the reign of Claudius or Nero or any of their successors, it would only be natural to expect a more liberal sprinkling of the coins of the monarch, viz., Claudius or Nero during whose reign these coins were brought to India. This not being the case, it may be concluded that the export of Roman money to India reached its peak during the reign of Tiberius.

The Julio-Claudian finds which account for around 80 per cent of the total early Roman coin finds in India are heavily concentrated in the western districts—Coimbatore, Erode and Salem—of Tamilnadu. The proximity of this region to the beryl mines, the large pepper and cardamom estates are the major reasons for this concentration. The Palghat pass, the sole land route through which Roman traders could travel from Kerala to the Coromandel region, is also located near Coimbatore.[8]

It may be noted that both pepper and cardamom, specially the former, were regularly exported to Rome throughout the period of trade. The highly prized beryl which was in great demand in the Roman world during the first century AD was then believed to be found only in India. Although the Karnataka region boasted of a few beryl deposits, the two major mines were in the Tamil country—one at Padiyur near Erode city and the other at Vaniyambadi in North Arcot district, not far from the border of Salem district. Besides the Romans, the people of north India and Andhra too would have procured beryl from the Coimbatore-Erode region by paying for it in Roman currency.

A little known factor which adds to the economic importance of the Coimbatore-Erode region is the presence of high quality magnetite ores at Chennimalai hills, just 18 km east of Kodumanal, an early historical urban site, close to Erode city. Surface collections from Kodumanal include a denarius each of Augustus and Tiberius. Excavations at the site have revealed that it was a major iron and steel production centre.[9] Huge quantities of iron slag, furnaces of different sizes as well as a large variety of iron objects such as swords, arrowheads and stirrups have been recovered. Karur, not too far from Kodumanal, has also yielded iron slag and remnants of huge ancient furnaces.[10] It is plausible that the iron and steel produced at Karur and Kodumanal were exported to Rome either through the port of Muziris on the Malabar coast or the port of Kaveripattinam on the east coast. Significantly, Kodumanal is strategically located on the banks of the river Noyyal, almost equidistant from the Coromandel and the Malabar coasts. Noyyal is a tributary of the river Kaveri that joins the sea at Kaveripattinam. Kodumanal lies on the ancient trade route linking Karur with Muziris via Sulur and Vellalur in the vicinity of Coimbatore city. Not surprisingly, all these sites have yielded Roman coins belonging to the Julio-Claudian period.

The number of coins in many of the Julio-Claudian hoards is large: Akkanpalle (Andhra) and Budinatham (Tamilnadu) contain over 1,000 coins each; the Kottayam and the Karur denarii hoards, discovered in 1847 and 1856, respectively, are much larger. There are at least four hoards that contain around 500 coins each—two denarii hoards from Vellalur excavated in 1841 and 1891, respectively, the denarii hoard from Karur discovered in 1878 and the aurei hoard from Pudukkottai (Tamilnadu). Smaller hoards have been unearthed as well, such as Akhilandapuram and Koneripatti (Coimbatore-Salem region)(Plates 3 and 4), Nasthullapur (Andhra) and Adam (Maharashtra). Due to the complex composition of the different hoards and the lack of details about the precise coin types in many of the finds, it is not possible to state whether the 'number' of coins in each hoard has any particular significance. However, a noteworthy feature is the predominance of two common types in both the smaller and the bigger hoards—the 'Gaius and Lucius Caesares reverse' type of Augustus and the 'Pontif Maxim' type of Tiberius. The high incidence of these two varieties may be either purely accidental or, at best, attributed to the easy availability of these common types to Western traders visiting India. These types do not seem to have been specially minted for trade with India because they have been found in considerable numbers throughout the Roman empire. Also, there is no reason to believe that Indians expressed a special preference for these two types.[11]

The death of Nero in AD 68 was followed by a bitter civil war which greatly undermined the Roman economy. The new emperor Vespasian (AD 69-79) passed a series of laws discouraging the ostentatious lifestyle of the Roman aristocracy. The demand for oriental luxuries including silks, ivory and beryl registered a slow but steady decline in most parts

PLATE 3. AUGUSTUS DENARIUS FROM
KONERIPATTI HOARD (TAMILNADU): OBVERSE AND REVERSE

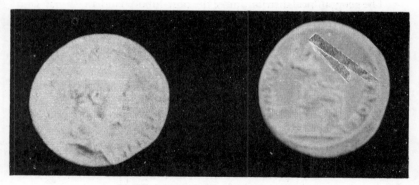

PLATE 4. TIBERIUS DENARIUS FROM
KONERIPATTI HOARD (TAMILNADU): OBVERSE AND REVERSE

of the empire. These luxury goods began to be traded, more intensely
and in increasing quantities, between the different regions of India as
also between India, Sri Lanka and South-East Asia. Thus, by the end of
the first century AD, maritime trade between India and the West was, to
a large extent, confined to comparatively inexpensive items such as cotton
fabrics and pepper. This was also the period when the Andhra coast saw
an unprecedented proliferation of trade activities and trade guilds. In
the earlier periods, the centralized organization of trade under the
Mauryans had hampered the rapid growth of local trade networks in
places like Andhra which were on the periphery of the far-flung Mauryan
empire. Further, this rather slow and late development of trade networks
in Andhra may also be ascribed to the survival of the 'primitive'
megalithic settlements in remote pockets of the lower Krishna valley
even at this late date. After the first century AD, however, Roman traders
frequented the Andhra ports in greater numbers. They obtained their
requirements of iron and steel not from Kodumanal but from Karim-
nagar area in Andhra. Similarly, besides pepper from south Kanara and
Malabar regions, pepper from Andhra also began to be exported to
Rome.

The geographical distribution of the post-Julio-Claudian Roman coin
finds in India bear testimony to this change in the trade pattern. There
has not been a single find post-dating Nero in the Coimbatore-Erode-
Salem regions. Numerous finds of this period have been reported from
the cotton-growing areas in Andhra Pradesh, Maharashtra and to a
limited extent, Gujarat; the majority of the finds are, undoubtedly, in
Andhra. In fact, according to Peter Berghaus, a large number of coins
of Antoninus Pius (AD138-61) have been discovered in the region lying
between the Krishna and Godavari rivers in Andhra.[12] Similarly, there
is a clustering of the coins of Marcus Aurelius (AD 161-80) in Gujarat.
Coins of Septimius Severus (AD 193-211), extremely rare in the
Tamilnadu-Kerala region, have been recurrently reported from Andhra,
Karnataka, Maharashtra and Gujarat.

Compared to the Julio-Claudian hoards, the post-Julio-Claudian ones
contain fewer coins. This may be due to the fact that the value of each
'commercial transaction' in the later period was comparatively less. Any
transaction involving cotton fabrics would certainly require fewer coins
as against the large numbers involved in trading in silk, ivory or precious
stones. Due to the lower value of the chief commodity of trade (cotton),
the number of Roman coins reaching India in the late first and second
centuries AD was less even though the volume of trade remained almost

the same. By the beginning of the third century, however, there was a marked decrease in the quantum of trade. Roman issues of the third century are very rare in India—a mere 17 odd coins.

The paucity of both the Julio-Claudian and the post-Julio-Claudian finds in eastern India as also in large areas of northern and western India is partially explained by the fact that the Kushans and the western Kshatrapas, who ruled over these regions during the period of Roman trade, melted some of the foreign coins to use the metal to mint their own coins. At a much later date, the Guptas could have melted, for the same purpose, not only the Roman aurei and denarii but also the Kushan gold coins accessible to them.

The earliest Roman coins that were brought to India were of silver. All the Republican issues found so far are of silver and even among the Augustan and Tiberian finds, silver coins predominate. Since the time of Gaius, however, there is a gradual increase in the number of gold issues vis-a-vis silver ones. One reason for this is that during the reigns of Gaius, Claudius and Nero, Roman gold coins were minted in greater numbers than silver coins.[13] Silver issues post-dating Nero are very few in India—a coin of Vespasian from Jabalpur (Madhya Pradesh); two denarii of Hadrian (AD 117-38)—one from the Pakli and the other from the Laccadive hoards—and a few other finds.[14] It is also clear that as soon as Roman gold reached India, Indians expressed a preference for the gold issues even before Nero's currency reform of AD 64 which reduced the purity of the denarius and the weight of the aureus. It is pertinent to note that the heavy pre-AD 64 aurei appear in large quantities compared to the later issues in India, even in hoards with a TPQ of the late first or second centuries AD. This is neither because Indians, who were mainly concerned with the bullion value of the Roman issues, desired to acquire the heavier aurei, nor because Roman traders themselves preferred to trade in the old heavy aurei in India for a profit instead of the new lighter ones, both of which had the same nominal value in the Roman market. On the other hand, as Indo-Roman trade reached its zenith much before AD 64, the majority, if not all, of the pre-AD 64 aurei reached India prior to the reform of AD 64. Thus, at no point of time, any special preference for the heavier aurei was expressed by either the Indians or Roman merchants.

Finds of early Roman issues in base metal are very few in India.[15] According to Paula Turner, indigenous gold and silver coins are very scarce in south India during this period but Tamil kings had a well-developed system of copper coinage and hence, Indians did not evince much interest in Roman copper issues.[16] This theory is unacceptable because there is ample evidence to show that silver punch marked coins were in circulation in the Andhra-Tamilnadu region during the period of Roman trade. Further, several silver coins issued by the Sangam Cheras have recently come to light. In such circumstances, the paucity of the early Roman base metal issues can be traced to the subtle link between the metal of the Roman coins of different periods in India and the type and quantity of Indian goods exported to Rome during those periods. Thus, in the first century AD when the volume of trade in precious goods was large, the use of copper coins in these 'high-value transactions' was not thought of. However, from the end of the first century AD when the trade was mostly confined to non-luxury items, there was a slow and steady increase in the number of Roman copper coins finding their way to India.

The preceding detailed survey of the early Roman coin finds in India reveals that the differences in the metal and quantity of Roman coins reaching the various regions of India, at different times, are related to the nature and quantum of trade during the different periods. MacDowall's arguments in support of his theory that Roman coins were brought to India only after AD 70[17] can be refuted on several grounds. First, the mere fact that the Republican and Augustan coins were in circulation in the Roman empire during the Flavian period (AD 70-98) cannot be a reason for the import of these coin types to India at such a late date. Further, he has argued that the Julio-Claudian denarii seen in hoards found in both India and Europe show similar loss of weight due to wear and tear and hence, Roman coins could have reached India after being reduced to this state of wear in the Roman empire itself. This is hardly an argument because any coin will show weight loss over a period of use whether in India or Rome and thus, many of the worn Roman coins in India could have shown weight loss due to their being used in India. Further, MacDowall's dating does not conform to the chronology of Indo-Roman trade furnished by archaeological excavations in scores of early historical sites spread throughout India.

As most of the early Roman coins in India are found in hoards, it is important to probe the factors which prompted people to bury such huge quantities of money in pots. Could some of the hoards represent 'reserve capital' saved by a trader? Wheeler has suggested that the hoards in the neighbourhood of Coimbatore may have been hidden or lost by travellers threatened by brigands operating in the area which, due to its hilly terrain and its being the 'border' of the Sangam Cōḷa, Sangam

Chera and Sangam Pāṇḍya kingdoms, provided ideal 'escape-routes' to the bandits.[18] More recently, in the same vein, MacDowall has opined that the hoardings may have been the result of panic or fear of a sudden attack or war or some natural calamity which forced people to hide their wealth, away from nature's fury and human attacks.[19]

K.V. Raman's contention that Roman coins could have been hoarded around AD 300 when the Tamil country faced the Kalabra invasions[20] is unacceptable because it has been conclusively proved that the maximum number of Roman coins reached India in the first century AD and most of them were buried long before AD 300. Further, Roman coin hoards, similar in composition to those found in Tamilnadu, have been discovered in many other regions of India not subjected to the Kalabra incursions.

It may be concluded that the early indigenous coins of south India were invariably thin small pieces of silver or copper whereas the Roman issues in gold and silver were heavier and artistically superior; hence, the latter were often hoarded in large numbers mainly for their bullion value. In this context, it is significant to note that hoards containing the issues of the early Tamil kings and chieftains are very rare, the only notable exception being the Āṇḍippaṭṭi hoard (Tamilnadu) of 143 lead coins. The recent discoveries of such dynastic issues are either those found on the banks of rivers or stratified finds. Among the stratified finds, are those reported from the excavations in the port towns of Arikamedu and Alagankulam. The find from Arikamedu is a square Sangam Cōḻa copper coin dated to the beginning of the Christian era. The two square copper coins from Alagankulam belong to the Sangam Pāṇḍya and can be assigned to the second century BC.

At this juncture, it may be pointed out that the composition of many of the Roman coin hoards in India is quite different from those found in the Roman empire. This is not surprising because the quantum and types of Roman coins in circulation in the empire were more than those in India. Similarly, the metal, denomination, level of wear and quantity of Roman coins found in India are different from those in other regions which were not part of the Roman empire but which carried on trade with Rome. These 'differences' may be explained in terms of the variations in the 'nature', 'volume' and 'period' of Roman trade in each of those territories. The varying monetary policies of the different Roman emperors and the consequent changes in the metallic composition and metrology of their coins had a direct bearing on the export of these coins to Free Germany, Scandinavia, Eastern Europe, Arabia as well as India and Sri Lanka.

## LATE ROMAN COINS

Finds of late Roman coins, viz., coins post-dating Constantine I are fewer than the early Roman issues in India. Also, as the majority of the late Roman finds in India are small, worn, unattractive copper coins, they have hitherto not attracted the attention of many scholars, museums and coin collectors. In almost all the studies on Indo-Mediterranean trade, these late coins are either simply ignored or at best, accorded cursory treatment.

There are over 30 well attested finds of late Roman coins spread over 27 Indian sites (Appendix I). There have been several inadequately recorded finds both from western and southern India, particularly from the Coimbatore region in close vicinity of the Palghat gap.[21]

Details about the precise number of late Roman coins in different regions are not available. In the towns of Madurai and Karur, thousands of copper coins issued from the mints of Antioch and Alexandria have been unearthed. But the finds from all the other places are extremely limited.

Unlike the early Roman coins which are mainly found in hoards, the later issues are largely surface finds of either a single coin or at the most, a small batch of not more than ten coins. However, at least five hoards contain late Roman coins—Weepangandla (Andhra Pradesh), Akkialur and Katryal (Karnataka), Puthankavu (Kerala) and Nathampatti (Tamilnadu). Nathampatti, Puthankavu and Katryal hoards contain only late Roman issues. Weepangandla has one early Roman coin—an issue of Constantine I, while Akkialur hoard contains three early Roman coins—two of Septimius Severus and one of Caracalla (AD 198-217). It should, however, be noted that all the foreign coins from Weepangandla and a few from Akkialur are imitations. In any case, the presence of both the early and late Roman coins together in the hoard proves that they were accorded a similar status and were used for the same purpose.

The stray find from Ahin Posh (Afghanistan) consists of five Byzantine solidi set in a 'modern' bracelet.

A few late Roman coins reported from the north-western part of the subcontinent are ritualistic offerings in Buddhist establishments. For instance, *stupa* no. 10 at Hadda or Hidda (Afghanistan) has yielded five solidi along with Kushan and Sassanian coins. Such *stupa* finds of late Roman coins are numerically far less than similar finds of the early period. A plausible explanation for this is that Buddhism itself was on the decline in those regions during this late period.

Alagankulam in Tamilnadu and Kudavelli, not too far from Weepan-gandla, in Andhra Pradesh have yielded late Roman coins in the stratified context. As Kudavelli lies close to the famous Eastern Chalukyan Sangameśvara Temple at the confluence of the rivers Tungabhadra and Krishna, it has been opined that the coins from this site may also be ritualistic offerings.[22]

Till date, no single site in the Indian subcontinent has yielded both the early and late Roman coins in the stratified context.

A notable observation is that although the finds of the late Roman coins are comparatively few, their overall geographical distribution compares favourably with that of the early Roman finds. Unlike the early Roman finds, the later coins are heavily concentrated in the southern part of the Coromandel coast from Nellore in Andhra to Alangankulam. Since the mid-nineteenth century, late Roman finds have been intermittently reported from several important sites including Mahabalipuram, Cuddalore, Tirukoilur and Bandarpattinam situated along this coastal stretch. Of all these sites, Bandarpattinam, not far from Tanjavur, has been recently discovered. Small-scale archaeological excavations have revealed that the site was occupied from the third century BC to the medieval times. The site has yielded a pearl bead, a punch marked coin and four late Roman copper coins— two of Arcadius (AD 395-408) and two of Honorius (AD 395-423), besides medieval Cōla coins and Chinese pottery.[23]

The limited occurrence of late Roman coins has to be viewed in the context of the frequent changes in the trade pattern—a process which, as discussed earlier, started towards the end of the first century AD itself. By the third-fourth centuries AD, all the Malabar ports including Muziris declined. Trade activities were now confined to Sri Lanka, the Pāṇḍyan capital of Madurai and to a lesser extent, the Chera capital of Karur. Thus, of all the Coromandel ports, Alagankulam alone, on account of its strategic location close to both Madurai and Sri Lanka, was regularly patronized by Western traders during this period.

Why is it that a large majority of late Roman coins in India are of copper? One reason, as discussed earlier, is that the chief exports from India, at that time, were non-luxury items for which payment in Roman copper coins sufficed. Another reason is linked to the law, passed in AD 396 by the Roman government, decreeing that the *nummus* (Roman copper coin), which had all along been a heavily overvalued token currency, would henceforth be worth its weight in copper.[24] In the subsequent period, the value of copper in relation to gold steadily increased in Rome. For instance, 1 solidus equal to 25 pounds of copper earlier, was equivalent to just 20 pounds of copper in the fifth century. Also, compared to the solidi, the *nummi* were available in greater quantities to Roman traders. Hence, they deliberately chose, for trade with India, copper coins instead of gold ones, both of which were accepted by Indians solely for their 'metal-value'.

The view, repeatedly expressed by many scholars, that trade ceased in the third century AD and was slightly revived during or soon after the reign of Constantine I (fourth century AD),[25] is erroneous. It may be noted that coins of almost all Roman rulers right from Augustus to Justinus I (AD 518-27) have been unearthed in India in varying numbers and there is no reason to believe that trade activities ceased in the third century AD. Instead, the process of decline beginning in the late first century AD, continued slowly but steadily till the sixth-eighth centuries AD when contacts finally ceased. It is difficult to determine the precise date of the end of trade activities. A solitary gold imitation coin of Leo III, a Byzantine ruler of the early eighth century, has been reported from Madurai. But late Roman copper coins and their imitations from Madurai and other Indian sites all belong to the fourth-sixth centuries AD.

The reasons for the final decline of trade are chiefly rooted in the changed politico-economic scenarios and ideologies not only in India and Europe but also in the countries lying between India and Europe. As far as south India is concerned, the scores of urban centres, which sustained the trade during the early historical period, declined by the early medieval times. Further, the ruling families, mercantile communities and guilds that had initiated the trade were no longer available. The decline of Buddhism and the consequent desertion of the monastic establishments set up on the major trade routes made these routes unattractive and unsafe for merchants.

## SLASHED COINS

One of the unusual features of Roman coin finds in India is the presence on some of the coins of slash marks, generally 1 to 2 mm long, effected by a knife, a chisel or a file. Such marks are totally absent on Roman coins found outside India including those reported from Sri Lanka, Africa and Central Asia.

Regarding a few Roman coins found in India but now lost, the published accounts are unclear as to whether these coins are slashed or not. For example, the famous Kottayam hoard contained a few coins which were 'partially obliterated' but there is no certainty whether this refers to slashes or not. Similarly, some of the coins preserved in a pot beneath an old Hindu temple at Nellore have been described as 'much defaced and perforated'. This, again, may refer to the state of wear of the issues rather than a deliberate attempt to disfigure the coins. Nevertheless, from the fact that all the coins from the Nellore hoard belong to the second century AD, it is possible to infer that these coins were not slashed because, with the exception of a few coins of the second and fourth centuries AD, all the known slashed coins are of the first century AD.

There are at least nineteen wellrecorded slashed finds in India. The largest number of finds (nine finds) is from the Andhra region, closely followed by Tamilnadu (five finds). Kerala, Karnataka and Madhya Pradesh have yielded one find each. There have been reports of some more slashed coins, specially the denarii, but neither the exact find-spot nor the circumstances of these finds are known.[26]

The site-by-site distribution of the known slashed coins is as presented in Table 1.

Almost all the slashed coins are part of either small or big hoards. The defaced coin from Chakherbedha (Madhya Pradesh) was, however, discovered along with a supposedly 'modern' ear ornament in a non-hoard context. Slashed coins from archaeological excavations are very rare, a notable instance being Peddabankur (Andhra) where defaced and non-defaced Augustan and Tiberian issues have been recovered together in stratified layers (Plate 5). Slashed coins are unknown among finds of single Roman issues discovered in many parts of India, specially the Coimbatore region. Slashed coins are also not found among coins deposited in Buddhist *stupas*.

Another peculiar feature is that only a few hoards contain all slashed coins. Nagavarappupadu, Peddakodamagundla, Adam and Belgaum are the only well attested specimens of such hoards. In the case of the other hoards, there is no discernible pattern in the quantity of slashed and unslashed coins in the various hoards. At Kaliyampattur, Nandyal and Eyyal, barely 10 per cent of the total coins in each hoard are incised. On the other hand, at Pudukkottai and Akkanpalle, over 90 per cent of the coins in each hoard are defaced. At Madurai Hills, the defaced coins constitute around 50 per cent of the total issues in the hoard. In many of these finds, the non-slashed coins are of the same ruler and sometimes of the same type as the slashed coins.

TABLE 1 **SLASHED COINS**

| Site | Number of Slashed Coins |
|---|---|
| *Tamilnadu* | |
| • Kaliyampattur | 4 |
| • Madurai Hills | 5 |
| • Pudukkottai | 461 |
| • Tondamanathan | 2 |
| 39 Soriyapattu  1992 N | 1 |
| *Andhra Pradesh* | |
| • Akkanpalle | 1505 |
| • Alluru | 1 |
| Gumada | 8+ |
| • Nagavarappupadu | 58 |
| • Nandyal | 17 |
| • Nasthullapur | 15  ok 39 |
| • Peddabankur | 2+ |
| • Peddakodamagundla | 3 |
| • Vinukonda | 2 |
| *Kerala* | |
| • Eyyal | 7 |
| *Karnataka* | |
| • Belgaum | 30+ |
| *Maharashtra* | |
| • Adam | 11 |
| N 139 Uppavahr | 1 |
| *Madhya Pradesh* | |
| 142 Chakherbedha | 1 |
| TOTAL | 2134+ |

The marks effected by a knife, a blade or a chisel are less than 2mm in depth and are mostly seen on the royal bust depicted on the obverse. Very few coins from such hoards as Akkanpalle, Nagavarappupadu and Pudukkottai carry marks on the reverse. A few coins from Akkanpalle and Pudukkottai and at least one coin from Nagavarappupadu are slashed on both sides. Usually, coins bearing marks on the reverse have a bust-type reverse but there are instances of slashes on the non-bust reverse also such as the 'Gaius and Lucius Caesares reverse' coins of Augustus from Akkanpalle.

Many coins bear two or more marks, usually intersecting each other but rarely running parallel to one another. A notable specimen of the

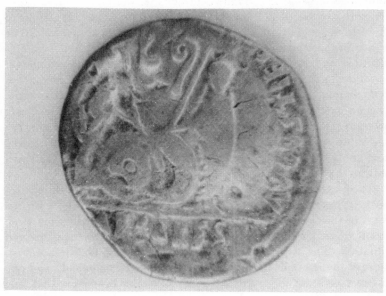

PLATE 5. SLASHED IMITATION AUGUSTUS DENARIUS FROM
STRATIFIED LAYERS–PEDDABANKUR (ANDHRA):
OBVERSE (ABOVE) AND REVERSE (BELOW)

latter category is a coin from Gumada bearing three slashes running parallel to one another. The slashes are generally vertical but horizontal slashes are also seen on some coins, specially those from the Andhra region.

It is not clear as to whether the differences in the types of slash marks found on the coins of various hoards have any significance. In the absence of more details about many of the relevant coins, it is difficult to arrive at any definite conclusion regarding the distribution pattern of the varied types of slashes, both region-wise and period-wise. None the less, differences in the types of slash marks found on the gold and silver coins have been reported by Paula Turner.[27] The gold coins, according to her, carry marks which are usually quite short and nearly as deep as they are wide, that is, 1 to 2 mm, but not deep enough to bend the coin. These marks are believed to have been effected by punching a dull blade on the issue. She has also pointed out that the gold coins normally have only one mark but an exception cited by her is an aureus bearing two slashes from the Adam hoard. The marks on the silver coins are attributed by her to a sharp knife and they are supposed to be longer, sometimes crossing the circumference of the coin twice. These marks are generally less than 1 mm wide and are thinner in comparison to those on the gold coins but are deep enough to almost cut the coin. The dissimilarities between the marks on the gold and silver coins are not, according to her, the result of the varying properties of the two metals.

Studying the types of slash marks on both gold and silver coins, Peter Berghaus has pointed out that the denarii rarely possess more than one mark.[28] At the same time, he has reported significant differences between the marks on the issues (gold and silver) of the first century and those on later coins (gold). According to him, slash marks on the later coins do not deface the emperor's portrait as much as the chisel cuts on the first century coins.

The present study, however, shows that these views on the differences in the types of slashes on coins of different metals and those on the coins of the first century and later, are not substantiated by the more recent finds. Considering the supposed differences between the gold and silver coins, it may be seen that the little known aureus from Alluru, most of the issues in the aurei hoard from Nagavarappupadu and one aureus each from the Gumada and Eyyal hoards bear more than one mark, and this does not substantiate the observations of Paula Turner. Again, the slashes on the gold issues from the Gumada, Nandyal and Pudukkottai hoards are as deep as those on some of the Akkanpalle silver coins. A good number of gold coins—at least five Gumada coins which seem to have been slashed with shears and a few more issues from other places including Pudukkottai and Chakherbedha—bear slash marks which have nearly cut and bent the coins, indicating that this phenomenon is not confined to silver coins alone. Further, several slash marks on the Gumada aurei are longer than those on some of the Akkanpalle denarii. Thus, slash marks on both gold and silver coins have several features in common, although in varying degrees. Regarding the differences in the earlier (first century AD) and later (second-fourth centuries AD) coins as pointed out by Peter Berghaus, there does not seem to be any major difference between the slashes on the coins of these periods. In fact, the mark on the Chakherbedha coin (second century AD) is almost identical in terms of length, depth and other features to the slashes on several of the Nagavarappupadu coins (first century AD). Hence, most of the marks on both the earlier and later coins seem to have been effected with the sole objective of damaging the royal bust as much as possible. Thus, if the heads on a few coins of the Gumada hoard (second-fourth centuries AD) have not been severely defaced, so are the heads on several coins of the Adam find (first century AD).

It is a little known fact that with the exception of Akkanpalle, slashes on coins belonging to a single hoard largely share certain features such as depth and size. Akkanpalle, which incidentally is the largest slashed hoard in India, has revealed three distinct types of slashed coins—issues with vertical slashes, those with horizontal slash marks, and those depicting a combination of both types. Slashes on the coins of this hoard also show wide variations in depth. On seven of the eight known slashed coins in the Gumada hoard, the mark is a single straight vertical line extending from almost the centre of the coin to the circumference below. The other slashed coin from this hoard has three such lines running parallel to each other. The only known slashed coin from Uppavahr, a Septimius Severus imitation, also has two marks, parallel to one another, extending from almost the centre of the flan down to the circumference below. Many of the slashes on the coins in the Nandyal hoard are short straight vertical lines but none of these lines ever touch the circumference of the coin. These marks are, as usual, on the royal head but do not touch the facial features such as the eyes, nose and lips, that is, these marks largely extend from the back or side of the head to the neck below but do not disfigure the face. Most of the coins from Nagavarappupadu have 'multiple marks' consisting of vertical and

horizontal lines intersecting at different angles. The find from Alluru
has only horizontal marks while those from Peddabankur bear only
vertical slashes. All the known slashed coins from Pudukkottai bear one
mark extending vertically from the head. The slashes on six of the seven
coins from Eyyal are almost identical to those on the Nandyal coins
mentioned earlier. The other slashed coin from Eyyal, a Tiberian aureus,
has two slashes—a vertical and a horizontal one intersecting each other
at right angles to form a 'cross'.

Significant variations in the size, shape, depth and number of slash
marks on the coins of different hoards seem to suggest that the practice
of slashing coins was followed by different persons/agencies using a
variety of instruments. Hence, it is impossible to accept Paula Turner's
suggestion that the slashing of the aurei was a 'one time incident' and
the coins thus slashed travelled to distant places where they were
hoarded.[29]

Regarding the chronology of the slashed coins, defaced specimens of
the Republican period (first century BC) or of the late Roman rulers
post-dating Constantine I are unknown. As indicated earlier, over
99.9 per cent of the slashed coins belong to the first century AD. In
many hoards containing coins both of the first and second centuries AD,
the first century coins alone have been slashed, even if the second century
coins outnumber those of the first century in the hoard. In fact, the
latest slashed coin in most of the hoards is that of Nero. These
observations may be further clarified by citing details of some of the
hoards: the Kaliyampattur hoard contains issues of Augustus (number:
?), Tiberius (6 coins), Gaius (1), Claudius (18), Nero (17), Domitian
(AD 81-96) (5), Nerva (AD 96-98) (2) and some other coins now lost.
All the known slashed coins from the hoard are of Claudius (2) and
Nero (2). In the Vinukonda hoard, only the 2 coins of Tiberius are
slashed although the hoard contains 13 post-Nero coins including those
of Hadrian, Antoninus Pius, Marcus Aurelius, Commodus (AD 176-
92) and Caracalla. Similarly, the Eyyal hoard comprises Republican issues
(5), coins of Augustus (47), Tiberius (14), Claudius (8), Nero (4), Trajan
(1) and unidentified types (4); here again, only 7 specimens—5 of
Tiberius and 1 each of Claudius and Nero—bear slash marks.

The majority of the slashed coins in India are of Tiberius, followed
by those of Augustus, Claudius, Nero, Gaius and Vespasian in that order.
The post-first century AD slashed coins, confined to three sites—
Uppavahr, Chakherbedha and Gumada—are imitations of the issues of
Septimius Severus, Marcus Aurelius, Commodus and Constantine I.

In the light of these facts, it may be concluded that the majority of the coins were slashed during the second half of the first century AD, viz., a few years prior to the burial date of the major slashed hoards.

Slashed coins are largely in silver or gold. Slashed base metal issues, until recently unknown, have been found in the stratified context at Peddabankur (Andhra). An imitation of the Tiberian 'Pontif Maxim' type in lead, from this site, has two slashes on the obverse. The coin was probably originally coated or plated with silver. From the same layer at Peddabankur, eight more issues of the Augustan and Tiberian types including a slashed issue of the Augustan 'Gaius and Lucius Caesares reverse' type have been recovered. These eight coins are of silver. Since some of them are broken/perforated, their lead core is clearly discernible.

Among the slashed gold and silver issues numbering over 2,132, over 70 per cent (1,540+ coins) are of silver. The number of slashed gold hoards is more than double that of the silver ones. The unusually large Akkanpalle hoard, which has revealed 1,505 incised coins, alone accounts for over 99.5 per cent of the slashed silver specimens in India.

The distribution of the slashed coins is in consonance with the general pattern of distribution of Roman coins in India. As previously mentioned, the earliest Roman coins to reach India were of silver, hence, the earliest slashed coins were also of silver. Roman gold issues are fewer in number but are more widely scattered in India than silver ones. Hence, it is not surprising that the slashed gold and silver coins show the same pattern of distribution in the subcontinent. In fact, all the three major slashed denarii hoards are confined to a limited geographical area: northern Andhra Pradesh and Belgaum region in Karnataka, whereas the slashed gold issues have been recovered from Adam and Uppavahr in Maharashtra down to Madurai and Eyyal in the south.

There are varied views on the significance of slash marks on Roman coins in India. The possibility that the slashes may have been effected to ascertain the quality of the metal of the coins is not accepted by most scholars because the marks are large, deliberately cut across the royal bust and have been effected with such force that often the coin is bent. Shroff's marks need only be tiny strokes and they are generally near the edge of the coin.

G.F. Hill initially opined that the early Indian kings may have ordered for the coins too worn for further use to be slashed before being melted; some such incised coins could have accidentally reached the hoarders.[30] Hill has subsequently argued that the slashing was done by Indian rulers to prevent foreign coins from circulating in India.[31] Both these viewpoints are, however, not tenable. It is highly improbable that the coins identified for melting were slashed on the royal head depicted on the obverse in such a manner as to almost cut or break the coin. Moreover, many coins in 'fair' or 'good' condition, thereby not warranting their being melted, also bear these incision marks. All the coins from Adam and the Nerovian aurei from Nandyal and Kaliyampattur are some of the specimens of slashed unworn coins.

Close on the heels of Hill's theories, Mortimer Wheeler has suggested that any aureus reaching the Kushan empire or even the states bordering Kushan territory was, as a policy, immediately incised with a view to prevent Roman gold issues from competing with the Kushan gold currency which was minted from the metal obtained by melting the aurei.[32] The discovery of a few non-defaced aurei on the fringes of the Kushan empire has been ascribed to administrative negligence. The fact that Roman gold coins, except the *stupa* find from Ahin Posh, are rare in Kushan territory lends support to this view. This theory, however, does not consider the distribution of slashed coins, many of which have been discovered in the Andhra-Tamilnadu region, at a great distance from the Kushan empire. Also, the Kushan emperors post-date the majority of the slashed coins found in India. Wheeler has contended that the slashing was reserved for the aurei alone. According to him, the denarii were not slashed because there were no silver coinages comparable to the denarii in India during the first two centuries AD and hence, the risk of the incoming foreign silver issues competing with the local silver currency did not exist. This line of argument is again not valid because of the subsequent discoveries of the major slashed denarii hoards of Akkanpalle and Nasthullapur. Moreover, as pointed out earlier, the silver punch marked coins, some of which were equal in weight to the Roman denarius, were in circulation, at least in south India, during the period of Roman trade.

According to W. Theobald, the slashes were effected, long after the Roman coins reached India, by Muslims who wanted to be hailed as the 'breakers' and not the 'sellers' of idols.[33] He has further stated that the coins buried within *stupas* were not incised because those shrines predate the Muslim conquest of India. This theory can be dismissed on the grounds that even the latest hoard containing defaced coins (Gumada hoard) was buried in the fourth century AD, nearly five centuries before Islam spread to India. Further, the limited number of Roman coins found in north and north-west India and the adjoining regions, where Islam was dominant almost throughout the medieval period, have not been slashed. On the other hand, most of the slashed coins are found in the extreme south where Muslim rule was not known until the fourteenth century AD. Paula Turner has opined that the chisel cuts on the coins are very different from the damage inflicted by Muslim iconoclasts on the sculptures of Elephanta (Maharashtra).[34]

Yet another opinion, not very widely known, expressed by T.G. Aravamuthan, is that the slashing was done in regions hostile to Rome such as Arabia and to a limited extent, Africa. The defaced Roman coins would have reached India along with other items of trade from these regions.[35] According to him, unlike Indians, the people of Arabia were well aware that the busts on the obverse of Roman coins were that of the Roman emperors or other members of the royal household while the figures on the reverse were those of gods and goddesses. Hence, the Arabians deliberately defaced the obverse bust to express their indignation against Rome. Aravamuthan has identified a number of specimens of slashed coins in Africa and in the Black Sea region. He has concluded that defacing the coins of a political rival was a common practice in these regions but was unknown in ancient India. However, the absence of slashed gold and silver Roman coins in all the countries lying between Rome and India makes it difficult to accept Aravamuthan's reasoning.

Another well known suggestion, proposed by P.L. Gupta, is that the early rulers of south India would have incised Roman coins merely to obliterate the denominational value of the issues and validate them as local currency.[36] This was done to save time, energy and expense involved in minting new coins. In the same vein, Ajay Mitra Shastri has argued that the obverse bust was obliterated so that the circulation of foreign coins as currency in India would not adversely affect the political prestige and status of the local rulers in the eyes of the public.[37] Here again, it may be noted that Indians would have had little knowledge, if any, of the Roman denominational system and, the punching of minute countermarks, instead of the unsightly slashes, would have been a far better and easier method of authenticating foreign coins as a local medium of exchange. Further, if there was a regular system of incising Roman coins immediately after their import into India, one would expect a larger number of slashed finds in all parts of the country, or at least a paucity of unslashed issues in a particular area—probably near a major port—where the practice of slashing all the incoming foreign issues would have been a regular feature. But in all areas of the country, including the Andhra-Tamilnadu region which has yielded the maximum number of slashed issues, unslashed coins far outnumber the defaced ones. Even among the known slashed hoards, there is hardly any find in the coastal areas where the arrival of foreign coins by sea could be expected. All this evidence clearly suggests that the slashing of coins was a localized phenomenon confined to a few pockets in the interior regions of India and was not a systematically organized practice.

According to Paula Turner, the reasons for the slashing of gold coins are entirely different from those of silver ones.[38] The defacement of the gold issues, according to her, can be directly linked to Nero's monetary reform (AD 64) that reduced the purity of the denarius by 11 per cent and the weight of the aureus by 4 per cent. Prior to Nero's reign, Indian traders would have readily accepted any Roman gold coin offered to them as they would have been sure of its purity and weight, specially because the weight of the aureus was stable during the early Julio-Claudian period. After AD 64, specimens of the new lighter aurei were brought to India along with the heavier pre-reform coins. At this juncture, a few Indian traders may probably have decided to slash the old heavier aurei to differentiate them from the post-reform aurei. Incidentally, this would have also checked the practice of sending the heavier coins back to Rome, for whatever reason, because such incised coins would have been viewed with suspicion even in Rome. The fact that most of the incised coins found in India were issued before AD 64 lends support to this view. In fact, a few of the defaced post-AD 64 coins such as the three Vespasian aurei from Pudukkottai are almost similar in weight to the pre-reform issues. This theory, however, does not account for the defacement of the royal heads portrayed on the coins and the presence of many non-defaced pre-AD 64 coins along with the incised ones in the various hoards. It should be noted that slash marks also appear on a few post-first century AD aurei of very low weight.

Regarding the silver coins, Turner has argued that they were mutilated to prevent their competing with the Sātavāhana silver coinage issued by Gautamiputra Sātakarṇi between AD 70 and 90. This argument can be supported by the fact that all the three known slashed denarii hoards—Akkanpalle, Nasthullapur and Belgaum—were in the Sātavāhana territory. This theory can be refuted on the grounds that non-defaced Roman silver coins are not uncommon in the Sātavāhana region. If the denarii were incised merely to ensure that they did not compete with the local silver currency, then one would expect that the Roman aurei would have been left untouched at least in south India where none of the local dynasties including the Sātavāhanas had an indigenous gold currency system. However, slashed aurei belonging to the same period as the denarii have been recovered in large numbers and interestingly, all the major slashed aurei hoards, except Pudukkottai, are in the Andhra region, very much within the Sātavāhana domain. Further, the Andhra region has also yielded slashed coins of the post-Sātavāhana period, viz., the fourth century issues from Gumada.

Turner has put forward the theory that the slashes on the Akkanpalle and Nasthullapur coins may be the result of Buddhist iconoclasm. The main flaw in this theory is the absence of slash marks on the figures of Greaco-Roman gods and goddesses invariably portrayed on the reverse of these coins. Moreover, the Sātavāhana coins depicting the royalty and Hindu deities were not defaced.

Another suggestion linking the slashing of the coins with Nero's reforms has been proposed by R. Champakalakshmi and R. Sumathi.[39] According to them, during the years following Nero's reign, there was a heavy demand, within the Roman empire, for the pre-reform coins which had a higher intrinsic value than the new issues. The nominal value of the Roman coins was not recognized by Indians who accepted these coins mainly as bullion. Hence, Roman merchants would have made special efforts to trade only in the older coins—the heavier aurei and the purer denarii—with India for a profit, instead of the new issues, both of which had the same nominal value in the Roman market. In these circumstances, it is likely that the Roman government decided to slash the pre-reform coins to invalidate them as legal tender not only to prevent their circulation within the Roman empire but also to positively discourage their export to Asia. A few Western traders who somehow managed to procure limited quantities of the slashed issues may have brought them to India. This view is not plausible because it is highly unlikely that the Roman government decided to deface some of its own issues merely to invalidate them as legal currency among its subjects, specially when it had other more effective means at its command to organize a total recall of the older coinage. Also, such slashed coins have not been found anywhere in the Roman empire. This theory is based on the erroneous assumption that all the defaced pre-AD 64 coins in India reached this country after AD 64. Further, this theory does not take into account the significant differences in the types of incision found on the coins of the various hoards.

Thus, each of these theories of the significance of slashing is flawed in one or more ways. Future discoveries and studies may shed light on the precise purpose of these chisel cuts.

Slashed coins, other than Roman coins, are extremely rare in India, specially in south India. The collection of the State Archaeological Museum in Hyderabad includes an Ikśvāku lead coin bearing a prominent chisel mark on the trunk of the elephant depicted on the obverse. This mark is strikingly similar to some of the slash marks on the Roman coins in Andhra.

## COUNTERMARKED COINS

Another peculiar characteristic of Roman coin finds in India is the depiction of countermarks on some of the coins. The marks include dots, crescents, circles, lines and letters of the Roman alphabet such as C and S (Fig. 1). All these marks are extremely small in size.[40]

Most of the earlier scholars either failed to observe these countermarks or chose to ignore them. It is indeed surprising that many coins of the wellknown hoards that have been extensively photographed and published bear interesting countermarks which have not been studied or described. The tiny marks are rarely discernible in the published photographs of these coins. In the course of this study, it was observed that these marks are fairly widespread; a re-examination of a number of hoards revealed several new types of marks on the coins. Many published hoards which may include countermarked coins are, however, not available for study.

There are instances, particularly in the case of worn silver coins, where it has been very difficult to ascertain whether some of the minute lines, curves and dots are actually countermarks or mere accidental scratches. Also, the countermarks are sometimes partially obliterated by slash marks.

There are around 1,500 well attested countermarked coins spread over 16 sites. In addition, the Government Museum in Madras has in its possession a few gold and silver coins of unknown provenance, bearing countermarks such as circles and crescents. Besides, a research article by Peter Berghaus has reported an unusual countermarked coin—an imitation of a Caracalla aureus countermarked on the obverse with the 'shell of Travancore' (conch symbol?).[41]

The maximum number of finds is from Andhra Pradesh. In Tamilnadu, most of the finds are from the Coimbatore-Salem region.

The site-wise break-up of the countermarked coins is given in Table 2.

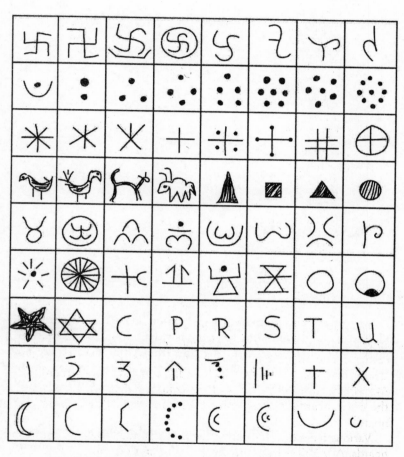

FIG. 1. SOME COUNTERMARKS ON ROMAN COINS IN INDIA

TABLE 2

| Site | Number of Countermarked Coins |
|---|---|
| *Tamilnadu* | |
| Akhilandapuram | 3 |
| Budinatham | 200+ |
| Koneripatti | 3+ |
| Pudukkottai | 1 |
| Madurai(?) | 1 |
| *Kerala* | |
| Nedumkandam | 1 |
| Valuvally | 1 |
| *Indian Islands* | |
| Kadmat Island | 2 |
| *Karnataka* | |
| Yeshwantpur | 1 |
| *Andhra Pradesh* | |
| Akkanpalle | 1279[42] |
| Darmavaripalem | 1 |
| Kudavelli | 2 |
| Nagavarappupadu | 10+ |
| Nasthullapur | 4 |
| Peddabankur | 4+ |
| *Uttar Pradesh* | |
| ? | 1 |
| TOTAL | 1514+ |

Many of the countermarked issues occur in hoards. At Kudavelli and Peddabankur, countermarked coins have been found in the stratified context. The circumstances of the find from Uttar Pradesh are not clear. There is no hoard in which all the coins are countermarked. At Akkanpalle, over 80 per cent of the coins are marked but in most of the other hoards, marked coins constitute a small percentage of the hoard.

Various types of marks have been noted on the coins of the different hoards. At Akhilandapuram, the countermarks are only on the obverse of the coins. An Augustan issue from this find bears the 'S' mark just beyond the royal head, near the lips of the emperor. Another issue of Augustus portrays a small scratch with the numeral '2' below it in front of the neck of the bust. The letter 'C' is marked near the chin of the bust on one of the Tiberian issues from this hoard.

The Koneripatti denarii have marks only on the obverse. All the marked coins of the find are of Tiberius. These marks include dots, curves and small strokes. Dots, lines and letters of the Roman alphabet appear on some of the coins from Budinatham. In the Pudukkottai hoard, a Nerovian aureus of the 'wreath reverse' type bears the countermark 'R' on the obverse. The worn slashed Augustan aureus from Madurai(?) bears a circle punch mark just below the chin of the bust on the obverse. The marks on the coins of the Kadmat island are small scratches while the Nerovian aureus from Valuvally has a semi-circle punched on the obverse.

The sole marked coin from Nedumkandam is a Republican issue minted in 50 BC. The coin has on the cheek of the obverse bust, two marks—a prominent crescent and below it, a much smaller crescent. This is the only specimen of a countermarked Roman Republican coin in India.

An Augustan denarius from Yeshwantpur (Karnataka) is reported to bear the countermark 'KARKH' in Persian language below the figure of a galloping horse of Gaius Caesar on the reverse. As Karkh is the name of a town in Persia built around the eighth century AD by Marufi Karkhi, a Sufi saint, it is believed that this coin was brought to India by a Persian horse dealer and the countermark, appropriately placed below the figure of a horse, may be the identification mark of the dealer.[43] However, the unworn condition of the coin is indicative of the fact that it was buried long before the eighth century AD.

As many as 59 distinct marks have been noted in the Akkanpalle hoard. These include 'dot within crescent', various forms of *svastika*, a wheel with 16 spokes, birds, a three arched hill, triangles, stars, circles of varying sizes, 'dot within circle', two dots, three dots, four dots, five dots, six dots and seven dots. The commonest mark is, however, the 'dot within crescent' which is depicted both alone as well as in association with other symbols. The majority of the coins of the hoard have marks only on the obverse but some issues have marks only on the reverse; a few coins are marked on both sides.

The Darmavaripalem hoard contains an aureus of Nero which has a mark resembling the letter 'P' punched close to the temple depicted on the reverse.

In the Nagavarappupadu hoard, the coins have marks on the obverse. A Tiberian aureus from the hoard bears a unique star-shaped punch mark (nine-petalled flower or wheel?) in front of the eyes of the royal bust. Another Tiberian aureus bears three punch marks, all circles; the circle on the royal head is slightly smaller than the one behind the bust; the third one which is almost equal in size to the one on the head appears in front of the neck. Some other coins of the hoard have circles and crescents of various sizes on or near the bust. On a few coins, the marks are obscured by the unsightly slashes.

At Nasthullapur, countermarks are seen on the obverse of two Augustan and two Tiberian slashed denarii. These marks are tiny circles punched on or near the bust. The Peddabankur coins depict dots and scratches.

Kudavelli is the only site where countermarked late Roman gold coins have been recovered. The two coins from the site are countermarked on the obverse. One of the coins, an issue of Constantius II (AD 337-61), bears the countermark 'X⊐⊐'. The other coin, an issue of Anastasius (AD 491-518), depicts small cross marks or scratch marks.

The Augustan denarius from Uttar Pradesh has the letter 'U' (or crescent?) near the lips of the royal figure on the obverse.

It is clear that the marks are usually on the obverse although not unknown on the reverse. These marks are generally seen on the obverse or reverse device or on the legends or in the space between the device and the legends. One cannot visualize any pattern in the depiction of the various marks or symbols. A large number of coins bear a single mark but several coins, mainly from Akkanpalle and Nagavarappupadu, have two, three or even four marks in various combinations. There does not seem to be any 'relationship' between the marks and no particular 'combination of marks' appears on more than a few coins.

It is, however, significant to note that certain types of markings predominate in a specific area or site. For example, religious symbols such as the *nandipāda*, *svastika* and *ćakra* are all confined to the Roman coins from Akkanpalle. Although these symbols are equally sacred to the Hindus, Buddhists and even the Jains, on the basis of circumstantial and contextual evidence, it may be inferred that these symbols on the Akkanpalle coins are undoubtedly connected with Buddhism.[44] All the denarii from the site are of the first century AD—a period when Buddhism was popular in the Andhra region. Further, as will be discussed later, Buddhist monasteries in Andhra and elsewhere actively participated in the maritime trade and Buddhist monks and pilgrims were familiar with and had access to Roman coins.

Again, religious symbols and other marks commonly seen on *kārśāpanas* are often countermarked on the Roman coins in the Andhra country but are rarely seen on the Roman coins from Tamilakam. A possible reason for this is that the punch marked coins were in more intense circulation and for a much longer time in the former region than in the latter. This view is corroborated by the fact that finds of *kārśāpaṇas* are more numerous in the Andhra territory than in the Tamil country. In this context, it may also be noted that many of the *kārśāpaṇa* finds in Tamilnadu appear to have been brought there from north India via Andhra as a result of inland trade. At Nasthullapur in Andhra, countermarked Roman coins are found in association with eight *kārśāpaṇas*. Surprisingly, the symbols on these eight *kārśāpaṇas* are not found among the countermarks on any of the Roman coins in India.

Roman coins countermarked with letters of the Roman alphabet and numerals are more common in Tamilnadu than in Andhra.

Among the other types of marks, circles and crescents of varying sizes are the most numerous. These are depicted on Roman coins from many sites in Kerala, Tamilnadu and Andhra.

Most of the countermarked Roman coins are of silver and are predominated by the issues of Augustus and Tiberius. Marked gold issues, restricted to a few sites, mostly belong to the period of Nero or later. The majority of the coins were countermarked in the second half of the first century AD—at a time when the slashing of some of the Roman coins was also in vogue.

The few countermarks on the post-first century AD Roman coins are mostly not Buddhist motifs or *kārśāpaṇa* symbols but mere dots and scratches. The apparent reason for this is that the second-third centuries AD saw a marked decline in the circulation of punch marked coins in all parts of India as also the decline of the early Buddhist centres in Andhra.

There are varying views on the precise significance or purpose of these countermarks. The likelihood of these marks being effected to test the quality of the metal is ruled out because many of the marks are intricate floral or geometric designs. According to P.L. Gupta, while the slash marks cancelled out the issuing authority, the countermarks were intended to authenticate these foreign coins as local currency and were thus 'authority symbols'.[45] Gupta's theory implies that the function of the countermark is complementary to that of the slash mark. According to him, the practice of counterstamping foreign coins to validate them as local money was known throughout history.[46] The close similarities between the countermarks on the Roman coins and the symbols on punch marked coins lend ample support to this theory.

Recently, T. Sathyamurthy has hinted that the countermarks on the Roman coins may be 'bankers marks' effected in India prior to the circulation of these foreign coins in the country.[47] He has pointed out that the semi-circle countermarks on the reverse of some of the *kārśāpaṇas* from the Angamali hoard (Kerala) and the same mark on the Nero aureus from Valuvally may be that of a local banking institution operating in the Kerala region.

N.C. Ghosh and K. Ismail's contention that these countermarks may have been devised as a simpler and aesthetically better substitute for the ugly slash marks[48] is not acceptable because several countermarked coins such as those from Akkanpalle, Nasthullapur, Nagavarappupadu and Pudukkottai are also slashed. One is, however, not sure whether the countermarking followed the slashing of each of these coins.

Many scholars like N.C. Ghosh, K. Ismail, Paula Turner and Peter Berghaus have described these countermarks as ownership or identification marks.[49] While broadly agreeing with them, it is important to add that the necessity of stamping one's ownership mark would arise only on specific occasions when the coins (wealth) belonging to different individuals were handed over for safe custody to a single moneylender or banking institution. Significantly, early Indian epigraphs allude to such deposition of coins with corporate bodies.[50]

Coins with only one countermark may have been deposited either once or on many occasions by one individual while coins with numerous marks may have been in the possession of various individuals during different periods of their circulation, each of whom would have stamped his own mark before placing the coins in the custody of a trader or a guild. Countermarks depicting letters of the Roman alphabet would have been inspired by the legends on Roman coins. The marks were effected not only by Indians but also by foreign traders residing in India.

Countermarked denarii are more numerous than the countermarked aurei because foreign silver coins would have circulated among a larger section of the population and consequently would have been more frequently deposited with moneylenders. The paucity of such marks on indigenous coins of south India is due to the fact that these coins were considered less valuable than the foreign ones for hoarding and depositing with banking agencies.

## IMITATION COINS

Imitations of Roman issues have been discovered in more than 25 sites mainly spread over Madhya Pradesh, Maharashtra, Andhra Pradesh, Karnataka, Kerala and Tamilnadu. Further, some coins vaguely labelled as 'found in India/south India/Andhra' are part of various private and public collections.[51] Thus, unlike the genuine Roman coins which are unevenly scattered over large areas of the Indian subcontinent, the imitations are confined to select 'pockets' of west and south India.

Numerically, the maximum number of imitation coins are from Madurai and Karur. They are, however, more widespread in the Andhra region where at least 15 sites have revealed imitations but the number of specimens from each find is comparatively small. The finds from all other regions are very few.

Many of the imitations are found in hoards, for instance Akkanpalle, Darmavaripalem, Gumada, Nagavarappupadu, Nasthullapur, Veeravasaramu and Weepangandla (Andhra); Uppavahr (Maharashtra); Akkialur (Karnataka); Valuvally (Kerala); and Soriyapattu and Malaiyadiputhur (Tamilnadu). Important sites where the imitations have been found in the stratified context are Peddabankur (Plate 6), Dhulikatta and Kondapur in Andhra. The remaining imitations are stray finds of two or three coins, mostly on the surface and rarely under the ground.

It is pertinent to note some general physical characteristics of the imitations. In many cases, the workmanship of the imitations compares favourably with that of the genuine coins. Imitations from such sites as Gumada and Valuvally are stylistically inferior to the original coins. In fact, the human figures on many of the Gumada coins appear like thumbnail sketches devoid of illusion of depth or sense of movement. This presents a sharp contrast to the gods and kings displaying robust physiognomy usually seen on the genuine Roman coins. The legends on many of the imitations of the first century AD Roman coins are, except for some minor errors, identical to those on the original issues. But the legends on the imitations of the later periods often appear to be meaningless combinations of letters of the Roman alphabet and in some instances, are mere dots, circles and tiny vertical lines, clearly indicating that the producers of these coins had absolutely no knowledge of the Roman script. Another significant feature is that while genuine Roman coins are invariably die-struck, the copies are both die-struck and cast. The imitations in gold reported from Nagavarappupadu, Gootiparti and Valuvally are die-struck while those from several other sites such as Darmavaripalem and Veeravasaramu appear to be cast. The imitations in silver are, however, largely die-struck. Both these techniques seem to have been simultaneously in vogue throughout the period when the imitations were produced. Due to the non-availability of many of the imitations for physical verification, it is not possible to determine

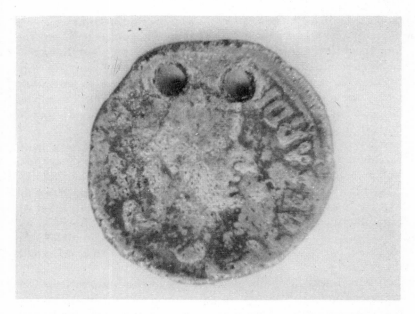

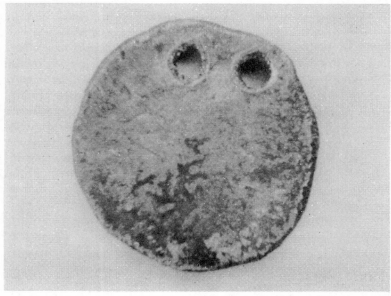

PLATE 6. PIERCED IMITATION TIBERIUS DENARIUS FROM
STRATIFIED LAYERS–PEDDABANKUR (ANDHRA):
OBVERSE (ABOVE) AND REVERSE (BELOW)

whether the copies produced through any one of these techniques predominated in any given region.

Very few hoards such as Nosagere in Karnataka and Gopalapuram in Andhra exclusively contain imitation coins. The number of coins in such hoards is normally very small, not exceeding four or five. In hoards such as Akkanpalle and Nasthullapur, genuine coins constitute over 95 per cent of the total coins of the find. On the other hand, in Gumada, Veeravasaramu and Darmavaripalem, over 90 per cent of the coins are imitations. In the Malayadiputhur hoard, the original and imitation coins are equally represented. In any given region or area, imitations constitute a small percentage of the total Roman coin finds in the region.

Imitations of the Roman Republican coins are unknown in India. The copies vary in date from the first century AD to the seventh–eighth centuries AD. The first century AD imitations are limited but there is a steady increase in the number of imitations of the second–fifth centuries. Imitations of the fourth-fifth centuries number in thousands, specially in Madurai and Karur. Imitations of a very late date, i.e. seventh-eighth centuries AD have been reported from a few sites such as Madurai and Weepangandla. Such finds are, however, very rare and they belong to a period after the cessation of regular commercial ties between India and the Mediterranean region.

There are certain similarities in the composition and chronology of the imitation and genuine Roman coin finds in India. As the earliest Roman coins brought to India were of silver, the earliest imitations were also of silver. All the known silver imitations are of Augustan or Tiberian types. Silver imitations began to be produced in the mid-first century AD. The manufacture of gold imitations also began, although on a very small scale, during the first century AD itself, a few years after the production of the denarii copies. Nagavarappupadu has yielded three first century AD gold imitations—two of Augustus and one of Claudius—while a gold imitation coin of Tiberius has been found at Nagarjunakonda. The maximum number of gold imitations were, however, produced during the second-third centuries AD—a period when the majority of genuine Roman coins exported to India were of gold. Again, just like the genuine Roman gold issues of the second century AD, the imitation aurei of this period are also found in small batches and are scattered throughout Andhra and Maharashtra—Gumada and Darmavaripalem are the largest among such finds containing 19+ and 23 imitations, respectively.

Lead imitations of Roman issues, unknown outside India, have been recovered during the course of archaeological excavations at Nevasa (one coin), Kondapur (two coins), Veerapuram (one coin) and Peddabankur (four+? coins). One of the issues from Kondapur is fully plated with gold. Some of the lead imitations from Peddabankur are also silver plated. It is significant to note that all these lead imitations are of Augustan or Tiberian type and are found within the Sātavāhana territory along with Sātavāhana antiquities.

As the export of genuine Roman copper coins was at its height in the fourth-fifth centuries AD, the majority of the imitations during this period in India were also of copper. Most of these imitations, as noted earlier, have been discovered in Madurai and Karur; the finds from Madurai far outnumber those from Karur. Reports of the finds from Madurai have been appearing regularly since the third quarter of the nineteenth century, while the finds from Karur have been discovered only after 1985. While imitation finds from the other parts of the subcontinent are either regular hoards mostly in an earthenware pot or accidental discoveries of two to four coins, at Madurai and Karur, imitation coins are frequently discovered in many parts of the old township and its surroundings, mainly in the river beds—river Vaigai near Madurai and river Amaravati in Karur. Most of the imitations in copper are small, worn out, irregular pieces of metal having lost their original circular shape probably due to decades of circulation before being finally buried or lost. It has, however, been argued by Peter Berghaus that the poor condition of the coins is the result of corrosion caused by the rivers (Vaigai and Amaravati) during the period when the issues were buried in the soil and also due to the improper methods of cleaning them, adopted by the finders.[52] The legends on most of these imitations are blurred and the royal bust on the obverse is hazy, making the task of identifying the Roman emperors represented on the specimens difficult. The reverse of many of these coins portray two or three Roman warriors standing with spears in their hands. Often, several genuine late Roman copper coins have also been found along with the imitations at both Madurai and Karur. It may be noted that such finds are common in Sri Lanka as well, although the number of imitations in the Ceylonese finds is higher than those in the Indian finds. Further, while the finds in India are mainly confined to Madurai and Karur, in Sri Lanka, they have been discovered in several coastal and inland sites in hoards and/or in stratified contexts.[53]

The origin and purpose of Roman imitations in India remains a debated issue. It has been repeatedly argued that these imitations were not minted in India but in the Roman empire itself.[54] It should be remembered that Roman imitation coins comparable to those found in India have not been discovered outside the subcontinent.

Genuine Roman coins circulated as money in several parts of ancient India and imitations were produced whenever there was a scarcity of genuine issues. There are no imitations of the early period of trade (second-first centuries BC), the first copy was, as already mentioned, produced in the middle of the first century AD. This is because the use of Roman coins as money in India would have taken place a few decades after the commencement of the export of Roman coins to India. Moreover, there ought to have been a further lapse of a few decades before there was a shortfall in the supply of the original coins and there was a consequent need to mint imitations. As the number of genuine Roman coins brought to India during the first century AD was very large, the need for imitation coins was minimal; thus the number of imitations in the hoards of the first century AD is less than those in the hoards of the subsequent periods. Again, unlike the first century imitations, the later copies depict different rulers and their distinct coin-motifs on the obverse and reverse in various 'impossible' combinations. This is because the coin producers of the later period had access to specimens of many genuine first century AD and later Roman coins, and they randomly selected the obverse and reverse devices on these for portrayal in several unusual combinations. In some cases, the imitations depict the known obverse and reverse types of a single ruler but in hitherto unknown combinations!

The most clinching evidence in support of the production of imitations in specific regions of India is provided by the distribution pattern of imitation and original coins of the various Roman emperors in India. All regions yielding the imitation issues of a particular ruler also reveal his original issues but the reverse is not always true, i.e. the genuine issues of a ruler are often found in those areas where his imitations are not known. If the imitations were produced abroad and were exported to India along with the genuine coins, then it would be expected that any region revealing the original issues of a ruler would also yield a few imitations ascribed to him. Since the imitations of a particular coin type are found in only a few of the various places which have revealed the originals of that type, it may be inferred that the copies were produced in or near the areas where they have been recovered, solely for the purpose of local circulation. For instance, there have been over fifty finds of Augustan issues in India of which only about six finds, all confined to the Andhra region, contain imitations. Similarly, Tiberian issues have been reported from more than fifty four finds spread across the subcontinent, from Taxila in the north-west to Eyyal in the south, but the imitations of this ruler are found in only seven sites of which six are in Andhra.

In all likelihood most of the imitations were produced in a few places in west and south India. All the imitations of gold coins from Darma-varipalem, Gumada, Veeravasaramu, Gopalapuram and Uppavahr show identical workmanship thereby indicating that all these coins were issued from a single mint which was probably located in Andhra. Regarding the silver imitations, most of which have been unearthed in the Andhra country, these were probably minted either in or near Akkanpalle which has yielded the largest number of denarii copies or at Dhulikatta where a single silver imitation coin was found in the course of archaeological excavations. The latter site was significantly a mint town. Although imitation coins were normally in circulation in limited areas, the solitary denarius copy from Arikamedu reached the site from Andhra possibly along the coast. Again, lead imitations may have been produced at Kondapur which was a major mint town; the site revealed hundreds of coins including Sātavāhana specimens in potin and lead, as also punch marked issues along with their moulds.[55] The site has even revealed a rare burnt dark grey terracotta 'proof piece' (model) of the reverse of the silver portrait coin of the Sātavāhana ruler Vāsiṣṭhiputra Śivaśri Puḷumāvi.[56] The lack of lead imitations of post-first century AD foreign coins may be because in south India, specially Andhra, even the local lead coins are very rare after the decline of the Sātavāhanas and the Ikṣvākus.

The copper imitations were produced in Madurai and Karur. As there are no copper deposits in or around these two places, it may be inferred that the copper mines in Andhra provided the raw material for these imitations. Both Karur and Madurai were royal capitals and mint towns. At Karur, two interesting bronze dies have been recovered—a cylindrical Roman coin die bearing the portrait and legend occurring on Hadrian's coins[57] and the die of a punch marked coin.[58] The latter die is similar to the *kārṣāpaṇa* die earlier discovered at Eran in Madhya Pradesh.

Until recently there were no copper mines in Sri Lanka and hence many scholars have asserted that the island imported copper for the production of imitations. In recent years, however, copper deposits have been located in the island and it has been proved that the smelting of copper was known to the local people even during the early iron age.

According to Sudharshan Seneviratne, South Asia's largest copper-magnetite deposit south of the Bihar–Orissa region is in Sri Lanka. Brāhmī inscriptions in the island specifically refer to guilds of coppersmiths.[59]

As the Indian imitations were probably produced with royal sanction, with the objective of using them as local legal tender along with the genuine ones but without any intention of criminal fraudulence, many of the Indian imitations equal not only in weight but also in the purity of the metal, genuine Roman coins. It is likely that the services of a Roman artisan who came to India or an Indian coinmaker trained by him in the skills of low relief die cutting, could have been utilized to make the copies which certainly exhibit a higher level of workmanship than most of the early Indian issues including the *kārśāpaṇas* and the early Chera and Sātavāhana coins. Indeed, these imitations have often been hailed as the best specimens of early south Indian numismatic art.

The view that imitation coins were treated as currency on par with genuine Roman coins is substantiated by the fact that the slash marks and countermarks seen on some of the genuine Roman coins in India are found on the imitations as well. Further, both the original Roman and imitation coins are often found together, sometimes along with the early Indian coins.

The paucity of imitations in many parts of India may be explained by the fact that the copies were not produced regularly or at frequent intervals but solely in response to a demand for more coins in a specific area during a given period and each such batch of newly minted coins was mainly used for circulation within that region alone and at the most, for trade with a neighbouring kingdom. Hence, although the imitations were accepted as legal tender on par with the genuine issues, they were not in circulation over large areas because of the very reason for which they were produced, i.e. to offset the shortfall in the supply of genuine coins in an area. Thus, regions not yielding Roman imitations may be of two types:

1. Regions where Roman currency was not used as a medium of exchange and therefore the need for local imitations of the foreign currency did not arise. For example, north-west India where genuine Roman coins were known but only Kushan and other local issues were used as money.
2. Places which did not face a scarcity of foreign coins for use as money, such as the Coimbatore region in Tamilnadu.

According to T.G. Aravamuthan, the legends on some of the Gumada imitations resemble the letters of the Brāhmī script.[60] Further, the letters forming the legend on the imitation Claudius aureus from Nagavar-appupadu have been described by Krishna Sastry as resembling Brāhmī.[61] However, physical examination of these hoards did not reveal a single Brāhmī letter on any of the coins; the legends in all these cases are similar to those on other imitation coins in India. After a lengthy and confusing discussion of the subject, Aravamuthan finally concluded that the resemblance between the Gumada coin legends and the Brāhmī script does not exclude the possibilities of resemblance of the legends to a system of writing which may have been used outside India![62]

## CIRCULATION OF ROMAN COINS IN INDIA

The most crucial question pertaining to Roman coin finds in India is whether any of these issues were in circulation as a medium of exchange in the subcontinent.

Opinions have been expressed both in favour of and against the theory of the circulation of Roman coins as currency in ancient India. Most of these views are based on certain characteristics such as slash marks and countermarks found on some of the Roman coins in India. The views supporting the 'non-circulation theory' may be examined first.

It is widely believed that the Roman coins—specially gold coins—were received in India purely for their intrinsic value. In fact, the *Periplus* (49) categorically states that at the port of Barygaza (Gujarat), Roman' gold and silver coins were exchanged for the local Indian currency at a profit. This, however, is surprising because all the known early Indian issues, barring the Kushan coinage, were tiny pieces of silver, lead or copper and were not a match for the foreign currency either in terms of purity of metal or aesthetic value. Most of the local coins were much lighter than the Roman issues; the few silver punch marked coins which are equal in weight to the Roman denarii being an exception. Thus, in normal circumstances, it is extremely unlikely that Roman traders expressed a desire to acquire the native Indian coins for any purpose whatsoever. However, on the basis of the *Periplus*' statement, it has been argued by David MacDowall and N.G. Wilson that the Roman denarii would have been received by the Western Kshatrapas, most probably during the reign of Nahapana, purely as bullion and later melted for minting the Kshatrapa silver specie and the resultant profit was shared between the suppliers of bullion (Roman traders) and the local minting authority.[63] They have added that this may be the only way in which Roman coins could have been exchanged with the native coins, to the advantage of the foreign merchants. This theory alluding to the non-circulation of foreign silver coins as money in India is silent on the aurei which too, according to the *Periplus,* were exchanged for a profit with the local issues. Further, it is unbelievable that the minting of silver coins by the Western Kshatrapas yielded huge profits for them and that even if profits had accrued, they would have been shared with the foreign merchants. A more plausible explanation is that the flourishing port of Barygaza may have like Ter in Maharashtra and Arikamedu near Pondicherry, supported a regular colony of Roman merchants who would have exchanged a few aurei and denarii for large quantities of the indigenous currency for their everyday transactions.

Some of the reasons propounded by scholars like G.F. Hill, Mortimer Wheeler and Paula Turner for the slashing of Roman coins in India, indirectly support the theory that these coins did not circulate as money in this country.[64]

Turner has observed that several Roman coins, specially the denarii, in the hoards, are unworn and seem to have been buried soon after they reached India.[65] She has reiterated that the Roman issues did not circulate as money but were hoarded as bullion. She has also cited the scarcity of Roman coins in excavated contexts as evidence that Indians did not use these issues as currency in their daily transactions.

In his recent study, David MacDowall has suggested that except the late Roman coppers of the fourth-fifth centuries AD found mainly in Madurai and Sri Lanka, none of the other Roman coins ever circulated as money in India.[66] A series of currency reforms in Rome, during the first century AD and later, steadily reduced the weight of the aureus and denarius and hence, he has argued that as these coins were valued in India, not as a denomination in the Roman monetary system but for their bullion content, older issues containing a greater proportion of gold or silver were carefully selected for export to the subcontinent. He has concluded that the large number of worn Roman coins found in India were exported to this country after being reduced to this state of wear due to decades of circulation within the Roman empire itself.

Another argument in favour of the non-circulation theory has been put forth by Balram Srivastava. According to him, as minting was under state control in early historical India, the local government would have thwarted all attempts of Roman traders to circulate foreign coins in the Indian markets, as it would have adversely affected the region's economy.[67] This view is merely based on the doubtful factor of royal control and its effectiveness on the minting and circulation of coins during the early period; in fact, the local coins may have been issued by merchant organizations or trade guilds. Further, there is no reason for the local ruler to object to the introduction of the readily available Roman gold coins as circulation money, specially in the light of the fact that such a move would have provided a boost to large-scale trade, in which most of the early ruling families evinced an interest.

It has recently been argued by I.K..Sarma that south Indians may have never thought of using the foreign coins as money but would have certainly preserved these coins as decorative objects.[68] In support of this line of argument, he has drawn attention to the extremely limited occurrence of these coins in a large and commercially important excavated habitation site as Nagarjunakonda (Andhra). Sarma has also suggested that the aurei may have been used by the kings and nobles in religious ritual.

The use of Roman coins as jewellery in ancient India, as evidenced by the occurrence of pierced coins meant to be used as pendants, also indicates that these coins did not circulate as legal tender in the sub-continent. But the pierced coin finds are so few that it is impossible to accept that Roman coins were mainly used as jewels.

Regarding the arguments in favour of the 'circulation theory', it is significant to note that the same characteristics such as slash marks which were used by scholars in favour of the 'non-circulation theory' have been differently interpreted by other scholars to support the theory that Roman issues did serve as legal tender in parts of ancient India. Interestingly, scholars like G.F. Hill and Wheeler have put forth several arguments both in favour of and against the 'circulation theory'. Many scholars favour the 'partial circulation theory', that is, certain varieties of Roman coins were used as money in specific regions of India.

Some of the interpretations of G.F. Hill, P.L. Gupta and Ajay Mitra Shastri regarding the slash marks on Roman coins admit, albeit indirectly, that these coins circulated as currency in India.[69] Even B.N. Mukherjee has opined that the slashing of coins may indicate an attempt on the part of the authorities in various regions of India to remind the people using these coins as money that the bust on the coins did not represent the local ruler.[70] It may be recalled that the countermarking of Roman coins has also been interpreted by P.L. Gupta as evidence that these coins circulated as money in India. [71]

According to Robert Sewell, among all the Roman coin finds in India, the late Roman coppers recovered from Madurai alone seem to have most effectively served as a local medium of exchange, mainly among the Roman, Syrian and Egyptian merchants residing at Madurai in the fourth-fifth centuries AD.[72] This view is substantiated by the fact that these foreign merchants would have been familiar with the Roman monetary system and hence, would have decided to use the Roman issues for their transactions within India.

A little known theory, put forth by T.G. Aravamuthan, refers to the 'limited circulation' of Roman coins in India. According to him, the coins were regularly brought to the country in batches through the port cities which were also market towns.[73] The native merchants who brought various products from the interior areas to the ports for export to Rome by sea, would have been the first to receive the foreign issues from Roman traders. The local merchants at the ports would have later passed on these Roman coins to the smaller merchants—the middle-men—in the hinterland who, in turn, would have given them to artisans and agriculturists in the remote villages in return for goods which were to be eventually sent to the ports for external trade; the foreign coins would not circulate any further. In other words, these coins would not be used as a medium of exchange among the common masses for their day-to-day transactions for which purpose they would use the thin and small local coins mostly in silver or copper. Further, it has been argued by him that as the Roman issues were mainly in gold and sometimes in silver and as they were much heavier than the indigenous coins, it is possible that a few of the Roman issues may have been, at each stage when they changed hands, melted or lost or bartered by the merchants themselves for their personal requirements. But at no stage would there have been a chance for the coins of a given batch, which may represent the payment received by Indians for a single consignment of goods meant for export to Rome, to be completely scattered or distributed over a wide area within India. Thus, Roman coins occur in significant numbers in each hoard but hoards of indigenous coins are much larger, the reason being that each of the Roman hoards may contain coins from one, or at the most, two batches of denarii or aurei reaching India whereas indigenous coins would be available in very large quantities for the hoarder.

Aravamuthan's arguments imply that Roman coins passed through certain specified trade routes: port city → big merchants → smaller merchants → producer of various products for export, in small towns and villages. This is consistent with the general pattern of distribution of Roman coins in the country. However, the fact that there are a few large Roman coin hoards such as Bamanghati in Orissa which are at a great distance from the main areas of concentration of Roman coin finds would militate against Aravamuthan's reasons for the theory of limited circulation of Roman coins in India. Moreover, the absence of die links among Roman coins belonging to different hoards for which die link analysis has been done, raises serious doubts about the contention that Roman coins were dispatched to India in specific batches which travelled, without being dispersed, through merchants to the remote sites where they were finally hoarded, because if all the coins of a single type belonging to one hoard had reached India together, then it would be expected that a few of those issues would be of the same die.

Wheeler's interesting theory states that a few Roman coins may have circulated as money in certain regions of India for a limited period, while the majority of Roman issues were procured and later buried simply as bullion.[74] Further, he has pointed out that even among the Roman gold and silver coins which served as legal tender, single specimens of these issues barely circulated in India. In most instances, a batch of coins, probably representing a unit of stamped silver or gold of a certain weight agreed upon for a specific wholesale purchase, changed hands amongst the merchants. Many of the Roman coin hoards probably represent the value of such a single commercial transaction. It has been further stated by him that the find from Chandravalli (Karnataka) which has revealed around six denarii—one (or two?) of Augustus, four of Tiberius and an unidentified type—sometimes in association with Sātavāhana coins, in the occupation strata of the site, may be part of a large Roman hoard, and these foreign coins circulated as high value currency in the area. This implies that the Roman aurei and denarii circulated only in 'batches' or 'bulk' within a very small, close-knit, prosperous business community. The non-occurrence of even a single Roman gold or silver coin in the stratified context in the port site of Arikamedu which has yielded several types of Roman antiquities has been cited by Wheeler in support of his theory. According to him, the late Roman coppers (fourth-fifth centuries AD) were used as 'token currency' by the common people of south India and Ceylon.

Recently, H.P. Ray has put forth the theory that in south-east India, Roman coins initially circulated as high value currency and were later used for local trade transactions.[75] The production of Roman imitation coins and the reference to the term '*dināri*' in Ikśvāku epigraphs have been cited by her in support of her argument. She has added that in Western Deccan, Roman coins were valued merely as bullion because this region had its own local currency. This, according to her, explains the comparative paucity of Roman coins on the west coast. However, her observation that during this period, the east coast had no local coinage is wholly incorrect, specially in the context of the discoveries of hundreds of Sangam Chera, Sangam Cōḷa, Sangam Pāṇḍya and Malaiyamān coins in many parts of Tamilnadu.

A thorough analysis of all these views on the circulation or otherwise of Roman coins as money in India leads to the conclusion that slash marks and countermarks do not have any bearing on the question of the circulation of these issues. Four other factors, which have till date not been collectively considered by scholars in the context of the 'circulation theory', are crucial to determine the extent to which these coins were in circulation in India:

1. Finds of Roman coins in archaeological excavations.
2. Finds of early indigenous coins in association with Roman issues in the hoards.
3. The state of wear of the coins, i.e. the incidence of worn coins in the various finds.
4. References to Roman coins in Indian inscriptions and literature.

ROMAN COINS IN EXCAVATIONS

The presence of foreign coins in archaeologically stratified layers facilitates in determining the exact period during which these coins along with the local issues were in use in the different sites. Many of the excavations yielding Roman coins remain unpublished. Even in the published reports, details regarding the precise layer in which the various coins have been discovered and the wear condition of the coins are seldom recorded. Some observations have been made on the basis of the meagre data obtained from these reports, the physical examination of some of the coins as well as personal discussions with a few of the excavators.

Around fifteen sites spread over Pakistan, Maharashtra, Karnataka, Andhra and Tamilnadu have revealed Roman coins in the excavated context. The maximum number of finds (at least nine) is from Andhra (Plate 7).

Most of the finds are from first-second centuries AD layers of habitation sites. Of all the indigenous coin series, the Sātavāhana issues

PLATE. 7. TIBERIUS DENARII FROM STRATIFIED LAYERS,
TOTLAKONDA (ANDHRA):
OBVERSE (ABOVE) AND REVERSE (BELOW)

occur most frequently along with Roman coins in the excavated context at Karnataka-Andhra sites such as Chandravalli, Peddabankur and Bavikonda. At Veerapuram (Andhra), a Roman imitation lead coin has been found along with at least one Sātavāhana coin and two+ Mahārathi coins.

In almost all the excavated sites where Roman issues have been found along with the local ones, the latter greatly outnumber the former, clearly indicating that the local coins constituted the main currency while the foreign issues merely supplemented the indigenous series. Also, in any region, stratified finds of Roman coins are very few compared to hoard finds and 'stray' finds.

The uneven geographical distribution of the stratified finds may provide a clue to the intensity of circulation of Roman issues in the different regions. Thus, compared to the Sātavāhana empire, the circulation of Roman coins in the Kshatrapa territory seems to have been less intense. Hence, it may be recalled that the foreign traders at Barygaza were compelled to exchange a few of their aurei and denarii for large quantities of local issues to be used for their daily living expenses. In the Tamilnadu-Kerala region, the occurrence of stratified Roman coin finds in merely two sites, viz., Karur and Alagankulam is, however, surprising because other evidence indicates that foreign money circulated extensively in the region.

The chronology of the excavated Roman coins also reveals certain interesting facts. No coin belonging to the Roman Republican period has, so far, been recovered in archaeological excavations. Most of the excavated coins are Augustan and Tiberian issues.

Among the excavated finds, silver issues predominate. This may imply that although the foreign gold coins were more numerous in India, the silver ones circulated more extensively probably even for day-to-day transactions. The excavated Roman gold coins are confined to three sites in Andhra—Kudavelli, Nagarjunakonda and Yellesvaram. Alagankulam near Madurai is the only site which has yielded genuine Roman copper coins in the stratified context.

Slashed, countermarked and imitation coins are not unknown among stratified finds. It may be noted that the occurrence of both genuine and imitation Roman coins in the same layer is rather rare, the finds from Peddabankur being the only well attested exception. Roman coins pierced to be used as necklace pendants have also been found in excavations.

## FINDS OF EARLY INDIAN COINS WITH
## ROMAN COINS IN HOARDS

Although the bulk of Roman coins found in India are in hoards, the presence of early Indian coins in these hoards is rare. Hoards containing Roman and Indian coins are almost unknown not only in north and north-west India where Roman coins were not in circulation as money, but even in west India where these coins did circulate as currency, albeit to a limited extent.

The hoards from Nasthullapur and Weepangandla (Andhra), Mambalam, Tondamanathan and Pennar (Tamilnadu) and Eyyal (Kerala) have revealed Roman issues along with punch marked coins. The Claudian aureus and more than six Sangam Chera portrait coins (first century AD?) recovered together from the dry bed of the river Amaravati at Karur (Tamilnadu) are believed to belong to a single hoard, emerging piecemeal. In all these hoards, the indigenous coins are invariably of silver while the Roman coins are of either gold (Weepangandla, Tondamanathan), or silver (Nasthullapur, Mambalam, Pennar), or both gold and silver (Eyyal).

Roman coins in most of these hoards belong to the first century AD. Among these, the issues of Augustus and Tiberius are the most numerous. Slashed, countermarked, imitation and rarely even pierced coins are found in these hoards.

## STATE OF WEAR OF ROMAN COINS FOUND IN INDIA

The state of wear of ancient coins is an indication of the extent to which the coins were in circulation before being lost or buried. Unlike indigenous coins, the state of wear of the foreign issues does not throw much light on the extent to which they were in circulation in India. This is because there is no certainty about the condition in which the foreign coins were transported to India. The occurrence of mint fresh Roman coins in a sizeable number of sites in India may imply that at least some of the worn Roman coins found in this country were reduced to this state of wear solely due to their being circulated in India.

The hoards from Eyyal, Kumbalam, Nedumkandam, Valuvally, Kaliyampattur, Nandyal and Nagavarappupadu exhibit a peculiar phenomenon: while the earliest coins are very worn, there is a gradual improvement in the condition of the later coins in each of these hoards, implying that the later coins did not circulate for long before being buried. No such pattern is, however, discernible in the case of most of the other hoards.

② The condition of the coins in the Kottayam, Madurai Hills, Nathampatti, Soriyapattu and Adam hoards is fairly good. The Kallakinar, Pudukkottai and Uthamapuram hoards and the *stupa* finds from Ahin Posh and Manikyala as also the stray finds from Bandarpattinam and Chakherbedha are extremely worn. Hoards such as Budhinatham, Akkanpalle and Nasthullapur contain worn as well as not-so-worn Augustan and Tiberian issues.

Worn specimens are very common among the late Roman copper coins found at Madurai and Karur.

A significant observation is that the limited number of coins, specially the denarii, obtained from archaeologically stratified layers are more ③ worn than the hoard finds. It may be surmised that the coins from the excavations circulated more extensively among the people whereas the 'hoard coins' would have been mainly used by wealthy traders who alone could afford to possess and stash huge quantities of foreign money.

It is evident that worn and unworn Roman coins occur in all the metals and regions. Similarly, worn and unworn specimens are found among the Roman coins of all periods—from the first century BC down to the eighth century AD.

Worn as well as unworn imitation Roman coins have been reported. Both worn and unworn coins have been slashed, countermarked and even pierced for use as jewellery.

REFERENCES TO ROMAN COINS IN INDIAN
INSCRIPTIONS AND LITERATURE

One of the most important but littleknown aspects pertaining to the circulation of Roman coins in India is the context in which these coins are referred to in inscriptions and literature.

It should be noted that epigraphs directly referring to the aurei or denarii or even Roman traders do not exist in India. Recent studies have revealed that some of the terms and phrases referring to certain types of coins in early Deccani inscriptions allude to the Roman coins which were very common in the Maharashtra-Andhra region during the same period. Similar lithic records referring to Roman money are surprisingly absent in the early Tamil country which has yielded the largest number of Roman coins.

The most relevant record is an inscription from Nashik (Maharashtra) dated Śaka 42 (AD 120) which mentions that 70,000 *kārśāpaṇas* is equivalent to 2,000 *suvarṇas*.[76] The *suvarṇa* mentioned here, no doubt, refers to a gold coin but its identification is problematic. The argument that the term may refer to a Kushan gold coin has been dismissed on the grounds that the site of the inscription was not a part of the Kushan empire and also, Kushan coins were not known in the region. In the absence of any other indigenous gold coin of the early historical period, the *suvarṇa* in the inscription has been, on circumstantial evidence, identified with the Roman aureus.

The integration of imported Roman coins with the local currency system in India is also indicated by a few Ikṣvāku epigraphs found at Nagarjunakonda. Two of the inscriptions here refer to the '*dināri*' and '*dināri-māśaka*' respectively. The *māśaka* is usually equivalent to 1/16th of a 'standard' coin. According to B.D. Chattopadhyaya, the reference to the *dināri* in the inscription may denote the Kshatrapa silver coins which may have circulated in the Ikṣvāku territory and the *māśaka* may refer to certain low weight punch marked coins.[77] On the other hand, Ajay Mitra Shastri has argued that the *dināri* denotes the Roman denarius while the *dināri-māśaka* may be the Ikṣvāku lead coin which would have been assigned the value of 1/16th of a Roman silver coin.[78]

The circulation of Kshatrapa silver coins as currency in the Ikṣvāku domain can, however, be ruled out because of the paucity of these coins in the Andhra country, specially in the stratified context. Hence, Chattopadhyaya's identification of the *dināri* with the Kshatrapa silver coin is unacceptable. Again, the *dināri* cannot be identified with the Roman denarius because while these Ikṣvāku inscriptions are of the third-fourth centuries AD, Roman silver coins were exported to India in the first century AD, and they were buried long before the Ikṣvāku rule. In these circumstances, it may be argued that while the *dināri māśaka* may be the Ikṣvāku lead coin, the *dināri* refers to Roman gold coins that were exported to India during the pre-Ikṣvāku, Ikṣvāku and post-Ikṣvāku periods. Also, the use of Roman aurei exported to India in the first century AD even during the subsequent period is amply attested by the fact that gold imitation coins portraying a combination of the motifs on the Roman aurei of the first century and later were produced in large numbers in the Andhra region. Thus, although Roman coins were used as a medium of exchange from the first century AD itself, it was only during the Ikṣvāku rule that the relative value of the base metal local currency and the foreign gold issues was fixed probably by the royal authority.

Besides the *dināri* and the *suvarṇa*, the term *hiraṇya* mentioned in the Ikṣvāku epigraphs also refers to gold coins which again should have been the Roman aurei alone.[79]

In this connection, the references to coins in the Tamil *Sangam* literature are also relevant. The *Sangam* works mention three distinct terms: *kāśu, kāṇam* and *pon,* all of which also find a place in the medieval inscriptions of south India[80]. *Kāśu* denotes both the coin and the jewel including the bead. *Pon* initially denoted any metal but mainly refers to gold; here again, whether the term *pon* in the *Sangam* literature refers to coins alone or other items of gold as well such as ingots and jewels is not clear. *Kāṇam,* however, definitely refers to a gold coin and as per the available evidence, seems to be the Roman aureus. The denominational relationship between the *kāśu* and the *kāṇam,* however, remians unclear.

In all likelihood, the gifts of gold coins bestowed by the Tamil kings on the *Sangam* bards were the aurei. Roman coins may also have been offered as *dakṣiṇa* to priests and scholars during the performance of Vedic sacrifices by the Tamil kings. These kings performed a number of such sacrifices including the *aśvamēda* (horse sacrifice) as evidenced by the recent discovery of 'aśvamēda type' coins of the Sangam Pāṇḍyas.

It is plausible that the term *paḷankāśu,* literally meaning 'old coin', mentioned in some Pallava inscriptions may also denote the Roman aureus.

The literary and epigraphical evidences confirm the circulation of foreign currency of different metals in early historical India. If the imported gold coins reached the king, he used them as 'gift items'. When these issues reached the traders, they used the coins both as 'money for immediate use' and as 'reserve capital' to be hoarded and used in future. The foreign silver and copper coins appear to have circulated more extensively among all sections of society. As the early epigraphs largely pertain to royal grants, they do not shed much light on these silver and copper coins.

## ROMAN COINS AS JEWELLERY

Some Roman coins appear to have been used as jewellery by the people of ancient India. The coin was converted into a jewel to be worn round the neck by drilling one or two small holes along its edge or by attaching a small metallic loop to it. Such pierced Roman coins are largely confined to select sites in the Tamilnadu-Andhra and Karnataka-Maharashtra-Gujarat regions. The maximum number of finds is from Andhra.

Many of the looped or pierced coins are found in hoards such as Malayadiputhur, Nathampatti and Soriyapattu (Tamilnadu); Bhagavan-pavam, Gootiparti (also known as Gaiparti or Gootipalle),

Gopalapuram, Gumada, Nellore, Upparipeta, Vinukonda and
Weepangandla (Andhra Pradesh); Akkialur and Nosagere (Karnataka)
and Dharpul and Uppavahr (Maharashtra). Pierced issues have been
found in the course of archaeological excavations in Kondapur, Kudavelli,
Nagarjunakonda and Peddabankur (Andhra). The finds from Arikamedu
(Pondicherry), Junagadh (Gujarat) and Chakherbedha (Madhya Pradesh)
are all stray or accidental discoveries. At Nagarjunakonda, apart from
the pierced genuine aureus and the pierced Roman imitation copper
coin found in the course of excavations, two pierced imitation Roman
gold coins or medallions have been unearthed along with other items of
jewellery as part of a ritualistic deposit within a *stupa*. Roman medals,
probably imitations in bronze and copper found in the Coimbatore-
Palghat area, have loops of various shapes attached to them.[81] Some of
these medals are linked to one another with a thin iron or silver chain.
A looped gold medallion from India (?) with the bust of Constantine I
on one side and Ardokśo, the Iranian goddess of wealth, on the other, is
part of the collection of the British Museum, London.[82] A unique twice
pierced gold coin (third century AD) depicting a standing Kushan king
on the obverse and a Roman bust on the reverse has been excavated at
Sisupalgarh (Orissa).[83]

    None of the Roman Republican issues found in India are pierced.
Pierced first century AD coins are fewer than those of the later periods.
An apparent reason for this is that the circulation of foreign coins as
'money' was maximum in the first century AD and, hence, the use of
these coins as jewels was limited during that period.

    The use of Roman and pseudo-Roman coins as jewellery is hardly
surprising because even the indigenous coins were often worn as pendants
of necklaces and chains. For example, a treasure trove from Lohardaga
(Ranchi district, Bihar) has brought to light two looped Kushan coins—
an issue each of Wima Kadphises and Vasudeva(?)—along with a lump
of gold. Belwadaga and Sultanganj (Bihar) have also yielded looped
Kushan coins; at Sultanganj, the Kushan coin was discovered together
with a looped 'standard type' of Samudragupta and some ornaments in
a pot. Looped or pierced imitation Kushan coins have also been reported
from archaeological excavations in Bihar.[84] Bonai (Orissa) yielded pierced
Kushan imitation coins along with a looped genuine gold issue of
Huvishka and broken pieces of a gold ring and a gold chain.[85] Double-
pierced coins are seen among the silver issues of Nahapana overstruck
on the Indo-Parthian coins. Even punch marked coins were sometimes
pierced for use as pendants. Whether these coins were used as ornaments

during the period when they were in circulation or after they had declined to be valid legal tender—having been replaced by the coins of a new ruling dynasty—is not clear.

The *uraṭhadināra mālaya* mentioned in *Kalpa Sūtra*, a Jain text, may refer to a garland of Roman aurei.[86] Necklaces made of coins are frequently depicted in early Indian stone sculptures. The gold *kāśu mā lai*—garland of gold coins—is still in use in the temples and households of Tamilnadu.

Pierced indigenous coins have not been found along with pierced Roman coins in the hoard context. However, both pierced and non-pierced Roman coins are often found either as part of or in association with other types of jewellery (Plate 8).

In some instances, the pierced hole(s) in the Roman coin is refilled either with metal or a peculiar reddish paste (lac?). The precise reason for 'refilling' remains a mystery. Such 'refilled' coins are found in the Gumada hoard and Peter Berghaus has reported similar coins from Akkialur and Vinukonda.[87]

Some of the Roman coins, have a small circular punch, slightly larger than a dot, close to the edge. These marks are not 'countermarks' but an indication of the unsuccessful attempt to pierce the coin at the point of the mark.

Moulds to produce medals or pendants in imitation of Roman coins have been discovered at Banavasi[88] and Talkad[89] (Karnataka), and Ujjain[90] and Besnagar near Bhilsa[91] (Madhya Pradesh), and Palanpur[92] (Gujarat).

The moulds from Karnataka depict the famous reverse device of Tiberian coins—Livia seated on a throne. Stylistically, however, the devices on the moulds are cruder than those on the genuine Roman coins. The mould from Banavasi is made of agate. The terracotta mould from Talkad, the famous capital of the Western Gangas, is reported to be of the same size as the gold and silver coins of Tiberius. The recovery of this mould from stratified deposits in association with an ancient kiln belonging to the first century AD has led the excavators to propose that the mould could have been used by a goldsmith for producing necklace pendants although unlike the Banavasi mould, it does not have a loop at the top. In stratified layers, a terracotta mould portraying the effigy of the Roman emperor Hadrian(?) has been found at Ujjain. The moulds from Besnagar and Palanpur are made of stone.

It is clear that the manufacture and use of such moulds is restricted to a few areas. Again, although Gujarat, Madhya Pradesh and Karnataka

*Symbols of Trade*

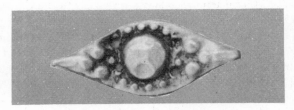

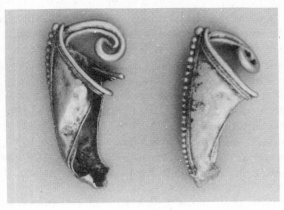

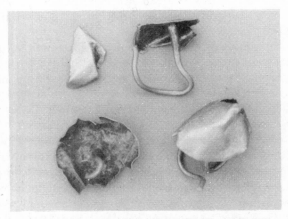

PLATE 8. EYE-SHAPED GOLD LEAF AND GOLD EAR
ORNAMENTS (*KUNDALAS*) IN THE DARMAVARIPALEM
AUREI HOARD (ANDHRA)

have revealed pierced imitation Roman coins, no metallic medal or pendant produced from these moulds is known to date. But looped or pierced clay bullae probably produced from such moulds have been recovered from a number of sites such as Rajghat and Kausambi (Uttar Pradesh); Garh (near Ujjain, Madhya Pradesh); Bhokardan, Brahmapuri, Karad, Kausam, Nevasa and Ter (Maharashtra); Chandravalli and Sannati (Karnataka); Sisupalgarh (Orissa) and Kondapur (Andhra).[93] Such bullae were probably not known in the Tamil country. The bullae are usually circular discs of baked clay. Some bullae like those from Sisupalgarh have a plain flat reverse. The bullae from Kondapur and a few other sites bear figures on both the sides: the obverse and the reverse are usually produced separately using two different moulds and later cemented together back to back. Many of the bullae may have been originally gilded to appear like gold jewels. In all the excavated sites, the bullae are usually found along with pseudo-Roman and Roman coins and pottery.

It may be inferred that these clay bullae were mainly used by the common people who could not afford genuine Roman coins and their metallic imitations. The indigenous coins were normally not imitated in clay because these coins were not of gold and hence were within the reach of even the poorer sections of society. Moreover, these coins were available in greater quantities than the imported ones.

## NOTES

1. Besides the Kallakinar coins, the Madras Museum has at least four Republican issues whose exact provenance has not been recorded. As most of the objects in this museum have been discovered in south India, it may be assumed that these coins too were recovered from the same region. Similarly, the British Museum, London, has three Republican coins from India whose precise find-spot remains unknown (India Office Collection [IOC] 1228, 1229 and 1230). For more details about the Roman Republican coins found in Maharashtra and other places in north India, see P.P. Kulkarni, 'Early Roman Coins in India', *JNSI*, vol. XLVI, 1984, pp. 37-8. For Republican coins found in Sri Lanka, see H.W. Codrington, *Ceylon Coins and Currency, Memoirs of the Colombo Museum,* series A, no. 3, Colombo, 1924, pp. 240-1.

2. D.W. MacDowall, 'Trade on the Maritime Silk Route—The Evidence of Roman Coins found in India', paper presented at the international seminar on *India and the Roman World Between the 1st and 4th Centuries A.D.*, Madras, 1990; idem, 'Indian Imports of Roman Silver Coins', in *Coinage, Trade and Economy (3rd International Colloquium, January 8th–11th, 1991)*, ed. A.K. Jha, Nashik, 1991, pp. 145-63; idem, 'The Evidence of the Gazetteer of Roman Artefacts

in India', in *Tradition and Archaeology—Early Maritime Contacts in the Indian Ocean*, ed. H.P. Ray and Jean-Francois Salles, New Delhi, 1996, pp. 79-95.

3. R. Krishnamurthy, 'Seleucid Coins from Karur', *SSIC*, vol. III, 1993, pp. 19-28; idem, 'Coins from Phoenicia found at Karur, Tamilnadu', *SSIC*, vol. IV, 1994, pp. 19-27; idem, 'Coins from Greek Islands, Rhodes and Crete found at Karur, Tamilnadu', *SSIC*, vol. V, 1995, pp. 29-36.

4. R. Gopal, 'A Greek Copper Coin from Hassan', *SSIC*, vol. III, 1993, pp. 51-2. Some scholars doubt the genuineness of this coin.

5. A. Burnett, 'Roman Coins from India and Sri Lanka', in *Origin, Evolution and Circulation of Foreign Coins in the Indian Ocean*, ed. O. Bopearachchi and D.P.M. Weerakkody, New Delhi, 1998, pp. 179-89.

6. V. Begley, 'Arikamedu Reconsidered', *AJA*, vol. 87, 1983, pp. 461-81; idem, 'Rouletted Ware at Arikamedu: A New Approach', *AJA*, vol. 92, 1988, pp. 427-40.

7. While Arikamedu has recently been re-excavated by the team led by V.Begley, Alagankulam has been excavated by the Tamilnadu State Department of Archaeology. For a detailed discussion on the date of origin of the trade, see the chapter on 'Roman Ceramics' in this volume.

8. The historical significance of the Palghat pass and the beryl mines with regard to the recurrent discoveries of Roman coins in the region has been discussed by several scholars since the late nineteenth century. See P.L. Gupta, *Roman Coins from Andhra Pradesh*, Hyderabad, 1965, p. 48; R. Sewell, 'Roman Coins found in India', *JRAS*, 1904, pp. 591-637; P.J. Turner, *Roman Coins from India*, London, 1989, p. 5.

9. The site was excavated in 1985, 1986,1989 and 1990 by the Department of Epigraphy and Archaeology of the Tamil University, Tanjavur. In 1997, the excavation was jointly conducted by the Tamil University and the Tamilnadu State Department of Archaeology. In 1998, the site was excavated solely by the latter agency. I am most grateful to Y. Subbarayalu and K. Rajan of the Tamil University for sharing valuable information about the site, and also for allowing me to examine many of the objects from the digs. I visited the site along with Bopearachchi of France when it was excavated in January-February 1998. A full report of the excavations is yet to be published.

10. These were noted during an exploration of the area undertaken by Bopearachchi and myself in 1998. Evidence of an ancient iron and steel industry in Karur has not been recorded earlier.

11. For an elaborate discussion of the predominance of these two coin types among the finds in India, see Turner, 'Roman coins from India', pp. 20-4.

12. P. Berghaus, 'Roman Aurei from Kumbalam, Ernakulam District, Kerala', *SSIC*, vol. III, 1993, pp. 29-42.

13. Burnett, 'Roman Coins from India and Sri Lanka', p.182.

14. The British Museum possesses at least eight post-Nerovian denarii which were apparently found in India. These include two issues of Vespasian (IOC 1253,

1254); two of Domitian (IOC 1255, 1256); one of Trajan (IOC 1257); two of Hadrian (IOC 1258, 1259); and one of Antoninus Pius (IOC 1260).

15. Museums in India including the Government Museum, Madras and the Indian Museum, Calcutta, have small collections of base metal Roman coins found in India. The precise find-spots of these coins are, however, not known.

16. Turner, *Roman Coins from India*, p. 19.

17. MacDowall, 'Trade on the Maritime Silk Route', idem, 'Indian Imports of Roman Silver Coins', pp. 145-63; idem, 'The Evidence of the Gazetteer of Roman Artefacts in India', pp. 79-95.

18. R.E.M. Wheeler, 'Roman Contact with India, Pakistan and Afghanistan', in *Aspects of Archaeology in Britain and Beyond: Essays Presented to O.G.S.Crawford*, ed. W.F. Grimes, London, 1951, pp. 345-81; idem, *Rome Beyond the Imperial Frontiers*, London, 1954, pp. 172-3.

19. D.W. MacDowall, 'Lecture' at the Tamilnadu Numismatic Society, Madras, 1990, quoted in K.V. Raman, 'Roman Coins from Tamilnadu', *SSIC*, vol. II, 1992, pp. 19-34. In 1994, I had a long discussion on this topic with MacDowall.

20. Raman, 'Roman Coins from Tamilnadu', p. 28.

21. Late Roman and Byzantine coins continue to be unearthed in large numbers in the villages around Coimbatore and also in Madurai and Karur. In recent years, the maximum number of finds has been from Karur. A visit to this town in 1998 revealed hundreds of such coins in the possession of local coin dealers and street urchins. I have also examined such coins in the personal collections of Vidwan I. Ramaswami, Boluvampatti and A. Sitaraman, Tanjavur. Some publications of the late nineteenth and early twentieth centuries refer to finds of such coins but the circumstances of the finds are rarely recorded. For a brief survey of some of these writings, see B.D.Chattopadhyaya, *Coins and Currency Systems in South India c. AD 225-1300*, New Delhi, 1977, pp. 116-17.

22. This opinion was expressed by I.K. Sarma during the course of my discussions with him at Madras in 1990 and at New Delhi in 1994. Also see I.K. Sarma, 'Roman Coins from Andhra Pradesh: Their Contexts, Chronology and Cultural Significance', *SSIC*, vol. II, 1992, pp. 35-50.

23. The site was excavated by the Archaeological Survey of India. See T. Sathyamurthy, 'Numismatic Finds from Bandar Pattanam in Tamilnadu', *SSIC*, vol. VII, 1997, pp. 49-55.

24. MacDowall, 'Trade on the Maritime Silk Route'.

25. K.V. Raman, 'Roman Contacts with Tamilnadu (South-eastern India): Recent Findings', paper presented at the international seminar on *India and the Roman World Between the 1st and 4th Centuries AD*, Madras, 1990; idem, 'Roman Coins from Tamilnadu', pp.19-34; Sarma, 'Roman Coins from Andhra Pradesh, pp. 35-50; Sewell, 'Roman Coins Found in India', pp. 591-637.

26. Turner, *Roman Coins from India*, p. 34; Wheeler, 'Roman Contact with India,

Pakistan and Afghanistan', p. 363. The sole slashed denarius in the Madras Museum mentioned by Wheeler, on the basis of the information that he received from T.G. Aravamuthan, Curator at the museum, is to date not traceable.

27. Turner, *Roman Coins from India*, p. 29.
28. P. Berghaus, 'Roman Coins from India and their Imitations', in *Coinage, Trade and Economy (3rd International Colloquium, January 8th-11th,1991)*, ed. A.K. Jha, Nashik, 1991, pp. 108-21.
29. Turner, *Roman Coins from India*, p. 33.
30. G.F. Hill, 'Roman Aurei from Pudukota, South India', *NC* (3rd series), vol. XVIII, 1898, pp. 304-20.
31. G.F. Hill, 'Untitled Note', *NC* (3rd series), vol. XIX, 1899, p. 82.
32. Wheeler, 'Roman Contact with India, Pakistan and Afghanistan', pp. 363-4.
33. W. Theobald, 'Note on Mr. G.F. Hill's Theory Regarding the Defacement of Roman Aurei from Pudukota', *NC* (3rd series), vol. XIX, 1899, p. 81.
34. Turner, *Roman Coins from India*, p. 32.
35. T.G. Aravamuthan, 'Catalogue of the Roman and Byzantine Coins in the Madras Government Museum', unpublished, 1942, pp. 17-21.
36. Gupta, *Roman Coins from Andhra Pradesh*, pp. 69-70.
37. A.M. Shastri, 'Imperial Roman Coins in Early Deccanese Inscriptions', *SSIC*, vol. II, 1992, pp. 77-87.
38. Turner, *Roman Coins from India*, pp. 33-6, 43-4.
39. R. Sumathi, 'Trade and its Impact on the Early Tamils—The Cōḷa Experience', unpublished M.Phil. dissertation, Jawaharlal Nehru University, New Delhi, 1984, p. 133.
40. Small countermarks are found even on Roman coins in European sites. These marks are totally different from, and cannot be compared with the marks on the Roman coins in India. Also, unlike the marks on the coins in India, the marks on the coins found in Europe have been extensively studied and published. See H. Mattingly, *Coins of the Roman Empire in the British Museum, Volume I: Augustus to Vitellius*, London, 1965, pp. xxviii-xliii.
41. Berghaus, 'Roman Coins from India and their Imitations', p. 112.
42. Many coins of the Akkanpalle hoard are in an extremely worn condition. In 1989, I examined the hoard in the Andhra Pradesh State Archaeological Museum, Hyderabad, and found countermarks on 1,279 coins although many of these marks were only faintly visible. I strongly believe that some more coins of the hoard bear countermarks which are to date not discernible. In Gupta, *Roman Coins from Andhra Pradesh*, p. 70, mention is made of 1,279 marked coins but Appendix A of the same book lists only about 1,123 marked coins.
43. E. Thurston, *Madras Government Museum, Coins-Catalogue No. 2: Roman, Indo-Portuguese and Ceylon*, Madras, 1894, pp. 26-7.
44. S. Suresh, 'Countermarks of Buddhist Symbols on the Roman Coins found in

Andhra Deśa', paper presented at the international seminar on *Contribution of Andhra Deśa to Buddhism*, Hyderabad, 1997; idem, 'Countermarks of Buddhist Symbols on the Roman Coins found in Andhra Deśa (Synopsis of the Paper)', *Contribution of Andhra Deśa to Buddhism—Souvenir*, Hyderabad, 1997, pp. 51-2; idem, 'Roman Coins found in India: A Study of the Countermarks', paper presented at the international seminar on *Trade and Economy of Ancient Sri Lanka, India and South-East Asia: Archaeological and Literary Evidence*, Colombo, 1999.

45. Gupta, *Roman Coins from Andhra Pradesh*, pp. 69-70.

46. P.L. Gupta, 'Coins in Rome's India Trade', in *Coinage, Trade and Economy (3rd International Colloquium, January 8th-11th, 1991)*, ed. A.K. Jha, Nashik, 1991, pp. 122-37.

47. T. Sathyamurthy, 'Angamali Hoard of Silver Punch-marked Coins', *SSIC*, vol. IV, 1994, pp. 45-50.

48. N.C. Ghosh and K. Ismail, 'Two Foreign Gold Coins from Excavation at Kudavelli, District Mahabubnagar, Andhra Pradesh', *JNSI*, vol. XLII, 1980, pp. 11-7.

49. Berghaus, 'Roman Coins from India and their Imitations', p. 112; Ghosh and Ismail, ibid., pp. 11-17; Turner, *Roman Coins from India*, pp. 34-6.

50. P.V. Parabrahma Sastry, 'Some Aspects of South Indian Numismatics', *SSIC*, vol. III, 1993, pp. 9-18. Chattopadhyaya, *Coins and Currency Systems in South India*, pp. 107-8.

51. I have seen such coins at the British Museum, London, the Madras Museum and in the personal collections of Vidwan I. Ramaswami, Boluvampatti, A. Sitaraman, Tanjavur, K.A. Thirugnanasampandam, Erode. Among the specimens in the British Museum are three silver imitations of Augustan or Tiberian denarii (IOC 1235, 1237 and 1239) and a very thin gold piece, weighing 4.184 g, attributed to Justinian I (IOC 1219). Also see P. Berghaus, 'An Indian Imitation of an Augustan Denarius', in *Prācī-Prabhā, Perspectives in Indology—Essays in Honour of Prof. B.N. Mukherjee*, ed. D.C. Bhattacharyya and Devendra Handa, New Delhi, 1989, pp. 101-5; idem, 'Three Denarii of Tiberius from Arikamedu', in *Indian Numismatics, History, Art and Culture—Essays in Honour of Dr. P.L. Gupta, I*, ed. D.W. MacDowall, Savita Sharma and Sanjay Garg, Delhi, 1992, pp. 95-8; P.D. Chumble, 'A Rare Roman Coin', *IIRNS Newsline*, 3, 1994, p. 7; P.V. Hill, 'A Puzzling Aureus of Septimius Severus from India', *Spink Numismatic Circular*, vol. XCII, 1984, p. 259; idem, 'Second Thoughts on the Severan Aureus from India', *Spink Numismatic Circular*, vol. XCII, 1984, p. 323.

52. Berghaus, 'Roman Coins from India and their Imitations', p.111.

53. The bibliography covering the late Roman copper coins in Sri Lanka is vast. In recent years, R. Walburg and O. Bopearachchi have compared these Sri Lanka finds with similar ones in south India. For more details about these finds and for a bibliography of the publications of these two and other scholars,

see O.Bopearachchi, 'Some Observations on Roman Coins found in Recent Excavations at Sigiriya', *Ancient Ceylon*, vol. 7, 1990, pp. 20-37; idem, 'Review of: R. Krishnamurthy: *Late Roman Copper Coins from South India—Karur and Madurai*', *Oriental Numismatic Society Newsletter*, vol. 141, 1994, pp. 3-4; idem, 'Archaeological Evidence on Changing Patterns of International Trade Relations of Ancient Sri Lanka', in *Origin, Evolution and Circulation of Foreign Coins in the Indian Ocean*, ed. O. Bopearachchi and D.P.M. Weerakkody, New Delhi, 1998, pp. 133-78; R. Walburg, 'Late Roman Copper Coins from Southern India', in *Coinage, Trade and Economy (3rd International Colloquium, January 8th-11th, 1991)*, ed. A.K. Jha, Nashik, 1991, pp. 164-7. I have learnt much about the finds in Sri Lanka through personal discussions with Bopearachchi at New Delhi in 1991 and 1992, at Paris in 1994, at Madras in 1997 and 1998 and at Colombo in 1999.

54. Gupta, *Roman Coins from Andhra Pradesh*, pp. 64-8; Turner, *Roman Coins from India*, pp. 37-41.

55. Kondapur was excavated around 1940. However, the full details have not been published. See Aloka Parasher, 'Kondapur: A Forgotten City (Reflections on the Early History of Telangana)', *Indian History Congress—Proceedings of the Forty-eighth Session*, Delhi, 1988, pp. 82-90; G.Yazdani, 'Excavations at Kondapur: An Andhra Town, c. 200 B.C.- A.D. 200', *Annals of the Bhandarkar Oriental Research Institute*, vol. 22, 1941, pp. 171-85.

56. A.M. Shastri, 'Kondapur: A Satavahana Silver Coins Mint', *SSIC*, vol. III, 1993, pp. 81-5.

57. R. Krishnamurthy, 'A Roman Coin Die from Karur, Tamilnadu', *SSIC*, vol. VI, 1996, pp. 43-8.

58. P.V. Radhakrishnan, 'A Punch-marked Die from Karur', *SSIC*, vol. IV, 1994, pp. 51-6.

59. S. Seneviratne, 'The Ecology and Archaeology of the Seruwila Copper-Magnetite Prospect, North East Sri Lanka', in *From Sumer to Meluhha: Contributions to the Archaeology of South and South West Asia in Memory of George F. Dales, Jr.(Wisconsin Archaeological Reports 3)*, ed. Jonathan Mark Kenoyer, Madison, 1994, pp. 261-80; idem, 'The Ecology and Archaeology of the Seruwila Copper-Magnetite Prospect, North East Sri Lanka', *The Sri Lanka Journal of the Humanities*, vol. XXI, nos. 1 and 2, 1995, pp. 114-45. I had fruitful discussions on the subject with Seneviratne at New Delhi in 1996.

60. Aravamuthan, 'Catalogue of the Roman and Byzantine Coins', pp. 25-32.

61. V.V. Krishna Sastry, *Roman Gold Coins—Recent Discoveries in Andhra Pradesh*, Hyderabad, 1992, p. 10, coin n.28.

62. Aravamuthan, 'Catalogue of the Roman and Byzantine Coins', pp. 25-32.

63. D.W. MacDowall and N.G. Wilson, 'The References to the Kuṣāṇas in the Periplus and Further Numismatic Evidence for its Date', *NC* (7th series), vol. X, 1970, pp. 221-40.

64. For full details of the opinions of these scholars, refer to the section on 'Slashed Coins' in this chapter.

65. Turner, *Roman Coins from India,* pp. 14-16.
66. MacDowall, 'Trade on the Maritime Silk Route'.
67. B. Srivastava, 'Economic Significance of Roman Coins found in India', *JNSI,* vol. XXVI, 1964, pp. 222-7.
68. I.K. Sarma, 'A Critical Study of the Numismatic Evidences from Nagarjuna-konda Excavations', *SSIC,* vol. IV, 1994, pp. 63-78.
69. For details, refer to the section on 'Slashed Coins' in this Chapter.
70. B.N. Mukherjee, *The Indian Gold: An Introduction to the Cabinet of the Gold Coins in the Indian Museum,* Calcutta, 1990, p. 14.
71. Gupta, *Roman Coins from Andhra Pradesh,* pp. 69-70.
72. Sewell, Roman Coins found in India, pp. 591-637.
73. Aravamuthan, 'Catalogue of the Roman and Byzantine Coins', pp. 37-9.
74. Wheeler, 'Roman Contact with India, Pakistan and Afghanistan', pp. 345-81.
75. I discussed this topic with H.P. Ray at New Delhi in 1990 and 1992. See H.P. Ray, 'The Yavana Presence in India', in *Athens, Aden, Arikamedu—Essays on the Interrelations between India, Arabia and the Eastern Mediterranean,* ed. Marie-Francoise Boussac and Jean-Francois Salles, New Delhi, 1995, pp. 75-95; idem, 'A Resurvey of "Roman" Contacts with the East', in *Athens, Aden, Arikamedu—Essays on the Interrelations Between India, Arabia and the Eastern Mediterranean,* New Delhi, 1995, pp. 97-114.
76. This inscription and the precise meaning of the term *suvarṇa* have been analysed by many scholars. See Chattopadhyaya, *Coins and Currency Systems,* pp. 104-5, 108; MacDowall and Wilson, 'References to the Kuṣāṇas', pp. 221-40; Sarma, 'Critical Study of the Numismatic Evidences', pp. 63-78; Shastri, 'Imperial Roman Coins in Early Deccanese Inscriptions', pp. 77-87.
77. Chattopadhyaya, *Coins and Currency Systems,* pp. 107-9.
78. Shastri, 'Imperial Roman Coins in Early Deccanese Inscriptions', pp. 77-87. For more details about the *suvarṇa* and the *dināri,* see Chandrashekhar Gupta, 'Foreign Denominations of Early Indian Coins', in *Foreign Elements in Indian Indigenous Coins,* ed. A.M. Shastri, Varanasi, 1982, pp. 109-23.
79. R. Subrahmanyam, *A Catalogue of the Ikshvaku Coins in the Andhra Pradesh Government Museum,* Hyderabad, 1979, p. 7. Also see Shastri, 'Imperial Roman Coins in Early Deccanese Inscriptions', p. 87, fn. 34. Subrahmanyam's book provides a fairly comprehensive account of the Ikṣvākus, their inscriptions and coins.
80. Chattopadhyaya, *Coins and Currency Systems,* pp. 112-13, 174-9; K.G. Krishnan, 'Some Aspects of South Indian Coinage', *SSIC,* vol. II, 1992, pp. 9-18; P. Shanmugam, 'Some Aspects of Monetary System of the Pallavas', *SSIC,* vol. III, 1993, pp. 101-8. I had a discussion on this subject with Krishnan at Madras in 1986.
81. I saw some such medals in the personal collection of Vidwan I.Ramaswami, Boluvampatti.
82. The medallion was originally in the Museum's Department of Greek and Roman Antiquities but is at present in the Department of Coins and Medals.

See R. Gobl, 'The Roman-Kushanian Medallion in the British Museum', *JNSI*, vol. XXXVIII, no. 1, 1976, pp. 21-6; P.L. Gupta, 'British Museum Romano-Kushana Medallion: Its Nature and Importance', *JNSI*, vol. XXXVIII, no. 2, 1976, pp. 73-81.

83. A.S. Altekar, 'A Unique Kushano-Roman Gold Coin of King Dharmadamadhara(?)', *JNSI*, vol. XII, 1950, pp. 1-4; B.B. Lal, 'Sisupalgarh 1948: An Early Historical Fort in Eastern India', *AI*, vol. 5, 1949, pp. 95-7, 100-1.

84. For a detailed survey of all these finds from Bihar, see P.L. Gupta, 'Kushana-Murunda Rule in Eastern India—Numismatic Evidence', *JNSI*, vol. XXXVI, 1974, pp. 25-53.

85. K.S. Behera, 'On a Kushana Gold Coin from Orissa', *JNSI*, vol. XXXVII, 1975, pp. 76-82.

86. Sarma, 'Roman Coins from Andhra Pradesh', p. 39.

87. Berghaus, 'Roman Coins from India and their Imitations', p. 110.

88. A.V. Narasimha Murthy, 'A Roman Coin Mould from Banavasi', *JNSI*, vol. XLVI, 1984, pp. 45-6.

89. A.V. Narasimha Murthy and D.V. Devaraj, 'A Roman Coin Mould from Talkad Excavations', *SSIC*, vol. V, 1995, pp. 59-62.

90. R.S. Sharma, *Urban Decay in India (c.300-c.1000)*, New Delhi, 1987, p. 68.

91. Wheeler, 'Roman Contact with India, Pakistan and Afghanistan', p. 351.

92. Gupta, *Roman Coins from Andhra Pradesh*, p. 77.

93. Lists of such finds have been included in several publications. See S.B. Deo, 'Roman Trade: Recent Archaeological Discoveries in Western India', in *Rome and India: The Ancient Sea Trade*, ed. V. Begley and Richard Daniel De Puma, Madison, 1991, pp. 39-45; Gupta, 'Roman Coins from Andhra Pradesh', p. 77; idem, 'Kushana-Murunda Rule in Eastern India', p. 39; Lal, 'Sisupalgarh 1948', pp. 101-2. The find from Sannati is a recent one and is not included in these lists. For details about the find from Sannati, see D.V. Devaraj, 'A Roman Terracotta Pendant from Sannati in Karnataka', *SSIC*, vol. VII, 1997, pp. 45-8.

# 3

## Ceramics

THE PRINCIPAL Roman ceramic types discovered in India are terra sigillata and amphora jars. The rouletted and the red polished wares were earlier considered as imports from the west, but recent studies have revealed that these are indigenous products.

Any study of Roman pottery in India is beset with two major problems:

1. Lack of sufficient information about the chronology of the ware: Many of the major archaeological excavations remain unpublished. Even in the case of published excavated sites, the stratified layers are, very often, not assigned any precise date but are merely termed as 'early-historical' or 'early-medieval', etc., leading to confusion in determining the exact date of the antiquities recovered from those layers.

Again, several important sites such as Kanchi (Tamilnadu) have been subjected to archaeological excavations more than once and by different teams. But full details of none of these excavations are forthcoming. On the basis of the available information, significant differences may be observed between the stratigraphy of different trenches within the same site, thus making it extremely difficult to assess the relative chronological sequence of pottery types, i.e. the sequence of their occurrence.

2. The non-availability of statistical data pertaining to the potsherds found in each of the sites: As the quantity of Roman and pseudo-Roman pottery in India is limited, the precise number of fragments from each site would assume considerable significance, particularly for the purposes of a comparative analysis of the quantity of one variety of ceramic vis-à-vis another in different regions of India. However, precise data on the number of sherds are not available for several excavated sites. In other words, exact numbers of the different varieties of potsherds obtained

from each layer have not been recorded. There is great ambiguity in the reports which use vague terms such as 'few', 'many', 'not much', 'a good number' and 'hundreds' to describe the quantity of the wares. It should be noted that non-quantified distribution patterns can lead to extremely distorted results by according the same importance to one sherd or hundreds of them.

## ROULETTED WARE

This refers to a pottery type which bears concentric bands of rouletted decoration usually effected by a toothed wheel. The rouletted designs include small triangles, parallelograms, ovals, dots, etc. The ware has a remarkably smooth surface and normally exhibits a metallic lustre. Such ceramics are common in early historical Europe.

Indians undoubtedly learnt the rouletting technique and designs from Western traders who would have definitely brought specimens of the Mediterranean ware to India. But all the rouletted sherds recovered from a number of Indian sites and presently housed in various private and public collections appear to be local products.[1]

Around a hundred sites spread over India have yielded rouletted ware (see Appendix II). The maximum number of finds, not surprisingly, is from the Andhra-Tamilnadu region. In fact, rouletted ware is found throughout the Coromandel coast and also in Sri Lanka, indicating a well established communication network linking the entire east coast of India with northern Sri Lanka. There is a marked paucity of this ware in most parts of the west coast, specially Kerala and Gujarat, though specimens have been recovered from a few sites in Maharashtra. Rouletted ware has not been found in Pakistan and north-west India. The ware occurs both in the course of archaeological excavations and also as surface finds. A good number of excavated sites have yielded rouletted ware on the surface as also in stratified layers.

It is clear that rouletted ware is widely distributed throughout the subcontinent both in the coastal regions and in the interior areas (Map 2). The general pattern appears to be that while Roman coin finds are more numerous in the coastal areas, rouletted ware sites are more in the interior. Rouletted ware seems to have been first produced in the coastal areas and some of the inland sites probably received the ware from the port towns. Almost all regions yielding rouletted pottery have also revealed Roman coins except West Bengal where rouletted ware has been recovered from eleven well attested sites but hardly any

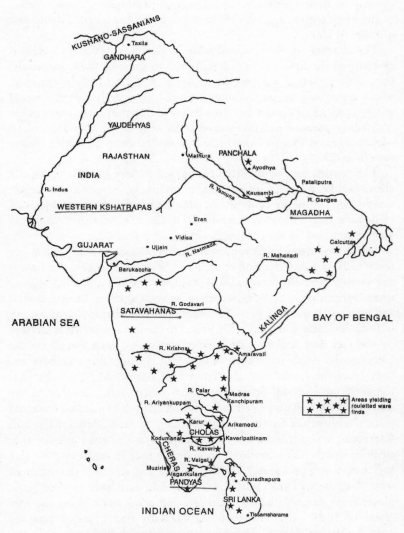

KUSHANO-SASSANIANS

• Taxila

GANDHARA

YAUDEHYAS

RAJASTHAN

PANCHALA ★

• Mathura

• Ayodhya

INDIA

R. Yamuna

Kausambi

Pataliputra

R. Indus

R. Ganges

WESTERN KSHATRAPAS

MAGADHA

Eran

• Vidisa

• Ujjain

R. Narmada

Calcutta ★

GUJARAT

R. Mahanadi

★ ★ ★
★

Barukaccha

★ ★

R. Godavari

ARABIAN SEA

SATAVAHANAS

KALINGA

BAY OF BENGAL

★
★ ★ ★ ★
R. Krishna
★ ★ ★
Amaravati

★ ★ ★

R. Palar

Madras

R. Ariyankuppam

Kanchipuram

★ ★ ★ ★ ★
★ ★ ★ ★ ★
★ ★ ★ ★ ★

Areas yielding
rouletted ware
finds

Karur

Arikamedu

Kodumanal ★

CHOLAS

★ ★

Kaveripattinam ★

CHERAS

R. Kaveri

R. Vaigai

Muziris

ALagankulam

Anuradhapura

PANDYAS

★

SRI LANKA

INDIAN OCEAN

★

• Tissamaharama

MAP 2: DISTRIBUTION PATTERN OF ROULETTED WARE
FINDS IN THE INDIAN SUBCONTINENT

Roman coin has been reported from the region. In all other parts of the country, rouletted ware sites are, compared to Roman coin sites, fewer in any given region, specially in the south which has revealed the largest number of coins.

The absence of the rouletted ware in Kerala is difficult to explain specially in the light of the fact that even in some of the Coromandel port sites, rouletted ware occurs in layers of second-first centuries BC which is precisely the period when Kerala's link with the Western world was at its zenith. It should, however, be noted that the maximum number of Mediterranean merchants visited India only in the first century AD when the main focus of the trade had shifted from Kerala to south-eastern India.

The reasons for the absence of rouletted pottery in Gujarat are not clear. Unlike Kerala, Gujarat has, surprisingly, revealed the largest number of amphorae finds in the whole of India. Bronze objects of Hellenistic origin have also been found in Gujarat. Moreover, rouletted ware is common in sites of neighbouring Maharashtra.

It may be inferred that rouletted pottery-making technique did not reach India through the land route across West Asia because the ware is not known in north-western India, Pakistan and the adjoining regions where various types of Roman antiquities such as coins, bronze objects and even amphorae have been discovered. The view that rouletted pottery in India is closely and specifically linked to the seaborne trade is attested by the fact that rouletted finds, very similar to those found on the Coromandel coast, have been reported in considerable numbers not only from Sri Lanka but also from East Africa, Maldives, Burma, Indonesia and several other South-East Asian sites.[2] Further, X-ray diffraction analysis and neutron activation analysis of selected rouletted ware sherds from Sembiran and Pacung in Bali, Arikamedu and Karaikadu in south India and Anuradhapura in Sri Lanka indicate that all these sherds had a common geological source in terms of their clay and temper compositions.[3] Thus, it is likely that several of the rouletted ware finds in Sri Lanka and South-East Asia may have reached those places from Alagankulam, Arikamedu and other ports along the east coast of India. Significantly, Arikamedu was a major pottery manufacturing centre. The active commercial exchange between Arikamedu, Sri Lanka and South-East Asia is further corroborated by recurrent discoveries in Sri Lanka and further east, of several other types of India related objects. For instance, glass and semi-precious stone beads believed to have been produced in Arikamedu have been unearthed in

Thailand. Recently, archaeological excavations at Khuan Luk Pat on the west coast of Thailand have even revealed a copper Sangam Cōḷa coin and a copper Pallava coin.[4]

It is interesting to analyse the probable routes through which rouletted pottery and the rouletting technique spread in India from the ports to the hinterland which has revealed the ware in large numbers. All the important port towns yielding rouletted ware are situated close to the spot where a major river joins the sea (Vasavasamudram: river Palar; Arikamedu: river Gingee and Ariyankuppam: Kaveripumpattinam: river Kaveri; Korkai: river Tamraparni; Alagankulam: river Vaigai). The reason for this is that the south-eastern coast of India is devoid of natural harbours and hence, most of the port sites are situated close to the estuaries of the rivers. Romans apparently travelled in India, from the coast to the interior, crossing the rivers in canoes. Hence, the location of the ports on the rivers would have certainly facilitated the spread of rouletted ware and the rouletting technique from the port towns, along the various rivers, to the hinterland where several rouletted ware sites have been discovered, for instance, Kanchi, not far from river Palar; Uraiyur on the banks of Kaveri; and Karur on the banks of Amaravati, a tributary of the Kaveri. There seems to have been some interaction between Arikamedu and Suttukeni situated, not far from Arikamedu, along the river Gingee, even though Suttukeni has not revealed any rouletted ware till date. In several cases, a group of sites, on either bank of a major river, has revealed numerous Roman objects as well as rouletted pottery thereby indicating that trade was very brisk along that river. Two such instances are the lower Kaveri valley in Tamilnadu (in the first century AD) and the lower Krishna valley in Andhra Pradesh (in the second century AD).

Even in the case of rouletted ware sites of north India, the pottery reached those places only through rivers. Ayodhya, on the banks of the river Sarayu, may be considered the innermost site (farthest from the sea) where rouletted sherds have been found in an archaeologically stratified context. Here, the trade would have been along the arterial riverine routes of the Sarayu and through it, the Ganga, after their confluence at Chapra, linking coastal sites such as Tamralipti (Tamluk) in eastern India with the hinterland. Rajghat, another important rouletted ware site, is also located on the banks of the Ganga. Till recently, both the Sarayu and the Ganga were used for water-borne trade between north and east India by means of *bagāras* (large boats). The rouletted ware sites of Maharashtra too are all located not too far from important rivers (Arni: river Arunavati, Nashik: river Godavari, Nevasa: river Pravara, Ter: river Terna).

In rare instances, the rouletted ware as well as the rouletting technique seem to have spread from trade centres, either on the coast or on the banks of rivers, even to remote inland sites which had no direct contact with the Roman world. Some of these sites have not yielded any Roman object and have been mentioned neither in the classical accounts nor in ancient Indian literature, and trade has not been a major activity in these places. Such sites are few in number and include Appukallu and Tiruvamattur in Tamilnadu.

It may be noted that there are several varieties among the rouletted ware sherds found in India. Broadly, the finds fall under two distinct categories—a finer variety which is almost identical to the Mediterranean rouletted ware, and an inferior variety which is invariably coarser in fabric, unpolished and unslipped and in which the rouletted designs depict crude workmanship. In bright light, minute mica particles can be seen on the finer variety. As the sherds from several sites are not available for physical examination, it is not possible to comment on the exact number of the inferior and finer varieties in the different regions. The available data, however, indicates that the finer varieties are more numerous in the coastal areas, specially the port sites. This may be explained by the presence of a larger number of Mediterranean traders and artisans proficient in the rouletting technique in the coastal towns. Vimala Begley has even suggested that the rouletted dishes in Arikamedu may have been originally meant for use by the Greek, Arab, Indian and other traders who flocked to the site.[5] It is plausible that the colony of Roman merchants at the site initiated the production of the ware here. Not surprisingly, the finer varieties of rouletted ware mostly occur in the site's 'Northern Sector' which is supposed to be the residential zone of the traders.

While most of the rouletted sherds in India, both of the finer and cruder varieties, are of varying shades of grey and black, the recent excavations at Arikamedu and Alagankulam have brought to light a fine bright red rouletted ware (Plate 9). At Alagankulam, all the rouletted sherds recovered from the third-fourth centuries AD layers are of the red variety. This red variety was, however, known even in the pre-Christian era. A sherd of this variety, collected from the surface at Alagankulam, depicts the Tamil Brāhmī legend 'ti-ca-a-n' (personal name?) palaeographically akin to the Tamil Brāhmī rock inscription at Māngulam (Tamilnadu) and dated to the second-first centuries BC. It

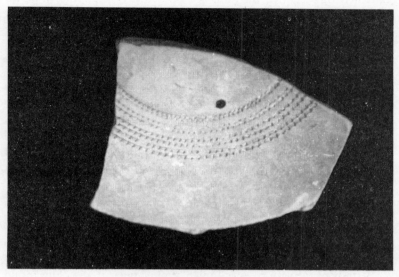

PLATE 9. RED ROULETTED WARE SHERD—FINE VARIETY,
ALAGANKULAM (TAMILNADU)

appears that the production of the grey, black and red varieties began almost simultaneously in the pre-Christian era although in the initial period, the production of the red variety was limited. Moreover, the red variety is not known in a large number of sites. In any case, the non-availability of data pertaining to the precise stratigraphic context of each of the rouletted ware sherds on a site by site basis makes it extremely difficult to draw any generalization about the precise chronology of the black, grey and red varieties of rouletted ware in India.

Regarding the centres or sites where rouletted pottery was produced in India, Vishwas Gogte has argued that it was manufactured at multiple production centres in the lower Ganga plains, mainly in the Chandraketugarh-Tamluk region of Bengal.[6] This view is based on the fact that the mineral patterns of select rouletted ware specimens from several sites such as Arikamedu and Alagankulam (Tamilnadu region), Sisupalgarh and Manikpatna (Orissa), Kothapatnam (Andhra) and Nashik (Maharashtra) are identical with the clay found in the Chandraketugarh area. Gogte's theory, however, fails to take into account the fact that the quantity of rouletted ware found in Bengal is far less than the finds in many south Indian sites, specially Arikamedu. It is extremely unlikely that the finds of a particular type of pottery would be far less in the vicinity of the production site than the finds in places where the pottery was exported. Further, there is concrete evidence in support of the fact that rouletted ware was produced in many sites outside Bengal. For instance, the rouletted sherds from Arikamedu and Brahmagiri (Karnataka) were originally believed to be identical but a recent re-examination of the finds reveals that although the surface treatment appears to be similar, the difference in the clay contents of the two sets of finds indicates that each of them was manufactured at a different centre. Again, an archaeo-chemical analysis indicates that there is no difference in the mineral content of both the megalithic black and red ware and the rouletted ware recovered from Satanikota (Andhra Pradesh) implying that both these wares were produced at this site itself.[7]

It is clear that rouletted ware has always been considered as 'precious' or 'deluxe' pottery, too precious to be discarded even if cracked or broken. For instance, at Vaddamanu (Andhra), broken or cracked rouletted ware dishes were, after being suitably rivetted with iron or copper, used by the people.[8]

A study of the various early Indian ceramic types as also coins found along with the rouletted ware, both in the stratified and non-stratified contexts, may be expected to provide a clue to the date of rouletted ware in India. Surprisingly, Roman coins have been found along with rouletted ware in stratified layers only in a few sites such as Karur and Alagankulam (Tamilnadu) and Nevasa (Maharashtra). The early Indian coins found along with rouletted pottery include the punch marked, Sangam-Cōḷa, Pūri-Kushan, Sātavāhana, Mahārathi and Ikṣvāku.

The black and red ware is the main type of pottery found to be associated with rouletted ware in almost all parts of India.

Rouletted ware has been recovered with the Russet Coated Painted (RCP) ware—erroneously termed 'Andhra ware'—at several sites such as Jambuladinne, Kambaduru, Mittapalli, Nilugondla and Satanikota (Andhra); Nashik and Nevasa (Maharashtra); Banavasi, Brahmagiri, Chandravalli and TNarsipur (Karnataka); Kodumanal and Uraiyur (Tamilnadu) and Arikamedu (Pondicherry). At Arikamedu, only a single sherd of RCP ware could be identified. At Kanchi, both rouletted and RCP wares occur together in period IB which varies from the first century AD to the third century AD. It is not clear whether RCP ware first appeared at Kanchi in period IB or IA which dates from the third century BC to the first century BC.[9] At Kodumanal, RCP ware was first identified in layers earlier to those of the rouletted ware. The case of Karur is not clear. According to one published account, the beginning of the use of RCP ware at Karur can be traced to around 300 BC, thus predating the appearance of rouletted ware at the site.[10] Another published account categorically mentions that the RCP ware phase at the site post-dates the rouletted ware phase and is datable to the third-fourth centuries AD.[11] At Perur near Coimbatore, RCP ware has been found in many of the layers of the early historical period but the site has not revealed any rouletted sherd. Rouletted ware has not been discovered at Nagarjunakonda (Andhra) either, although the site has been repeatedly excavated.[12] As both Perur and Nagarjunakonda have yielded Roman coins, and amphora has also been recovered from Nagarjunakonda, and as many places in the vicinity of these two sites have revealed rouletted ware, the reasons for the absence of this ware in these two sites are not clear.

Incidentally, the geographical distribution of RCP ware is very wide from Nevasa in western India to Madurai in south-eastern India. In different sites, the ware occurs in layers dating from 400 BC to AD 400. According to K. Rajan, contrary to popular belief, the ware originated in Kongunadu (Coimbatore area) and not in the Karnataka-Andhra region.[13] The non-occurrence of the ware in numerous early historical urban commercial centres in Karnataka-Andhra including Nagarjuna-konda may be cited in support of Rajan's view. However, V. Begley's contention that the RCP ware, common in Coimbatore and Malabar regions, is normally not found on the Coromandel coast[14] is true only with regard to the southern part (Tamilnadu) of the east coast as sites in the eastern districts of Andhra have revealed the ware.

Rouletted ware has been found along with Northern Black Polished (NBP) ware at Alagankulam (Tamilnadu); Chebrolu, Daranikota and Vaddamanu (Andhra); Sisupalgarh (Orissa); Chandraketugarh, Hariharpur and Tamluk (chalcolithic NBP?) (West Bengal) and Arni and Ter (Maharashtra). The NBP ware, as is well known, originated in the Ganga valley around 500 BC and was extensively used throughout the Mauryan empire. Hence, its occurrence in the extreme south of India initially came as a surprise. It may, however, be noted that Alagankulam is not the first Tamilnadu site to reveal the ware, as six NBP sherds have been unearthed earlier, most probably along with rouletted pottery, during archaeological excavations at the Pāṇḍyan secondary capital and port town of Korkai, close to the peninsular tip of India. NBP pottery has also been recovered from Anuradhapura in Sri Lanka in layers of the pre-Christian era.[15] At Alagankulam, more than 10 fragments of NBP ware have been found from a depth of 2.90 m. to 6 m. suggesting the use of the ware at the site from almost the third century BC to the second century AD. The recent discoveries of NBP ware all along the Coromandel coast, specially in the Nellore region of Andhra, provide valuable clues to the precise route along which the ware travelled from north India to the Tamil country and thence, across the sea, to Sri Lanka.

Recent studies and excavations at Arikamedu have indicated that the main period of rouletted ware is from around the second century BC to the late first century AD.[16] This early period during which rouletted pottery was introduced in India is corroborated by finds from a number of other sites.[17] Daranikota has yielded a wharf and a navigational channel together with multicoloured foreign glass objects, earrings, bangles and a seal of the second century BC. Both at Daranikota and at Amaravati (Andhra), rouletted ware has been recovered from the post-Asokan levels (period III). At Salihundam (Andhra), rouletted ware has been found in the mid-second century BC layers. Some of the sherds at this site also contain inscriptions palaeographically belonging to this date. At Vanagiri, near Kaveripumpattinam, black rouletted ware has been recovered along with a silver punch marked coin from the second century BC deposits. Alagankulam has also yielded rouletted ware in layers of the pre-Christian era. From a depth of 4.10 m., an interesting inscribed rouletted sherd has been found at Alagankulam. The legend on this sherd reads '*pi-ti-u-ra-y*'(?) meaning 'handle-cover'(?). Probably this sherd, assigned to the beginning of the Christian era, was the lid of a vessel. In all the excavated sites, the quantity of rouletted ware in the first century AD levels is far more than that of the earlier period.

It is obvious that rouletted ceramics were produced in India mainly during the period of maritime trade. When the trade began to slowly decline from the late first century AD, there was a corresponding decrease in the popularity, production and use of the ware, Alagankulam being the sole recorded site where the ware was in vogue as late as the fourth century AD.

In conclusion, the ceramic traditions of the early Tamil country where several rouletted ware sites are located may, with minor deviations in the case of a few sites, be summed up as follows:

| | | |
|---|---|---|
| Phase I | Black and red ware of thin fabric | 400 BC–200 BC |
| Phase II | Black and red ware of thick fabric, RCP ware, NBP ware, rouletted ware | 200 BC–AD 100 |

Phase III    Black and red ware of thick fabric,    AD 100–AD 400
             red polished or red slipped ware,
             brown slipped ware

## AMPHORAE

Amphora is a Latin term derived from the Greek 'amphoreus' or 'amphiphoreus', 'amphi' meaning 'on both sides' and 'phoreus' meaning 'bearer'. The term usually denotes an ancient jar or vase with a large oval body, a narrow cylindrical neck and two handles rising almost to the level of the mouth. The earliest amphorae were made by the Greeks but later different versions of such jars were produced almost throughout Europe.

Amphora finds have been reported from around forty sites scattered all across the Indian subcontinent from Taxila in the north-west to Alagankulam in the extreme south (Appendix III). Many specimens have been obtained from the early historical sites of Maharashtra and Gujarat. Finds from the east coast are comparatively less (Map 3). The majority of the finds are from archaeological excavations while a few are surface collections.

Mortimer Wheeler has argued that the import of amphorae into India began in the early years of the first century AD.[18] Recent studies and discoveries, however, have indicated that the amphorae began to reach Arikamedu from the second century BC.[19] At Arikamedu, almost half the number of sherds are of genuine Greek Koan amphorae of the second century BC. Many amphorae pieces from Alagankulam, too, are from layers of the pre-Christian era. A significant observation is that in all the excavated amphora sites such as Arikamedu, Karaikadu, Karur and Alagankulam which have also revealed rouletted ware, the rouletted ware pre-dated the amphorae by half a century. The contention that both rouletted ware and amphorae appear from almost the beginning of the human settlement at Alagankulam[20] is flawed. Here, rouletted pottery has been discovered from layers dating to around 200 BC while NBP ware has been assigned to around 150 BC. All these three types of pottery, viz., amphorae, NBP ware and rouletted ware have been found together at Alagankulam in layers of the late first century BC. In most of the excavated sites, the number of amphorae is maximum in the first century AD layers. With the gradual decline in the volume of sea trade, the import of amphorae into India also began to steadily decline from around the late first century AD. Amphorae sherds from the post-first

MAP 3: DISTRIBUTION PATTERN OF AMPHORA
FINDS IN THE INDIAN SUBCONTINENT

century AD layers, restricted to a few sites in India, are generally limited in number. Alagankulam alone, however, has yielded a sizeable number of fragments even from layers of the third-fourth centuries AD.

Contrary to general belief, most sites in India have yielded very few amphora sherds, except Arikamedu where a single excavation (Wheeler, 1945) has revealed 116 fragments representing approximately the same number of vessels. Excavations at the site by the French have brought to light 77 fragments. Recent excavations have yielded many more pieces including body sherds and handle fragments. At Nevasa, 63 sherds have been found. Although archaeological excavations were conducted in different parts of Karur, only six fragments have been reported. Taxila, Mathura, Vasavasamudram and some other sites have each revealed a single fragment. Information about the precise number of sherds from many other sites is not available.

The distribution pattern of the amphora presents a contrast to that of rouletted ware. While around 100 sites have revealed rouletted ware, barely 40 sites have yielded the amphora. Most of the rouletted ware sites are on the east coast, whereas the amphora sites are heavily concentrated in the west, mainly in Gujarat (15 sites) and Maharashtra (9 sites) which together account for over 60 per cent of the total amphora finds in India. The Coromandel coast has barely 7 amphora sites including Arikamedu which has yielded the largest number of sherds among all the Indian sites. Even on the west coast, no amphora has been found in the southernmost part (Kerala). In fact, this region has not yielded any type of Roman or pseudo-Roman pottery.

Barring a few single specimens of amphorae in places such as Taxila and Mathura, there are two distinct concentrations of amphora sites— one in the west (Maharashtra, Gujarat) and the other in the south-east (mainly Tamilnadu).

Among the finds from Tamilnadu, those reported from Vellalur (near Coimbatore) and Vijayamangalam (near Erode) are not widely known. Doubts have been expressed about the identification of the amphorae from these sites.[21] Yet, the fact that these sites lie within the region where evidence for the Roman trade of the first century AD in terms of Julio-Claudian coin hoards is numerous, makes these amphora finds assume special significance. It may be noted that among all the sites of India, Vellalur has yielded the maximum number of Roman coin hoards—six major hoards, totalling over 1,000 coins ranging in date from Augustus to Nero, besides some of the finest specimens of Roman gold jewellery of the first century AD. Recently, rouletted sherds have been collected from the disturbed habitation mound locally known as Uppiliappanmēdu at this site.

The amphorae finds from Vasavasamudram, Arikamedu, Karaikadu and Alagankulam do not come as a surprise because all these sites were important Indo-Roman trading ports of the first century AD when trade in amphorae was at its peak. Although the excavated materials from Vasavasamudram have been dated to the third-fourth centuries AD, it may be noted that the site was badly damaged before the small-scale archaeological digs and the amphora, probably bearing the trademark stamp, from the site, is not from the stratified context.

Karur, on the banks of the Amaravati, although not a port-city, was a flourishing capital of the Sangam Cheras and a famous market town. It was well connected with several other trading centres such as Uraiyur which supplied muslin to the Romans, and the port of Kaveripumpattinam. Karur has yielded hundreds of Roman coins and early historical jewellery revealing classical influence, mostly of the first century AD. Hence, the discovery of the amphorae at Karur is not surprising. The amphora finds from the site are confined to two trenches, lying close to one another, almost at the summit of the mound representing the old township. In both these trenches, a habitational deposit of about 5 m. has revealed that the site was in continuous occupation from the pre-Christian era to the medieval times. One of these trenches has yielded three amphora pieces: a rim at a depth of 1.10 m., another rim at a depth of 1.85 m. and a double handle at a depth of 1.75 m. The other trench has also yielded three fragments: a (body?) sherd and shoulder portion with a part of the handle at a depth of 4.30 m. and another small sherd at a depth of 4.50 m. It is therefore clear that the use of the amphora in the latter trench pre-dated its use in the former trench by a few decades. All the amphora finds have, however, been assigned to period II of the site, i.e. to the first two centuries of the Christian era. The associated finds include rouletted, black and red and red slipped wares. Some of the black and red ware sherds bear short legends in Tamil-Brāhmī script palaeographically akin to the famous Tamil-Brāhmī rock inscription at Pugalur, about 15 km. from Karur. Significantly, the inscription at Pugalur mentions the names of three generations of Chera rulers who are believed to have lived around the first century AD. The two other relevant discoveries from the excavations at Karur are the badly corroded Roman silver coin found at a depth of 52 cm.(?) below ground level as well as a square copper coin bearing an elephant on the obverse and a bow and arrow on the reverse. The latter coin, probably minted in the first century BC, is obviously an issue of the Sangam Cheras whose royal insignia was the bow. It may be noted that the solitary Roman coin was found in a trench which did not reveal the amphora.

Archaeological confirmation for the trade in amphorae between south India and Rome has come from the recent finds at the coastal site of Leukos Limen (Quseir al-Qadim) in Egypt. Of all the Roman Red Sea ports in Egypt, Leukos Limen is the closest to the river Nile and the most important from the point of view of trade. The finds from the site include two potsherds bearing Tamil-Brāhmī legends, huge quantities of amphorae and the remnants of an ancient glass-making industry.[22] The amphorae from the site are so large that it is not possible to accept that all the specimens were meant for use by the inhabitants of the area. Some of these amphorae would have been intended for trans-shipment to the ports of the Tamil country. This hypothesis is corroborated by the finds, in several Egyptian sites, of innumerable Rhodian and Knidian amphorae, identical to those seen in Arikamedu. Begley's recent excavations at Arikamedu have even revealed Tunisian amphorae of the fifth century AD. R. Nagaswamy has also reported Tunisian red ware from Alagankulam.[23] Berenice, the southernmost Egyptian Red Sea port, has also yielded a first century AD amphora fragment bearing a Tamil-Brāhmī inscription.[24]

Among all the amphora sites of western India, Ter is very important as it lies on the trade route linking Eastern Deccan with the port of Barygaza (Broach) via Paithan (an amphora site) and Nashik. Ter was also well connected with Kondapur, Nevasa and Nagarjunakonda. Amphorae have been recovered from the latter three sites. It is quite likely that the amphorae reached many sites in Gujarat and Ter from the port of Barygaza. From Ter, the amphorae would have been carried further east, may be even to Nagarjunakonda. Bhokardan, another amphora site in western India, also lies on the caravan route linking Ter, Paithan and Ujjain, the only amphora site in Madhya Pradesh. Bhokardan was well linked with Junnar (an amphora site), Karle, Kanheri and Kalyan. Thus, all the amphora sites in western India constitute a well knit group of commercial centres and Roman artifacts from one site could have easily been carried to the other sites as part of the trade process. Significantly, many of these western sites were also mint towns. The mint at Paithan, the capital of the Sātavāhanas, was obviously a Sātavāhana mint.[25] Junnar also had a mint used by the Sātavāhanas and later by the Western Kshatrapas.[26]

The amphora find at Chandravalli (Karnataka) has to be viewed in the context of the discovery of several first century AD Roman coins and rouletted ware from the site. The site has yielded a fragment of an original amphora in an unstratified context and another red ware jar, comparable to the amphora, probably in a stratified layer.[27]

The discovery of the amphora from Manikpatna (Orissa), lying at a distance of 50 km. from Puri, is puzzling because the Orissa region has hardly yielded any notable Roman or pseudo-Roman vestiges apart from the gold coins at Bamanghati, which were never fully published and are now lost, and rouletted pottery from Sisupalgarh. Recent explorations along the Orissa coast have, however, brought to light a number of ancient port sites that may have participated in the Indo-Roman trade.

Taxila and Mathura, two amphora sites, have each revealed a Roman coin of the first century AD. The strategic location and consequent commercial importance of Taxila are too well known.[28] Three major trade routes, one from northern and eastern India, the second from western Asia and the third from Kashmir and Central Asia, converged at Taxila. The amphora and the Roman coin found at Taxila would have reached the site from Rome over the land route across Central Asia. It is not clear how a fragment of an amphora handle recovered from stratified layers during excavations at Ambarish Tila, a mound in the northern part of Mathura city, reached the site. According to M.C. Joshi and A.K. Sinha, the sherd reached Mathura from the port of Barygaza.[29] This is a very circuitous route and evidence for any direct trade between Barygaza and Mathura is scanty, besides, Roman artifactual finds in the region between these two important trade centres are extremely limited. A more plausible explanation is that the amphora could have reached Mathura from Taxila. The close contacts between Taxila and Mathura are attested by the discovery of Mathura red sandstone in Taxila. It may also be noted that Mathura, on the banks of the river Yamuna (or Jamuna), lies almost midway on the long trade route linking Central Asia and Taxila with the port of Tamralipti (or Tamluk) in eastern India.

As wine was an important item of export from Rome to India, archaeologists and historians have, till recently, presumed that all the amphorae in India are wine jars and that the very presence of the amphorae in any part of the subcontinent indicates that it was engaged in trade in wine. Recent studies on the amphorae from Arikamedu, however, have revealed that all the amphorae in India are not of the same type.[30] Different versions of the jar showing subtle variations in size, shape and surface treatment and manufactured at different times at various European sites reached India. Moreover, items other than wine such as olive oil and *garum* (a fish sauce) were also exported to India in the amphorae. At Arikamedu, a few specimens of olive oil jars from Spain and from the Istrian Peninsula in the Northern Adriatic and more than nine fragments of the Spanish *garum* amphorae have been identified. Some of the amphorae are believed to have been used for the storage of fruits, mainly apples. The majority of the amphorae fragments are, however, of wine jars. The amphorae physically examined by me in different collections in Tamilnadu may be Greek Koan wine amphorae or Italian pseudo-Koan wine amphorae, most probably the latter. It should be stressed here that many of the amphorae finds in India are too fragmentary to determine the original shape of the vessel. The amphora sherd from Mathura bearing the inscription 'M. CAVSTR SVR' is of a wine amphora probably manufactured in or near Pompeii or Sorrento in Italy in the late first century BC. Further, many of the amphorae, both in western and southern India, are lined on the inside with a resinous substance. Such a practice, normally confined to wine amphorae, was intended either to reduce the porosity of the vessel and/or to flavour the wine with the resin. In some cases, the incrustation may merely constitute the hardened sediments in the liquid stored for long periods in the amphora. Xinru Liu's contention, not supported by any evidence, that the resinous material may be the residue of some kind of medicine[31] is unacceptable. The available evidence, although in 'bits' and 'pieces', is enough to indicate that wine was the chief, although not the only, item carried to India in the amphorae. The *garum* jars in Arikamedu simply confirm the existence of a Roman colony at the site since the early Romans considered *garum* as an important culinary delicacy.

What could be the reasons for the concentration of amphora finds in the Maharashtra-Gujarat region? Could the popularity of Mahayana Buddhism in the region during the early historical period be indirectly related to these amphora finds? By the middle of the first century AD, the rigid rules governing the lives of Buddhist monks may have been considerably relaxed, and, hence, the use of wine and also olive oil may have become common in the *vihāras*. This, in turn, could have resulted in a sudden increase in the demand for the Mediterranean wine that was carried to the ports of Western Deccan in the amphorae. This explanation[32] is not convincing but is supported by the fact that a good number of amphora sites such as Taxila, Mathura, Devnimori, Rajbandar

(near Bombay), Ter, Daranikota and Nagarjunakonda were major
Buddhist centres of the early centuries of the Christian era. In fact,
Devnimori, on the banks of the river Meshvo in Gujarat, yielded
amphorae sherds within the monastery premises. In the north-west, at
Shaikhan Dheri, the Kushan site of the city Pushkalavati, a workshop
or storeroom of distillation apparatus was found in a Buddhist shrine.
Here, the pottery used for making and storing liquor has been identified
and it has been suggested that the shrine was associated with the
consumption of wine for a very long period of time.[33] The Buddhist
monasteries may have participated in the far-flung wine trade chiefly
with the objective of helping the merchants who passed through these
establishments many of which depended on the generosity of the traders
for their very survival.

Another explanation for the greater number of amphora sites in
western India is that in Gujarat and the adjoining regions, Roman trade
followed a barter system; in other words, Roman amphorae and other
objects like bronze statuettes and glass vessels were obtained in exchange
for Indian products. The people of south India, on the other hand,
insisted on payment in the form of gold and silver coins from Rome in
exchange for the goods from India. The discovery of several Roman
bronze and glass antiquities in western India and the absence of
significant Roman numismatic finds in the region, specially in Gujarat,
and the large number of aurei and denarii hoards in the four southern
states of Andhra Pradesh, Tamilnadu, Kerala and Karnataka lend support
to this view.

It may also be suggested that the paucity of amphora finds in south
India may be because some of the jars brought here may have been
filled with Indian spices and taken back by the foreign traders.

At this point, it is important to examine some interesting evidence,
from both the Mediterranean region and India, regarding the export of
wine to India. In this connection, the possibility that a few ports of
south India occasionally received foreign wine in containers other than
the amphora, cannot be ruled out. Such containers may include Roman
bronze vessels some of which have been discovered both in west and
south India. This may partially account for the paucity of amphora
finds in south India, specially Tamilnadu where Roman wine was
popular. It may also be noted that besides the amphorae, other types of
containers including huge wooden barrels were sometimes used to
transport wine over long distances in the Roman empire.[34]

During the reign of Augustus, there was a sudden spurt in the production of wine in the empire.[35] As there was an unprecedented increase in the volume of trade between Rome and south India during Augustus's time, wine exports to India during his reign and that of his successors are not surprising. The *Periplus* (56) lists wine as an item of export to India but adds that the quantity of such export is 'not much'. In any case, it is clear that the wine exported to India was mainly but not exclusively Italian. Wines from several other places including Laodicea in Syria and the Greek islands of Kos and Knidos were also known in India.

Early Indian literary works, both in Tamil and Sanskrit, contain information about wine trade. In ancient Sanskrit works, the term *kusula*, denoting a ceramic vessel with a conical base resembling the human leg, may refer to the amphora.[36]

Mediterranean wine, known for its fragrance and high quality, was in great demand in ancient India. The greater demand for foreign wine in the west and south than in the north and north-west may be because the wine produced in the north-west, especially in Begram, was of a better quality than the wine produced in other parts of India.

The amphorae and the wine contained in them were very expensive and it may be inferred that the demand for these items in India was restricted to certain specific regions enjoying political stability and economic prosperity. Unlike the Roman coin or rouletted ware sites, many of the amphora sites are early historical urban centres of political and/or commercial and/or religious importance. Hence, each of these towns had an 'elite' class of people who were regular consumers of imported wine. In this connection, it may be pointed out that the more important port towns such as Arikamedu and Alagankulam would have certainly had a higher proportion of 'elite' population. Amphorae finds have been recovered from different layers of many of the excavation trenches in these sites. In the lesser known inland trade centres including Karur, the amphorae finds are confined to just one or two layers in one or two neighbouring trenches. This clearly indicates that in the inland sites, the ware was used on a very limited scale for a shorter period of time. Even the Tamil *Sangam* literature contains a pointed reference to the sweet-scented Roman wine enjoyed by the ruling elite—the kings and nobles (*Purananūru*, 56,17-21). Roman wine is nowhere mentioned in relation to the common people who could probably afford only the local brands.

A bas-relief (date unknown) of a camel loaded with amphorae found in Central Italy may be part of the funerary monument of an Italian family trading with the east, particularly India.[37] Again, several sculptures of the later Sātavāhanas and Ikṣvākus depict the drinking of wine in Roman(?) goblets, both by men and women. Such drinking scenes are also seen in the sculptures of Gandhara and Mathura as well as in the Ajanta murals. Terracotta pedestal cups betraying classical influence and believed to be used for drinking wine have been reported from Kanchi. Karur has revealed a small red slipped ware cup probably used for serving or drinking wine. The cup with a diameter of 6.2 cm. is a surface find. The cup bears a Tamil-Brāhmī inscription reading *'ku ra kal'* meaning 'little cup'. The inscription is palaeographically dated to the second century AD.

Imitations of the amphorae, besides the find from Chandravalli noted earlier, have been recovered from a few more sites. Such finds are concentrated all along the east coast from Bengal to the tip of the peninsula.

B.N. Mukherjee has published four such handleless imitations varying from 15 cm. to 18.3 cm. in height, from Hadipur in West Bengal.[38] All of them bear Kharoṣṭi or Kharoṣṭi-Brāhmī inscriptions. Like the trademark stamps on the original amphorae, the legends on the Hadipur jars, too, bear the names of the owners/potters. Palaeographically, the Hadipur jars are dated between the first and fourth centuries AD. Significantly, the first century AD jar is stylistically closest to the original amphora. Similar carrot-shaped amphora-like vessels have also been found at other sites like Chandraketugarh and Tamluk. A double handled imitation(?) amphora (height 66 cm.) has recently been reported from Karanji village, not far from Jayarampur, a historic site on the West Bengal-Orissa border.[39]

No details are available about some such jars recovered from the village of Pudur in the Nellore district of Andhra.[40]

Regarding the finds from the Tamilnadu region, conical jars erroneously termed as 'amphorae' in a few of the earlier publications, have been reported from Tiruverkadu, Kanchi, Vasavasamudram, Nerumbur, Arikamedu, Karaikadu and Sendamangalam.[41] Interestingly, these sites all lie in the Chingleput-South Arcot-Pondicherry region.

Unlike the amphorae, these conical jars from Tamilnadu do not have either a neck or handles and are in different shades of red including reddish yellow and greyish red. Some of the jars are grey or black inside. Jars from different sites as also those from the different layers of the same site show minor variations in size, shape and lip-type. The vessels are usually around 1m. in height. Broadly, there are two distinct varieties of jars: one is thin, brittle with a smooth lustrous surface and is bright red on the outside and black inside (Plate 10); the other is of a much thicker and coarser material and is generally dull red in colour (Plate 11). While the coarser variety has been found in all the sites, the finer variety is restricted to Arikamedu and Vasavasamudram. Even in these two sites, the sherds of the finer variety are scarce. In fact, most of the finds from the recent excavations at Arikamedu are of the coarser variety; the interior of some of these crudely made jars are often rough with lumps of clay adhering to the surface.

Normally, these conical jars do not have a slip but a few specimens from Arikamedu have a slip which is invariably confined to the portion above the shoulder. While some conical jars are completely handmade and others completely wheel-turned, a number of jars, particularly from Arikamedu and Vasavasamudram, are handmade up to a certain height from the base, above which they are wheel-turned. Smaller conical jars placed within bigger ones have been found at Arikamedu and Kanchi but not at Vasavasamudram. Due to their very shape, the smaller conical vessels could be easily and neatly fitted into the larger ones to add to the thickness, strength and durability of the container. This was not possible in the case of the imported amphorae which had large handles.

The mouth of many conical jars from Kanchi and one from Vasavasamudram is closed except for a tiny circular hole measuring 4 to 7 cm. in diameter at the centre (of the 'lid' portion). This hole seems to have been covered with a small terracotta stopper. Several such stoppers have been found along with the jars at Kanchi.

Among the conical jar sites in the Tamilnadu region, Nerumbur, Kanchi, Tiruverkadu and Sendamangalam have not yielded even a single specimen of the original amphora. The other three sites have revealed varying numbers of amphora specimens: a single sherd from Vasavasamudram; a few sherds from Karaikadu and hundreds of sherds from Arikamedu. The exact number of conical jars in Arikamedu is not known (definitely 100+). Among the other sites, Kanchi has revealed the maximum number (50+ jars) closely followed by Vasavasamudram (30+ jars).

These conical jars, modelled on the imported amphorae, could have been produced only after the first batch of the amphorae reached the Tamilnadu region. At Arikamedu, these jars have often been found in many trenches almost throughout the occupation of the site. Thus, the production of the jars started in the second century BC and continued

PLATE 10. CONICAL JAR—FINE VARIETY,
VASAVASAMUDRAM (TAMILNADU)

PLATE 11. CONICAL JAR—COARSE VARIETY,
VASAVASAMUDRAM (TAMILNADU)

up to the first century AD. It is likely that the earliest conical jars were produced in Arikamedu.

These conical jars, like the amphorae, were used to store wine. This is confirmed by the black discolouration, probably due to the action of wine, on the interior of one of the jars unearthed during the recent excavations at Arikamedu. At Kanchi and Arikamedu, the arrangement of a series of jars in rows may be the remnants of a small wine cellar or an ancient bar.

Of all the sites in the Tamilnadu region, Tiruverkadu, on the outskirts of Madras city, is a recent discovery. Located on the banks of the river Cooum, the earliest human settlement at the site was around the fifth century BC. The site had easy access to the port of Manarpha, identified with modern Mylapore (part of present day Madras), through the Cooum which, in pre-modern times, was navigable. Hence, Tiruverkadu would have participated in the maritime trade.

Large urns vaguely resembling the amphora, but not necessarily inspired by the latter, have been recovered from a few south Indian sites. In the early years of the twentieth century, A.H. Longhurst has recorded a very large ancient burial urn (date?) under a rock-cut tomb, 9 km. from Calicut. But for the absence of handles, the urn is not unlike the Roman amphora, having the same type of pointed base for insertion in a stand or in the ground.[42]

The amphora had limited influence on early Indian sculptural art. The Roman amphora depicted in a sculpture-panel (third century AD?) from Nagarjunakonda is a stray example. The site boasts of innumerable stone sculptures betraying Mediterranean influence.[43] The amphora may also have inspired the vase motif frequently occurring on several early coins of west and south India.[44]

## TERRA SIGILLATA

Wheeler, in his report on his excavations in Arikamedu, has mentioned a red glazed ware, some sherds of which have been decorated by being pressed into a mould.[45] For all these sherds, he has used, the term 'arretine' derived from the Latin place-name Arezzo, a famous centre for the production of such pottery in Italy. Later scholars, both European and American, have repeatedly emphasized that the sherds from Arikamedu are not exclusively from Arezzo; sherds from many other pottery centres in Italy including Pisa have been identified. Hence, the general term 'terra sigillata' which refers to a class of ancient pottery including mould-made decorated vessels as well as undecorated wheel-made ones produced in Italy or in imitation of such Italian wares, would be more appropriate to describe this class of finds in India. Indian publications including excavation reports and university textbooks, however, continue to use the term 'arretine'.

Apart from Arikamedu, terra sigillata has been found in some other sites such as Rajamundry, Arasankuppam, Karur, Kodumanal and Alagankulam (Plate 12), all in south-east India. It has been ascertained that reports about such finds from other sites including Chandravalli, Kanchi and Uraiyur are not true.[46]

The circumstances of the sigillata find at Arasankuppam are not clear. At Karur, fragments of the ware were picked up from the surface, but archaeological excavations did not reveal the ware at all. At Arikamedu and Alagankulam, sigillata has been recovered from the surface as well as in the stratified context. At Kodumanal and Rajamundry, it has been found in stratified layers only.

Many of the sherds from Arikamedu bear the potter's stamp and it is therefore possible to identify the place of their origin. Unfortunately, the finds from all the other sites are tiny fragments.

Among all the Roman and pseudo-Roman ceramics in India, sigillata has been reported not only from the least number of sites but also in

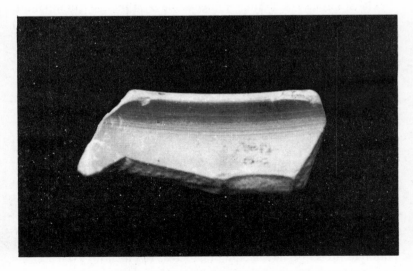

PLATE 12. SIGILLATA SHERD, ALAGANKULAM (TAMILNADU)

extremely limited quantities. Even at Arikamedu, Wheeler's excavation yielded only 31 fragments representing a smaller number of vessels. Of these, only 22 fragments are from a stratified context. Surface collections and excavations at the site before and after Wheeler have revealed some more sherds. The finds from all the other sites are far less. Karur has yielded just three fragments while Arasankuppam has revealed a single sherd along with unidentified red and thick black wares.

It is evident that sigillata reached Arikamedu and Alagankulam after crossing Africa. The other Indian sites would have received the ware from either of these two port towns. According to recent studies, different varieties of sigillata were sent to India mainly during the first half of the first century AD.[47] At Arikamedu, the ware has been found in stratified layers along with amphorae, conical jars, rouletted and other indigenous wares. It is most likely that at Karur and Kodumanal too, sigillata was in use only during this period. The precise stratigraphy of the finds from Kodumanal can be known only after the publication of the series of large-scale excavations at the site undertaken by different agencies. Rajamundry, on the banks of the river Godavari, has yielded sigillata along with red polished ware in an early second century AD layer. This Buddhist settlement with a *stupa* and a monastery, at a great distance from Alagankulam and Arikamedu, lies in the heart of the Andhra region whose trade contacts with Rome, it may be recalled, reached the peak only during the second century AD. In any case, it is clear that the cessation of the flow of sigillata into India pre-dates the cessation of the import of the other types of foreign objects.

Wheeler has assumed that sigillata was a regular item of Indo-Roman trade and he has attributed the sudden decrease in the import of the ware at Arikamedu to the decline in the production of the ware in the west.[48] In recent years, however, many scholars, both in India and outside, have expressed the view that the ware was brought to India as part of the personal belongings of western traders who visited the country in large numbers.[49] This line of argument is strengthened by the fact that there was a Roman colony at Arikamedu. Significantly, most of the stratified fragments of sigillata are from the site's 'Northern Sector' which is widely believed to be the residential locality of the foreigners, probably because they would not have resided far from the 'warehouse'. It must, however, be remembered that the 'warehouse' itself was constructed only towards the end of the 'sigillata phase' of the site. Further, the abnormally fragmentary condition of the sigillata, not only in Arikamedu but in all the other Indian sites as well, implies that the ware was continuously used for a good number of years. At Arikamedu, some of the best specimens of the 'superior' or 'finer' variety of rouletted ware have also been from the 'Northern Sector'. The fact that the Roman settlement at Arikamedu continued for a few decades beyond the 'sigillata phase' may be explained by the suggestion that the early groups of Mediterranean traders visiting Arikamedu would have carried the sigillata with them but after a lapse of a few years, the ware would have become scarce as it was not an object of regular trade and at this stage, the traders residing at the site would have been compelled to seek local substitutes for the imported sigillata. This, again, would not have posed any problem as Arikamedu was a pottery-manufacturing centre.

Like Arikamedu, Alagankulam also had a Roman settlement. Alagankulam, located in the delta of the Vaigai, on the northern bank of the river, is locally referred to as 'Kōttaimēdu' or 'fort mound'. The mound measures over 1 km. in diameter and is enclosed by a ruined brick fort from which the place gets its name. During the early historical period, the Vaigai was a perennial river, a fact corroborated by the early Tamil literature.[50] The location of the site is geographically and historically very important because of its close proximity to the Pamban channel through which ships could cross Adam's bridge between the Indian mainland and Sri Lanka. Interestingly, Mantai at the other end of Adam's bridge, on the north-west tip of Sri Lanka, has also yielded the sigillata.[51] Unlike Arikamedu, which declined in the second century AD, Alagankulam continued to flourish till the fourth-fifth centuries AD. The precise stratigraphy and the types of sigillata at Alagankulam are not known.

The non-occurrence of sigillata at several other well known trading ports of south India including Muziris on the west coast may be attributed to the fact that unlike Arikamedu and Alagankulam, many of the other coastal sites did not support a regular settlement of Roman merchants who would have needed the prized sigillata for their domestic use.

## RED POLISHED WARE

A red polished ware (RPW), closely resembling the Mediterranean Eastern Sigillata A, has been reported from several sites in India. The Indian ware is wheel-turned and is of fine fabric and has been made from well levigated clay. A burnished slip is usually seen both on the inner and outer surface. The colour of the slip is mostly bright red and in rare cases, it is brownish red. Decorations on the ware, though not common, include lines of black paint and finger pinches.

Over 500 sites spread from Punjab and Haryana in the north to Andhra-Tamilnadu in the south have yielded the ware both in the stratified and non-stratified contexts.[52] Over 400 of these sites are concentrated in the Gujarat region, mainly along the Sourashtra coast. The date of the ware ranges from the first century BC to the eleventh-twelfth centuries AD, although an overwhelming majority of the specimens are from the early historical period.

Subbarao, one of the earliest scholars to discuss the RPW in detail, has mentioned that the ware is an Indian ceramic whose finish and technique of manufacture betray Mediterranean influence.[53] According to S.R. Rao, as the technology of well fired finely made pottery was known in India even before the beginning of Roman trade, the RPW may be an indigenous ceramic type instead of an imitation of any of the Roman wares.[54] In support of his argument, he has cited evidence obtained from the excavated site of Amreli (Gujarat), which has yielded the largest number of RPW vessel shapes. At Amreli, the RPW was preceded by a locally produced black ceramic, identical to it except in colour. An archaeo-chemical analysis of these sherds has revealed that both black and red polished wares were made from the same clay and the difference in their colour was due to their being fired under reducing and oxidizing conditions respectively. As all the RPW vessel forms are strictly Indian in character and as almost all these forms also occur in coarser Indian associated wares, it has now been established that the RPW is an indigenous ceramic without any foreign influence on it. The ware has certain peculiar characteristics in terms of its distribution pattern, associated finds and chronology.

There are a few similarities between the RPW and rouletted ware finds in India. In many instances, both these pottery types have been found along with authentic Mediterranean objects such as amphorae and to a lesser extent, terra sigillata. In most of the sites where the RPW has been discovered along with other Indian ceramics, specially in the stratified context, the latter is more numerous than the former, implying that the RPW was a 'luxury' item, sparingly used.

Generally, the RPW in the coastal sites is of a finer material and higher workmanship than that of the inland sites. Similarly, while the RPW of the period between the first century BC and the third century AD is of a very fine fabric, there is a slow but steady decline in the quality of the pottery in the later centuries. This change in quality is discernible even in those sites which have revealed the ware in layers of both the early historical and later periods.

Like rouletted ware, the RPW also exhibits distinct regional variations in form, fabric and colour. RPW finds are, however, more widespread than rouletted ware sites.

The predominance of RPW in Gujarat and to a lesser extent, in Andhra may be directly related to the presence of a large number of Buddhist establishments in these areas. In fact, many of the RPW sites, like the amphora sites, are early historical Buddhist centres and some of the RPW finds have been recovered from within the premises of the monasteries, for example, Devnimori (Gujarat), Chandavaram (Andhra) and Kaveripattinam (Tamilnadu). It is likely that in addition to the amphorae containing wine or oil, the red polished pottery and/ or the contents therein were in demand in the Buddhist establishments. The most common shape of the RPW is the sprinkler, a flat-based elliptical jar with a narrow neck and a vertical spout at the shoulder (Plate13). As there is no knowledge of the practical use of the sprinkler, it has been surmised that the vessel was used in Buddhist ceremonies. In this connection, it may be noted that a sprinkler has been sculpted along with a tripod on the pedestal of the *Mahāparinirvāṇa* Buddha in Ajanta cave no. 26.[55] Again, the painting on the ceiling of cave no. 1 at Ajanta portrays a foreign(?) lady holding a wine flagon resembling the sprinkler.[56] Sculptures of Buddhist deities carrying sprinkler-like vessels are known in both the Gandhara and Mathura schools. The vessel is also described in early Buddhist literature.[57] Monks and traders who travelled long distances may have carried this impractical pottery-type from the Maharashtra-Gujarat region not only to the Buddhist centres of Andhra, but also to the Gangetic plains. This is attested by the fact that many of the RPW finds in Andhra have not been found in stratified layers earlier than the late first century AD whereas in Gujarat, the ware has often been discovered even in layers of the first century BC and the early first century AD. According to Begley, the RPW spread from Maharashtra to the east and south and from Gujarat to the north and north-east.[58]

Outside India, the RPW has been discovered in various sites in the Persian Gulf as also in Mantai, Anuradhapura and a few more sites in Sri Lanka.[59] Significantly, the Anuradhapura find is from a Buddhist monastery, i.e. Abhayagiri Vihāra. In many of the Lanka sites, the ware occurs in layers of the late second century AD and later. The quantity of the ware in both Sri Lanka and the Persian Gulf region is far less

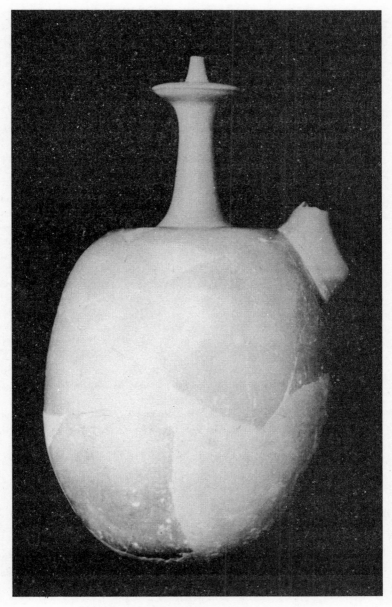

PLATE 13. SPRINKLER, YELLESVARAM (ANDHRA)

compared to the finds in India. Hence, India would have exported the RPW to these two regions. In this context, mention may also be made of a sherd of black ware, identified to be Indian but may not be of the NBP variety, reported from the archaeological excavations at Failaka, an island off Kuwait.[60]

## NOTES

1. Initially, like many other scholars, I was under the impression that rouletted pottery found in India was imported from the Mediterranean region. However, physical examination and comparison of the relevant ceramics in Indian and European collections, undertaken between 1993 and 1997, has convinced me that the finds from India are local products. I discussed the subject with V. Begley at New Delhi in 1992 and at Pondicherry in 1994.

2. For details about some of the rouletted ware finds outside India, see F.R. Allchin et al., *The Archaeology of Early Historic South Asia: The Emergence of Cities and States,* Cambridge, 1995, pp. 159-73; V. Begley, 'Ceramic Evidence for Pre-*Periplus* Trade on the Indian Coasts', in *Rome and India: The Ancient Sea Trade,* ed. V. Begley and Richard Daniel De Puma, Madison, 1991, pp. 157-96; O.Bopearachchi, 'Archaeological Evidence on Changing Patterns of International Trade Relations of Ancient Sri Lanka', in *Origin, Evolution and Circulation of Foreign Coins in the Indian Ocean,* ed. O. Bopearachchi and D.P.M.Weerakkody, New Delhi, 1998, pp. 133-78; S.U. Deraniyagala, 'The Citadel of Anuradhapura 1969: Excavations in the Gedige Area', *Ancient Ceylon,* vol. 2, 1972, pp. 48-169; M.J.Walker and S. Santoso, 'Romano-Indian Rouletted Pottery in Indonesia', *Asian Perspectives,* vol. 20, no. 2, 1977, pp. 228-35. For a survey of the close links between south India and Sri Lanka, see K.K.Pillay, *South India and Sri Lanka (Sir William Meyer Lectures, 1958-59—University of Madras),* Madras, 1975.

3. I.W. Ardika, P.S. Bellwood, R.A. Eggleton and D.J. Ellis, 'A Single Source for South Asian Export-Quality Rouletted Ware?' *Man and Environment,* vol. XVIII, no. 1, 1993, pp. 101-9.

4. P. Shanmugam, 'Two Coins of Tamil Origin from Thailand', *SSIC,* vol. IV, 1994, pp. 95-100.

5. V. Begley, 'Rouletted Ware at Arikamedu: A New Approach', *AJA,* vol. 92, 1988, pp. 427-40.

6. Vishwas D. Gogte, 'The Chandraketugarh-Tamluk Region of Bengal: Source of the Early Historic Rouletted Ware from India and Southeast Asia', *Man and Environment,* vol. XXII, no. 1, 1997, pp. 69-85.

7. For the comparison of the finds from Arikamedu and Brahmagiri, see Begley 'Rouletted Ware at Arikamedu', p. 428, fn. 11. For Satanikota, see N.C. Ghosh, *Excavations at Satanikota 1977-80,* New Delhi, 1986, pp. 107-13, 150-1.

8. T.V.G. Sastri, M.Kasturi Bai and M.Veerender, *Vaddamanu Excavations (1981-85),* Hyderabad, 1992, pp. 94-6.

9. For an analysis of the chronology of the ceramic finds in Kanchi, see S. Suresh, 'Roman Vestiges in Kanchipuram', in *Kanchi—A Heritage of Art and Religion*, ed. Nanditha Krishna, Madras, 1992, pp. 56-61.

10. K. Rajan, 'Stratigraphical Position of Russet-Coated Painted Ware', in *Indian Archaeological Heritage—Shri K.V. Soundara Rajan Festschrift I*, ed. C. Margabandhu, K.S. Ramachandran, A.P. Sagar and D.K. Sinha, Delhi, 1991, pp. 241-6.

11. I.K. Sarma, *Religion in Art and Historical Archaeology of South India: Contacts and Correlations*, Madras, 1987, p. 12.

12. For a general survey of the ceramic finds in several early historical sites of south India, see I.K. Sarma, 'Historical Archaeology of Tamilnadu and Kerala', *Tamil Civilization*, vol. V, nos.1 and 2, 1987, pp. 48-60; K.R. Srinivasan, 'Archaeology of Tamilnadu and Kerala—Accomplishments and Prospects', *Tamil Civilization*, vol. V, nos. 1 and 2, 1987, pp. 10-29.

13. Rajan, 'Stratigraphical Position of Russet-Coated Painted Ware', pp. 241-6.

14. V. Begley, 'Arikamedu Reconsidered', *AJA*, vol. 87, 1983, pp. 461-81.

15. Jan Bouzek, Jiří Břeň and Petr Charvát, 'The Chronology of the Local Pottery and Other Finds and Features Uncovered in the SW Sector of the Abhayagiri Vihara (Anuradhapura, Sri Lanka)', *Archeologické Yozhledy*, vol. XXXVIII, 1986, pp. 241-62.

16. Begley, 'Arikamedu Reconsidered', pp. 461-81; idem, 'Rouletting and Chattering, Decoration on Ancient and Present-day Pottery in India', *Expedition*, vol. 28, no. 1, 1986, pp. 47-54; idem, 'Rouletted Ware at Arikamedu', pp. 427-40. The main results of the recent excavations at Arikamedu are compiled in V. Begley et al., *The Ancient Port of Arikamedu— New Excavations and Researches, 1989-1992 I*, Pondicherry, 1996. I am grateful to the members of the excavation team, specially K.Kumar, for sharing with me information about the digs.

17. Sarma, *Religion in Art and Historical Archaeology of South India*, p. 13.

18. R.E.M.Wheeler, A. Ghosh and Krishna Deva, 'Arikamedu: An Indo-Roman Trading-Station on the East Coast of India', *AI*, vol. 2, 1946, pp. 17-124.

19. Begley, 'Arikamedu Reconsidered', pp. 461-81; K.W. Slane, 'Observations on Mediterranean Amphoras and Tablewares found in India', in *Rome and India: The Ancient Sea Trade*, ed. V. Begley and Richard Daniel De Puma, Madison, 1991, pp. 204-15; E.L. Will, 'The Mediterranean Shipping Amphoras from Arikamedu', in *Rome and India: The Ancient Sea Trade*, ed. V. Beglay and Richard Daniel De Puma, Madison, 1991, pp. 151-6. For a general discussion on the different types of amphorae and their dates see V.R. Grace, *Amphoras and the Ancient Wine Trade*, Princeton, 1979.

20. R. Nagaswamy, 'Alagankulam: An Indo-Roman Trading Port', in *Indian Archaeological Heritage—Shri K.V.Soundara Rajan Festschrift I*, ed. C. Margabandhu, K.S. Ramachandran, A.P. Sagar and D.K. Sinha, Delhi, 1991, pp. 247-54. There are discrepancies between Nagaswamy's descriptions and his diagram showing the cultural sequence of the site.

21. Officials at the Tamilnadu State Department of Archaeology, Coimbatore, expressed the doubt that the so-called 'amphorae' from Vellalur and Vijayamangalam may be Venetian jars of a late period. This, however, has not been confirmed. The whereabouts of the jars are not known. It is rumoured that they have been smuggled out of India.

22. For more details about the site see D.S.Whitcomb and J.H. Johnson, eds., *Quseir al-Qadim 1978 Preliminary Report*, Princeton, 1979. Also see S.E. Sidebotham, 'Ports of the Red Sea and the Arabia-India Trade', in *Rome and India: The Ancient Sea Trade*, ed. V. Begley and Richard Daniel De Puma, Madison, 1991, pp. 12-38.

23. Nagaswamy, 'Alagankulam', pp. 247-54.

24. I am grateful to I. Mahadevan for this information.

25. A.M. Shastri, 'Three Satavahana Mint-Towns', *SSIC*, vol. IV, 1994, pp. 57-62.

26. A.M. Shastri, 'Junnar: A Mint-Town of the Satavahanas', *SSIC*, vol. V, 1995, pp. 51-6.

27. Precise details about the imitation amphora from Chandravalli are not available. See R.S. Sharma, *Urban Decay in India (c.300-c.1000)*, New Delhi, 1987, pp. 85-6.

28. For more details about Taxila, see J. Marshall, *Taxila*, vols. I, II, III, Cambridge, 1951.

29. M.C. Joshi and A.K. Sinha, 'Discovery of an Amphora-Handle from Mathura', in *Indian Archaeological Heritage—Shri K.V. Soundara Rajan Festschrift I*, ed. C. Margabandhu, K.S. Ramachandran, A.P. Sagar and D.K. Sinha, Delhi, 1991, pp. 255-9.

30. Slane, 'Observations on Mediterranean Amphoras and Tablewares found in India', pp. 204-15; Will, 'The Mediterranean Shipping Amphoras from Arikamedu', 151-6.

31. Xinru Liu, *Ancient India and Ancient China: Trade and Religious Exchanges, A.D. 1-600*, New Delhi, 1988, p. 122, fn. 11.

32. Such an explanation has been hinted in R.N. Mehta, 'Urban Centres of Western India and the Western World', in *India and the West (Proceedings of a Seminar Dedicated to the Memory of Hermann Goetz)*, ed. Joachim Deppert, New Delhi, 1983, pp. 139-48.

33. Xinru Liu, *Ancient India and Ancient China*, pp. 122-3. I discussed this topic with F.R. Allchin in 1994.

34. Peter Garnsey and Richard Saller, *The Roman Empire—Economy, Society and Culture*, London, 1987, p. 54.

35. Garnsey and Saller, ibid., pp. 58-9.

36. Joshi and Sinha, 'Discovery of an Amphora-Handle from Mathura', pp. 255-9.

37. André Tchernia, 'Le Dromadaire Des Peticii Et Le Commerce Oriental', *Mélanges De L'École Française De Rome-Antiquité*, vol. 104, no. 1, 1992, pp. 293-301.

38. B.N. Mukherjee, *Indian Museum Bulletin XXV—Kharoṣṭī and Kharoṣṭī-*

Brāhmī *Inscriptions in West Bengal (India)* Calcutta, 1990, pp. 56-57, 71, Figs. 40, 41, 44, 48A and 48B.

39. For a general survey of some of the finds from the Bengal-Orissa region, see Gautam Sengupta, 'Archaeology of Coastal Bengal', in *Tradition and Archaeology— Early Maritime Contacts in the Indian Ocean,* ed. H.P. Ray and Jean-Francois Salles, New Delhi, 1996, pp. 115-28. B.N. Mukherjee shared much information about these finds, during my discussions with him at Calcutta in 1991, 1992, 1993 and 1994, at New Delhi in 1993 and 1994 and again when he visited me in Madras in 1996 and 2000.

40. The site was excavated during 1994-6 by the Birla Archaeological and Cultural Research Institute, Hyderabad. Full details of the excavation await publication. Members of the excavation team whom I met at Hyderabad in 1997 and 1998 informed that the finds include sherds of conical jars in imitation of the amphora.

41. None of these finds are adequately published. For a brief description of the finds from Arikamedu, see Wheeler, Ghosh and Deva, Arikamedu, p. 77. For Vasavasamudram, see R. Nagaswamy and A. Abdul Majeed, *Vasavasamudram (A Report on the Excavation Conducted by the Tamilnadu State Department of Archaeology),* Madras, 1978, pp. 11, 21-2, Fig. 14. Also see Suresh, 'Roman Vestiges in Kanchipuram', pp. 56-61; idem, 'Early Roman Finds in Madras City', in *Aspects of Madras—A Historical Perspective,* ed. G.J. Sudhakar, Madras, 1993, pp. 13-6. Between 1991 and 1998, I physically examined selected specimens from each of the sites.

42. A.H. Longhurst, 'Rock-Cut Tomb Near Calicut,' *Archaeological Survey of India Annual Report, 1911-12,* pp. 159-60.

43. For a general account of the history, monuments and sculptures of Nagarjunakonda, see H. Sarkar and B.N. Misra, *Nagarjunakonda,* New Delhi, 1980. Also see R.M. Cimino and F. Scialpi, *India and Italy—Exhibition Organized in Collaboration with the Archaeological Survey of India and the Indian Council for Cultural Relations,* Rome, 1974, pp. 36, 42.

44. Such vase motifs are seen on the coins issued by a number of dynasties including the Vishnukundins. See Sobhana Gokhale, 'Junnar in Trade during Satavahana Period', in *Coinage, Trade and Economy (3rd International Colloquium, January 8th-11th, 1991),* ed. A.K. Jha, Nashik, 1991, pp. 55-7.

45. Wheeler, Ghosh and Deva, 'Arikamedu', pp. 17-124.

46. See S.Gurumurthy, *Ceramic Traditions in South India (Down to 300 A.D.),* Madras, 1981, p. 299; Suresh, 'Roman Vestiges in Kanchipuram', pp. 56-61; idem, 'Early Roman Finds in Madras City', pp. 13-16.

47. Begley, 'Arikamedu Reconsidered', pp. 461-81; H. Comfort, 'Terra Sigillata at Arikamedu', in *Rome and India: The Ancient Sea Trade,* ed. V. Begley and Richard Daniel De Puma, Madison, 1991, pp. 134-50.

48. Wheeler, Ghosh and Deva, 'Arikamedu', pp. 17-124.

49. Many scholars including David MacDowall, I. Mahadevan and K.V. Raman expressed such a view during personal discussions with me at Madras between

1987 and 1990. See Comfort, 'Terra Sigillata at Arikamedu', pp. 134-50; Slane, 'Observations on Mediteranean Amphoras and Tablewares found in India', pp. 204-15.

50. For details regarding the references to the river in early Tamil poems, see Nagaswamy, 'Alagankulam', pp. 247-54.

51. R. Silva and J. Bouzek, 'Mantai—A Second Arikamedu', *Antiquity*, 1985, pp. 46-7. Also see Slane, 'Observations on Mediterranean Amphoras and Tablewares found in India', pp. 204-15.

52. The finds from various sites are to date in the possession of different institutions. Between 1987 and 1994, I physically examined the sherds recovered from sites in north India, Andhra and Tamilnadu. Finds from specific regions have been selectively listed and sometimes briefly described in a number of publications. See Nancy Pinto Orton, 'Red Polished Ware in Gujarat: A Catalogue of Twelve Sites', in *Rome and India: The Ancient Sea Trade*, ed. V. Begley and Richard Daniel De Puma, Madison, 1991, pp. 46-81; Xinru Liu, *Ancient India and Ancient China*, pp. 29-30, 189-90, Map 4, Fig. 2. For further bibliographic citations for RPW see Begley, 'Ceramic Evidence for Pre-*Periplus* Trade', p. 189, fn.5.

53. B. Subbarao, *Baroda Through the Ages*, Baroda, 1953, pp. 32, 56-64. Also see H.D. Sankalia, B. Subbarao and S.B. Deo, *The Excavations at Maheshwar and Navdatoli, 1952-1953*, Poona, 1958, pp. 161-2.

54. S.R. Rao, *Excavations at Amreli, A Kshatrapa-Gupta Town*, Baroda, 1966, pp. 51-9, 80.

55. M.N. Deshpande, 'Roman Pottery in India', in *Potteries in Ancient India*, ed. B.P. Sinha, Patna, 1969, pp. 275-84.

56. A. Ghosh, ed., *Ajanta Murals*, New Delhi, 1967, Pl. XLI; G. Yazdani, *Ajanta I*, Delhi, 1983, pp. 48-51. Also see Deshpande, ibid., pp. 275-84.

57. Arun K. Nag, 'Identification and Origin of the Sprinkler', in *Śri Dineśacandrika Studies in Indology*, ed. B.N. Mukherjee, D.R. Das, S.S. Biswas and S.P. Singh, Delhi, 1983, pp. 389-95. Nag's statement that the sprinkler is not seen in the southernmost part of the country is incorrect as the vessel form has been unearthed even in Kaveripattinam (Tamilnadu).

58. Begley, 'Ceramic Evidence for Pre-*Periplus* Trade', p. 192, fn. 48.

59. For the find in the Persian Gulf see D.Whitehouse and A.Williamson, 'Sassanian Maritime Trade', *Iran*, vol. 11, 1973, pp. 29-49; Jean-Francois Salles, 'The Periplus of the Erythraean Sea and the Arab-Persian Gulf', paper presented at the international seminar on *India and the Roman World Between the 1st and 4th centuries A.D.*, Madras, 1990. For the Anuradhapura find, see Bouzek, Břeň and Charvát, 'The Chronology of the Local Pottery and Other Finds', pp. 241-62. For the Mantai find, see John Carswell, 'The Port of Mantai, Sri Lanka', in *Rome and India: The Ancient Sea Trade*, ed. V. Begley and Richard Daniel De Puma, Madison, 1991, pp. 197-203.

60. Salles, ibid.

# 4

# Other Objects

ROMAN OBJECTS such as metal artifacts, glassware, jewellery and clay or terracotta figurines are not very common in India. Nevertheless, such objects have been discovered in a few sites spread throughout the subcontinent. Each of the finds is small in number—often a single, enigmatic specimen of a particular type of object. The antiquities occur in both the stratified and non-startified contexts, and mostly vary in date from the first century BC to the second century AD, although finds of a later period are known.

While Roman coins and ceramics found in India have been the focus of numerous studies, most of the other antiquities have, till date, not been properly catalogued or studied. An apparent reason for this is that the small number of finds of the latter types of antiquities has led to the assumption that these objects are not of much historical significance.

A major problem pertaining to the study of these minor antiquities in India is that it is extremely difficult to ascertain whether a particular object is an authentic import from the Mediterranean region or a local product betraying foreign influence. Imitations are fairly common even among Roman coins and ceramic finds in India. In the case of coins, a comparison of the legends, stylistic features of the obverse and reverse devices, weight and specific gravity of the Roman issues found in India with those of similar coins reported from within the Roman empire, facilitates in identifying the genuine coins among those found in India. Regarding pottery, a comparative study of the fabric and texture of the Roman ceramics obtained in India and those of similar wares discovered in Europe aid in differentiating the original Mediterranean pottery from their local copies among the various Indian finds. Also, as the number of Roman ceramics and coins found in India is large, an archaeo-chemical analysis, even of a destructive nature, could be attempted on a few selected specimens of these coins and pottery, with a view to ascertain whether the chemical composition of these objects is identical to that of the corresponding finds within the Roman empire. In the case of most of the other types of Roman antiquities such as glass and terracotta objects discovered in India, the finds are meagre and are too precious to be subject to a destructive analysis. Further, many of these objects are extremely small and fragile to permit such an analysis. Thus, almost all the Roman objects, other than coins and ceramics, discovered in India have been labelled as 'Roman' solely on the basis of stylistic considerations and hence, the identifications are open to debate. In this context, it should be remembered that several of the Indian imitations of the minor Roman antiquities are almost identical to the genuine objects in terms of their workmanship and finish, strongly suggesting that the copies were manufactured by Graeco-Roman craftsmen settled in India.

## METAL ARTIFACTS

Metal artifacts, mostly in bronze, constitute an important class of finds. These include statuettes of Graeco-Roman deities, various types of vessels and mirrors. There is a marked concentration of such finds in the western (Maharashtra-Gujarat) and north-western (Pakistan-Afghanistan) regions of the subcontinent. Surprisingly, very few objects have been recovered from south India.

Brahmapuri (Maharashtra) is particularly rich in Roman bronzes. It is situated in the western part of the modern town of Kolhapur, on the right bank of the river Panchganga. However, it has not been mentioned in the *Periplus*.

Archaeological excavations at Brahmapuri have revealed that the historical settlement at the site began around 200 BC; several NBP sherds, Roman pottery (?), terracotta and kaolin objects, iron implements, bangles, Sātavāhana coins and clay bullae in imitation of Roman coins have been unearthed. Apparently, the site was a manufacturing centre for beads and kaolin figurines. The structures comprised brick houses with stone foundations. The site was destroyed by a fire probably during the reign of SriYajña Sātakarṇi (AD 152-81) but was soon reoccupied. The historical settlement finally declined around the fourth century AD.[1]

The most important and well known find from the site is a large hoard of bronzes. The precise stratigraphy of this find was, unfortunately, not recorded and the whereabouts of several of the objects are to date not known. Also, a few of the artifacts have been damaged due to improper methods of cleaning them. According to the available information, two large bronze pots have been unearthed at a depth of about 3 m. below the surface, in a 'house' of the Sātavāhana period (first to third centuries AD). Both the pots were found together in the south-eastern corner of a room, close to a well. A total of 102 smaller metal objects including iron tools, 55 Sātavāhana lead coins, and a variety of bronze artifacts such as animal figurines, lamps, vases, toy carts and mirrors were found within and around these two pots. Many of the bronze items, including the two pots containing most of the antiquities, are indigenous products but around 13 of the objects are authentic imports.

Important Roman metal objects found in Brahmapuri and other sites in India are discussed in the following paragraphs.

EMBLEMA

One of the finds from the Brahmapuri hoard is the repousse copper emblema, depicting the legend of Perseus and Andromeda. As the Perseus-Andromeda theme was fairly common in the Roman art of the first two centuries of the Christian era, it has been very difficult to pinpoint the date of the Brahmapuri specimen. Initially, the find was believed to be of the second century AD[2] but a recent re-examination of the object has tentatively ascribed it to the second half of the first century AD.[3]

STATUETTES AND ALLIED OBJECTS

One of the most publicized finds from Brahmapuri is the bronze statuette of Poseidon, the Roman god of the sea. The contention that this is a surface find,[4] implying that the object was not part of the large hoard unearthed during excavations, is erroneous. The statuette is around 13 cm. in height and is well preserved. In the Mediterranean region, Poseidon frequently appears in metal and even stone (marble) sculptures from around 300 BC to AD 200. The Brahmapuri statuette was originally assigned by K. Khandalavala to the second century AD.[5] R. De Puma, however, has asserted that this find may be dated slightly earlier because it is stylistically closer to the specimens of the Hellenistic period (second-first centuries BC) than those of the imperial Roman period (first-second centuries AD).[6] It may be pointed out that there are hardly any major stylistic differences between the Poseidon figures of the Hellenistic and later periods and hence, it is hazardous to determine the precise date for any of the Poseidon sculptures solely on the basis of stylistic features.

A fine bearded muscular bronze statue of Atlantes(?) has been recovered from the bed of the river Meshvo at Devnimori (Gujarat). It may be noted that the site has also yielded red polished ware and Roman amphorae.

Taxila (Pakistan) and Begram (Afghanistan) have revealed innumerable metal artifacts of Hellenistic origin. An important find from Taxila is a bronze statuette of Harpocrates, the Graeco-Egyptian god (first century AD).

An almost similar bronze statuette of Harpocrates has also been found at Begram. This figure is 13.3 cm. in height and has been assigned to the first-second centuries AD. Other notable finds from Begram are a bronze head of Silenus (height 9.5 cm.) also of the first-second centuries AD, and a second century AD bronze statuette of Hercules crowned with Egyptian calathus (height 24 cm.).

At Ai Khanoum (Afghanistan), an imported bronze statuette of the beardless Herakles has been found. Significantly, Ai Khanoum is strategically situated at the junction of two important rivers—the Amu-Daria and the Kokcha.

A Roman bronze statue has been reported from Brahmagiri (Karnataka) but the absence of other details about this find, that too, from an area where such artifacts—whether imported or indigenous—have hitherto been unknown, makes one doubt the authenticity of this discovery.

The hilly area of the Nilgiris (Tamilnadu) has revealed a few metal artifacts including statuettes which may be of Roman origin. It may be noted that one of the earliest recorded finds from the area is a large hoard of bronzes which have not been precisely dated; the view that these objects are imported has been disputed. Among the recent discoveries from the Nilgiris is a brass (or bronze) sculpture portraying a Roman priest sitting in a chair and holding a thunderbolt in his left hand. The agitated folds of his garment are clearly discernible. The figure is mounted on a pedestal bearing the legend ROMAE. The exact date of this object is, however, uncertain.

In recent years, Karur (Tamilnadu) has yielded a series of small statuettes of Graeco-Roman personages in brass and bronze. One such find is the brass figure of a Roman soldier which may originally have been part of a jewel. These finds from Karur have, so far, not been published.

# BRONZE MIRRORS

Metal mirrors, mostly in bronze, are among the most interesting and rare finds in ancient sites throughout the world. In the Indian subcontinent, the earliest bronze mirrors have been reported from Mohenjodaro (2500 BC).

The Brahmapuri hoard has revealed three bronze mirrors. These are small circular objects with a tang for insertion into ivory or bone or metal handles. Surprisingly, no fragment of any such handle, whether attached to the mirror or otherwise, has been recovered from the site, although a few fragmentary metal pieces in the hoard may be part of such a handle.

It was originally believed that the larger mirror in the Brahmapuri hoard was an authentic Roman import while the other two may be Sātavāhana copies inspired by Alexandrian mirrors.[7] De Puma has recently pointed out that certain features of all these three mirrors such as the presence of tang, central protrusion on the reverse and rippled rims are unknown among Roman mirrors.[8] De Puma's study has also revealed that while the Brahmapuri mirrors would certainly have been inspired by the Mediterranean traditions, these specimens bear closer affinity to Egyptian mirrors of the Pharaonic period, which are largely tanged. On the basis of the fact that the Brahmapuri mirrors are stylistically very similar to those found in several sites in Pakistan, Afghanistan and Iran, he has suggested that the Brahmapuri specimens may be local copies influenced by types found in the Pakistan-Iran region or even direct imports from the north-western part of the Indian subcontinent. This view is strengthened by the fact that the north-west and west did maintain commercial contacts with each other during the ancient period not only by land routes but also by the sea route, specially along the coastline from Barbarikon to Barygaza.

Bronze mirrors similar to those found at Brahmapuri have been recovered from a few other sites. Ter, lying to the north-east of Kolhapur, has revealed two heavily corroded bronze mirrors in the stratified context.

Metal mirrors have also been reported from a few sites in the north-western region such as Taxila and Tillya-tepe. Taxila has yielded the largest number of mirrors varying in size from 5 cm. to 15 cm.

Three specimens of bronze mirrors have been found at Adichanallur (Tamilnadu). These mirrors range in diameter from 12.6 cm. to 15.4 cm. and have a plain convex rim.

VESSELS

*Wok-shaped basins.* The Brahmapuri hoard has revealed two Roman specimens of this type but one of them is a badly damaged fragmentary piece. Such basins usually have ornamental handles and a lathe-turned foot and, therefore, could not have been used for cooking purposes. The foot of one of the Brahmapuri basins, probably the better preserved one, has been unearthed separately and was originally mistaken to be the base of a Roman candlestick. These foreign basins are strikingly similar to the Indian *kaḍhāi* (frying pan) and were initially believed to be local products. The *kaḍhāi*, a cooking vessel, does not have a foot and often, it does not have handles. The Roman wok-shaped basin is widely found all over Europe. These vessels belong to the first century AD.

*Oinochoai and related objects.* Among the well preserved vessels of the Brahmapuri hoard, is a Millingen-type oinochoe with a squat belly, a short flat foot and a lion-faced handle. The vessel, though small, is impressive because of its simplicity and the perfectly symmetrical features. The handle of the vessel ends in a medallion depicting floral designs. Such vessels were in vogue in Europe mainly during the first two centuries of the Christian era. The Brahmapuri specimen was initially dated to the second century AD but, according to De Puma, stylistic features indicate that the vessel may have been produced in the middle of the first century AD. The Brahmapuri hoard has also revealed two identical bronze vessel handles which end in a large medallion depicting the figure of Amor.

An oinochoe find has also been reported from the Punjab region. It was originally identified as a Corinthian vessel but a recent examination of this object has confirmed that it has several Roman features and is stylistically very similar to the Millingen-type oinochoe from Brahmapuri. The heavy solid cast handle of the oinochoe from Punjab is of a type which is not usually seen in vessels of such shapes. Such handles are invariably found on the Alikaria-type oinochoe characterized by a swollen ovoid body and a trumpet-shaped foot. Hence, the Punjab oinochoe is suspected to be a forgery probably produced at Naples in imitation of an ancient vessel from Pompeii or Herculaneum, during the late nineteenth century.

A fragmentary bronze handle has been excavated at Akota in western India. This handle has been identified as part of a Millingen-type Roman oinochoe. The size and shape of the Akota handle is almost identical to the Brahmapuri handles featuring Amor. The Akota handle and fragments of the oinochoe recovered along with it were originally assigned to the second century AD. De Puma has recently pointed out that the closest parallels to the Akota objects have been discovered in stratified layers of the second half of the first century AD at Pompeii.

Yet another fragmentary oinochoe, now lost, also seems to have been found in the Gujarat region. Details about this find are not known.

*Other vessels.* The Brahmapuri hoard has revealed a small imported bronze cup, almost like the modern tumbler, depicting a pattern of parallel flutes. Another object in the hoard is a broken circular bronze strainer with a metal handle which ends in a small circular projection. The strainer measures 17.4 cm. in diameter while the length of the handle is 9.1 cm. The object was originally believed to be of local origin but recent studies have indicated that it is imported.

The finds from Begram include, besides an array of bronze objects, an important and unique Roman alabaster jug with a handle and a trefoil rim. The height of the jug is 17 cm. and it has been assigned to the second century AD.

A rare imported bronze vessel from Tamilnadu is a unique jug discovered at Avanasi near Coimbatore. Details of the find are not known to date. It was found along with a bronze globular oil container with a straight tapering spout and a bronze lamp stand with one wick(?). The latter two objects, the types of which are used in Tamilnadu to this day, may have been local products. The exact date of the imported Avanasi jug is uncertain. Its identification as early Greek or Phoenician and not Roman is somewhat intriguing. It should, however, be remembered that although authentic Greek artifacts are rare south of the Vindhyas, several recent studies have indicated a pre-Augustan or pre-Roman phase of trade between the Mediterranean region and south India. Recently, a few Phoenician coins have been recoverd from Karur.

Some of the coins of the large aurei hoard from Kottayam (Kerala) were reported to have been contained in a Roman brass (bronze?) vessel. However, no other details about this vessel are available. The abnormally massive size of the hoard, its proximity to the coast and the good condition of the coins have led to the belief that the hoard belonged to a Roman trader who had just arrived and was compelled to bury his treasures due to adverse circumstances, probably a shipwreck.[9] The fact that this is the only find in the country of Roman coins being found in a Roman vessel adds support to this view.

Among the other finds of foreign vessels in India is a collection of thirty-five ancient Greek vases, probably from western India. A bronze wine cup depicting a Bacchanalian scene and belonging to the fifth-sixth centuries AD is another notable specimen; the occurrence of this find in India is, however, unconfirmed.

MISCELLANEOUS OBJECT

A horn-shaped bronze object, apparently a cornucopia used in rituals, was discovered in Posheri (Maharashtra). The object has been traced to the early centuries of the Christian era. The decorative motifs on this object include a lion face on its lowest band. Stylistically, this object has much in common with the lion headed handle of the Millingen-type oinochoe from Brahmapuri.

GENERAL OBSERVATIONS

It is very difficult to ascertain the precise date when all the known Roman bronzes found in India reached the subcontinent. None of the foreign bronzes found in India bear signature trademarks which could be easily dated. Some of the finds are from non-stratified contexts; even in the case of finds from archaeological excavations, the precise stratigraphic position of the objects has not been properly recorded. Some finds from archaeological excavations have been simply assigned to the 'Sātavāhana period' which covers a very long time span from the first century BC to about the third century AD. Most of the imported metal artifacts, however, belong to the first century AD and seem to have reached India either in the late first or the second century AD.

Several interesting observations can be made on the basis of the analysis of the distribution of all the foreign metal artifacts found in India. It is evident that unlike Roman coins and ceramics, these metal artifacts are mainly confined to three specific pockets or regions of the Indian subcontinent: (a) Pakistan-Afghanistan, (b) Gujarat-Maharashtra, and (c) Nilgiris-Coimbatore (Tamilnadu).

The imported artifactual finds from north-west India may be, as indicated earlier, the result of overland trade rather than of maritime commerce. Although the finds from the other regions of the country undoubtedly arrived by the sea route, it is interesting to note that coastal sites, whether in Maharashtra, Tamilnadu or elsewhere, have not yielded foreign metal artifacts. Significantly, almost all the sites revealing these artifacts have yielded other types of Roman objects as well such as coins and ceramics, and many of these sites were important early historical commercial centres and were actively involved in the trade with the west.

Were these metal artifacts commodities of trade regularly shipped to India along with other merchandise? A close scrutiny of all the available evidence indicates that some of these objects were brought to India as 'items of gift' while others were merchandise. The same types of objects (statuettes, vessels, etc.), on some occasions, were sent as gifts and on others, as trade items.

First, the evidence supporting the flow of these objects as gifts into India will be examined. The paucity of such objects both in arch-aeological excavations and as stray occurrences almost throughout the Indian subcontinent, except perhaps in the north-west, has led many scholars to ignore these artifacts in the context of Indo-Roman trade.[10] Further, a large number of these objects are statuettes of Graeco-Roman deities which would hardly have been of any interest to most Indians. As the culinary habits of Indians were markedly different from those of Romans, Indians would not have been aware of the significance and use of many types of Roman vessels found at Brahmapuri and elsewhere and, hence, there would not have been any specific demand for such exotic foreign utensils among the local people. Even indigenous bronze utensils do not seem to have been in daily use among the common people of early historical India; the few such finds from a limited number of sites seem to suggest that they were used by the upper strata of society. Many of the local bronze objects of this period are jewellery items such as bangles and bracelets. The few foreign bronze objects reaching India would have been considered very precious and would have been beyond the reach of the common people. All these factors collectively indicate that there would not have been a large-scale market for Roman metal artifacts in India.

In these circumstances, the predominance of Roman bronze finds in the Maharashtra-Gujarat region may be explained in the context of the large number of early Buddhist establishments in the region. Many of the foreign bronze items, particularly the cornucopia and the mirrors, may have played a role in Buddhist rituals. It is also plausible that there was a specific demand in the *vihāras* for products such as wine or oil contained in the Roman bronze vessels. The fact that Mediterranean traders often made lavish donations to Buddhist establishments of Western Deccan is attested by several early epigraphical references[11] and hence, it is not unlikely that some of the foreign traders may have occasionally carried with them bronze artifacts as gifts to the monasteries.

This line of argument is in consonance with the fact that Roman bronze finds in any given region of India including Maharashtra, number far less than the finds of other Roman objects (such as coins and pottery) because items of gift would definitely be numerically much less than goods which were regularly traded on a large-scale. This theory of the association of Roman bronzes in India with Buddhism is also supported by the fact that many of the sites yielding bronzes have also revealed structural remains associated with the Buddhist faith as for example, Taxila and Devnimori. Although no Buddhist structures have been found in Kolhapur so far, there is no reason to believe that the site was not a Buddhist centre specially because it was a very large and flourishing urban settlement situated on a very important trade route frequented by foreign merchants who may have been patrons of Buddhism.

It is also important to examine the evidence that at least some of the Roman metal objects reached India during the course of trade. The metals mentioned by the *Periplus* as being imported into India include antimony, copper, tin and lead (*Periplus* 56). Interestingly, the copper repousse emblema depicting Perseus and Andromeda from Brahmapuri may be among the 'copper imports' into India. According to a recent study, the *yavana* or Roman lamp which was exported to the Tamil country and which has been vividly described in the Sangam classics (*Perumbāṇārruppaḍai* 316-18; *Neḍunalvāḍei* 101-3) may also have been in copper or bronze and may be part of the 'metal imports' into India, listed by the *Periplus*.[12] Specimens of such lamps have till date not been found anywhere in India.

An important piece of evidence, not considered so far, pertaining to the role of Roman metal objects in India as 'trade items' is that many of the imported bronzes in the subcontinent are associated with either the production or storage or distribution of wine which was a major item of export to India. For example, the bronze sieve from Brahmapuri is reported to have been used to strain wine. The fragmentary bronze handles recovered from Brahmapuri and Akota are believed to have been part of wine pitchers; in fact, the Akota handle appropriately depicts Amor straddling a wine amphora. The famous oinochoe from Brahmapuri was of a type usually used to store wine. The imported jug from Avanasi may also have been used for the same purpose. The small basket-shaped bronze cup from Kolhapur was probably used for drinking wine. Many of these bronzes in India are believed to have been manufactured at Capua in Campania (southern Italy), a region famous for its excellent wine. Significantly, Capua is barely 15 km. north of Puteoli, the well known Italian port which carried on trade with Alexandria, which was a major 'transit port' in the commerce between Rome and India. It may thus be concluded that the export of most, if not all, metal objects took place along with the export of wine to India. It may be recalled that Roman wine was in great demand mainly in two regions of India, viz., Maharashtra-Gujarat and the Tamil country which are also the regions yielding a large number of metal objects. Several sites that have revealed imported bronzes have also yielded the earthen amphorae mainly used to store wine. For example, Taxila, Devnimori, Akota, Ter and Karur. Although Avanasi is not an amphora site, Vellalur, a neighbouring site, has revealed the amphora.

It has been established that almost all the amphora sites in India are early historical urban centres housing a prosperous 'elite' class which regularly consumed wine. Naturally, this 'elite' class would have evinced an interest in acquiring the various types of imported metal vessels used for straining, storing and serving wine. The same 'elite' class would also have liked to possess exotic foreign objets d'art including artistic mirrors and statuettes, for 'personal collection' and/or for display as 'showpieces' or 'status symbols' and/or for conferring the objects as 'gifts' to Buddhist institutions and others. Thus, Roman bronze icons seem to have had essentially an 'ideo-technic' or 'socio-technic' value in India. The large Brahmapuri hoard found systematically arranged in a house may represent the carefully preserved treasure of one of the leading local traders of early historical Kolhapur. In fact, it has been argued that the concentration of Roman bronze finds in Maharashtra-Gujarat was primarily due to the fact that the people there were culturally conscious and had an artistic bent of mind.[13]

It is clear that foreign metal artifacts in India, both 'gift items' and 'trade items', catered to the needs of a very small section of the Indian population, viz., the Buddhist clergy and the 'urban elite'. Unlike Roman coins and pottery, foreign bronzes, specially statuettes, would have rarely been part of the local trade network, and hence, may not have been transported from one region of India to the other. This, again, partially accounts for the concentration of imported bronze finds in just a few sites confined to three distinct 'pockets' in the subcontinent.

The contention that the items in the Brahmapuri hoard were deliberately amassed for disposal at a neighbouring foundry[14] is unacceptable because the hoard contains antiquities of three different metals—lead, iron and bronze—and it is extremely unlikely that objects of varied metals were sought to be melted together. Also, the 55 local lead coins in the find were used as currency when the hoard was buried. Moreover, the hoard includes several utility objects such as indigenous iron and bronze implements in a 'good' condition, thereby not warranting their being consigned to the melting pot. Even the worn items in the find would have been reduced to this state of wear during the centuries when the hoard was buried underground.

## GLASSWARE

Mediterranean glass antiquities have been discovered in a few sites in north-west, west and south India. The finds from most of the sites, except Taxila and Begram in the north-west, are limited in number and are often fragments of various types of vessels. The finds mostly belong to the period between the first century BC and the first century AD.

The *Periplus* contains copious references to the import of glass to India. References to glass in early Indian literature are, however, meagre. Although Roman glassware has been discovered in sites in the Tamil country, there is no reference to 'glass objects', 'glass production' or 'glass-trade' in the Tamil Sangam literature. A few of the early Sanskrit and Pāli works—most of which seem to have been written in north India—do refer to glass objects but it is not clear as to whether all or some of these references are to 'Roman glass' because Indians were adept in the art of glass-making long before the commencement of Indo-Roman trade.[15]

The important imported glass objects found in the subcontinent are as follows.

### GLASS VESSELS

These have been discovered at Begram (Afghanistan), Taxila (Pakistan), Paithan, Ter and Nevasa (Maharashtra), Daranikota and Kothapatnam (Andhra) and Arikamedu. Details about the find from Kothapatnam are not available.

Among the imported glass finds from Begram is an amphora-shaped vessel with two handles; the outer surface of the vessel has ornamental meandering designs in relief. The site has also revealed a Roman cut-glass vessel in the shape of a tall goblet decorated with a 'bee-hive' design and a Roman ribbed bowl. Taxila has also yielded similar bowls.

According to Wheeler, the various objects including foreign glassware in the large hoard unearthed between 1937 and 1939 at Begram, the western outpost of the Kushans, may constitute the 'tributes' exacted by the local ruler from traders of different nationalities who passed through the city.[16] However, this theory is considerably weakened by the fact that this hoard includes several local products, viz., objects manufactured within the Kushan empire such as ivory carvings. Another view, put forth by Wheeler, is that the Begram hoard may be part of the Kushan royal treasures originally housed in the Kushan palace at Peshawar or Taxila or Mathura and later brought to the frontier city of Begram by one of the last Kushan princes sometime during the fourth century AD when the empire had almost declined. However, it is extremely unlikely that a defeated prince while fleeing from his royal capital would have decided to carry with him a motley collection of sculptures and vessels including small glass bowls, and later would have buried all these objects in the distant city of Begram. A more plausible explanation is that the Begram hoard, like the Brahmapuri hoard of bronzes, may represent the well preserved collection of a single wealthy individual, probably an indigenous trader, who was involved in cross border trade in which both Taxila and Begram actively participated. This line of argument is supported by the fact that unlike the Roman glass finds in west and south India, the imported glass vessel finds from Begram are not only unusually large but also consist of almost complete vessel forms instead of tiny fragments. Moreover, these glass vessels form part of a 'compact' and intact hoard comprising objects arranged in two small rooms, one of which had been walled up, within a house. The hoard includes besides glassware and ivory, other exotic luxury items such as Chinese bronzes and lacquer ware.

A notable find from Paithan is the rim portion of a mould-made cobalt blue vessel probably of the first century AD. Marianne Stern has opined that this object may have been manufactured at Mouza, the Arab port which carried on trade with Barygaza.[17]

Ter has yielded fragments of glass cups, the base of a small bowl as also a bulbous glass bottle or flask. A bulbous bottle or flask has also been discovered at Taxila. All these objects may be dated to the first century AD. All the foreign glass vessels from Nevasa comprise broken pieces of mould-made bowls of the first century AD.

Small pillar moulded glass bowls found in Bahrain, Begram and Taxila have also been reported from Arikamedu and Daranikota. Several such specimens have been found at Arikamedu during the course of various archaeological excavations. The bowls are around 6 cm. high and the diameter of the rim is about 4.5 cm. These bowls may also be dated to the first century AD. Recently, Jean-Francois Salles has put forth the suggestion that the Roman glass bowls may have reached Bahrain through the port of Barbarike in the Indus delta in north-west India.[18] It has also been argued that some of the Roman merchandize, including metals such as copper, reaching the Indian port of Barygaza, were re-exported along with Indian products such as red polished pottery to the Gulf region, through Arab-Persian sailors. Even the solitary Tiberian coin found at ed-Dur in the United Arab Emirates would have been routed through India.

RAW GLASS

Although raw glass was a major item of import into India, it has been discovered only in few of the excavated sites, mostly along the Coromandel coast. Probably, raw glass was converted into finished products such as beads by the local craftsmen, shortly after it reached India. The fact that several sites, both in the Deccan and in the Tamil country, yielding Roman antiquities such as coins and pottery, have also revealed, in the same stratified layers, enormous quantities of glass beads, lends support to this line of argument. The most noteworthy among these sites are Paithan, Nevasa, Brahmapuri, Ter, Peddabankur, Kondapur, Maski, Brahmagiri and Chandravalli (Sātavāhana sites) and Arikamedu, Karaikadu, Kanchi, Uraiyur, Kodumanal and Alagankulam (sites in Tamilakam); all these were important trade centres in the early historical period.

Archaeological evidence indicates that although Roman raw glass first reached the different sites of western and south-western India, the glass industry was more prosperous in south-eastern India. Stern has argued that much of the imported raw glass reaching the ports of the west coast of India may have been transported to the east coast through the Palghat pass.[19] The coastal sites of Arikamedu and Karaikadu, as also the Pāṇḍyan port town of Alagankulam were major glass bead production centres. At Arikamedu which housed the largest bead-making industry, sizeable quantities of raw glass were also manufactured indigenously.

The bulk of the glass beads manufactured in the Tamil country were for local use but large quantities were apparently exported not only to Andhra, but also to Sri Lanka and South-East Asia.[20] The hexagonal green-coloured glass beads produced at Arikamedu may have been meant to be sold as genuine beryl stones to unsuspecting Western traders. A late second century BC Chinese record mentions the export of glass from Kanchipuram, a flourishing early historical trade centre, to China.[21] This Kanchipuram glass would undoubtedly have been routed through either the port of Arikamedu or Mahabalipuram or Vasavasamudram as all of them are not too far from Kanchi. China would have received Roman and Indian glass through Begram and Taxila as well. Although the Chinese themselves manufactured glass from the fifth century BC, the Chinese glass, till the third century AD, was of a very poor quality.

GLASS BEADS

The reference to 'several sorts of coloured glass' in the *Periplus* (6, 7, 17) may include glass beads of various colours. A few glass beads from the Arikamedu collection have been identified as imports from the Roman empire. Some of these are reported to be imitation of onyx beads which were manufactured at Arikamedu and sold to Rome. Glass beads from none of the other sites in India are believed to be authentic imports from the Mediterranean region. It should, however, be noted that the bead finds from many of the Indian sites, specially those in the extreme south, have not been thoroughly investigated. It is plausible that some of the glass beads discovered at Karaikadu, Kodumanal and Alagankulam may have been imported from the west. Glass beads imported from Rome have been recently found in the stratified context at Mantai (Sri Lanka).[22] In any case, the import of glass beads into India was on a small scale.

GENERAL OBSERVATIONS

The reasons for the uneven distribution of imported glass objects in different parts of the country are many. It is plausible that some other types of Roman glass vessels, a few of them containing wine, were regularly sent to India but were destroyed during the medieval period or even earlier. Again, although glass bottles and beads were often buried under Buddhist *stupas*, both in India and China, the use of glass utensils was generally prohibited in the monasteries and hence, the monks may not have evinced as much interest in the 'glass trade' as in the 'amphora trade'. Throughout ancient India, glass was mainly used for producing jewels such as beads and bangles rather than vessels. Therefore, the demand for foreign glass vessels would have been limited. Moreover, the fragile nature of glass would not only have restricted its use but also the probability of its being transported from one region to another across rough terrain.

## TERRACOTTA ANTIQUITIES

Clay or terracotta objects such as human figurines and lamps depicting Graeco-Roman features have been discovered in various sites throughout the subcontinent. Most of these objects, apart from some of the specimens from Arikamedu and a few other sites, are not from stratified layers. The available evidence, however, indicates that the majority of these objects belong to the first century AD. Arikamedu is the only site to have yielded a terracotta female figure revealing Graeco-Roman influence from a pre-sigillata layer which may be dated to the end of the first century BC; this is definitely the earliest object of its kind in the Tamil country.

The important terracotta objects include lamps unearthed at Arikamedu, Kanchipuram and Ter; the unique Hellenistic head from Kodumanal; the jar from Yellesvaram (Andhra) and seals with Roman letters from Rajbadidanga (West Bengal).

Of all these items, lamps are definitely imports from the Roman empire. Arikamedu has yielded several specimens of such lamps but many of them are not stratified finds. At this juncture, the interesting references to the *yavana* (Roman) lamp in the Tamil Sangam literature may be examined. The *Perumbānārruppaḍai* (311-19) describes a *yavana* lamp in the shape of a swan. Here, the poet uses the term *yavanar* in connection with the city of 'Nīrppeyarru', belonging to Iḷantiraiyan of Kanchi. The work also describes an interesting episode: a group of damsels go to the tank for their bath and the fish-shaped gold earring of one of the girls accidentally falls into the tank. The kingfisher, in search of its prey, takes the earring, mistaking it for a real fish, only to throw it away in disgust. The earring rolls down through the leaves of the palmyra tree and finally comes to rest on a pillar near the sacrificial altar of the Brahmins. The earring, reflecting the rays emitted by the fire within the altar, appears to the poet, like a real gold coloured fish atop the swan lamp of the *yavanas*. It is likely that metallic swinging lamps were specifically designed in the shape of a swan with the fish placed at the top as if to lure the swan below. Dorai Rangaswamy has commented at length on this passage from the *Perumbānārruppaḍai*. According to him, the fire within the sacrificial altar may have appeared, to the poet, like the flame of the lamp while the sacrificial pillar at whose base the fire was lit may have appeared like the chain of the swinging lamp.[23] He has indicated the possibility that this description in the *Perumbānārruppaḍai* may be a simile referring to the light hanging atop a ship in mid-sea;

even a star in the sky might appear, to the people on the coast, an earring on top of the ship. It seems that these exotic swan lamps were not commonly used in Tamilakam and the few imported specimens were, according to the *Perumbāṇārruppaḍai* (316-18), a novelty for the local people. The *Neḍunalvāḍei* (101-3) describes another variety of *yavana* lamps shaped like women, holding, in their folded palms, a *tahaḷi* or shallow bowl containing oil for lighting the lamp. Such foreign lamps may have been the prototype for the *pāvai viḷakku*—a metallic female figure, holding a lamp in her hands, fairly common in the Tamil country during the later periods. Even during the Sangam age, according to the bard, the damsel-shaped lamps were lighted every evening in all the homes of Madurai. The *Maṇimēkalai* (1:45) refers to the practice of installing *pāvai viḷakku* as offerings to the deities. The idea underlying such lamps may either be to perpetuate the memory of the female donor by depicting her holding the lamp gifted by her to the Lord or to give the donor, a representation of her offering the lamp to the deity, before her very eyes.

Surprisingly, the *Periplus* does not mention Roman lamps but Champakalakshmi has opined that some of the different metals listed in the *Periplus* as imports to India may have been in the form of finished products such as lamps.[24] Lamps similar to those mentioned in the Sangam classics have not been discovered anywhere in the Tamil country and K.V. Raman's identification of the lamps mentioned in the *Neḍunalvāḍei* with the finds from Arikamedu[25] is erroneous. It should be noted that the Tamil literary evidence implies that the *yavana* lamps were huge metal objects but all the finds from Arikamedu are small, plain terracotta specimens and can in no way be compared to the lamps mentioned in the literature.

Interestingly, a terracotta lamp closely resembling the lamp described in the *Neḍunalvāḍei* has been recovered from Ter. It is shaped like a female bust; the head is hollow and has a central knob with a transverse perforation for suspension. The face is oval unlike the squarish-round physiognomy of the Sātavāhana terracottas common in the Deccan. The anatomical features of this terracotta lamp are typically Roman. It is pink in colour and is made of fine well levigated clay, quite different from the other terracottas of Ter, and hence it is believed to be an import.[26]

Incidentally, lamps similar to the *pāvai viḷakku* are not known in north and north-west India but are in use in Bengal even to this day. Although the east has hardly yielded any such lamp finds, whether indigenous or foreign, in the early historical archaeological context, it is possible that the use of such lamps in Bengal was the result of the region's contact, through Tamiḷakam, with ancient Romans.

Among the other types of pseudo-Roman terracotta objects found in India, the well preserved bust of Apollo(?) from Kodumanal is noteworthy (Plate 14). The clipped beard, moustache and the spiked helmet indicate that the figure is a warrior. The figure has a typical Roman nose, long and sharp, thin elongated lips, half-closed eyes and a smiling countenance. The Hellenistic elements are discernible in the shape of the helmet as also in the type of the moustache which closely resembles those on Gandhara sculptures. Similar terracotta human figurines portraying Graeco-Roman features from Arikamedu are local imitations.

A unique terracotta find unearthed at Dhulikatta in Andhra is a red slipped and polished human figure wearing a discular hat with a prominent brim and a rosette attached to the right; the eyes and ears are added applique and the mouth is open to simulate a laugh. The figure identified as that of a Roman trader seems to be part of a spout of a water jar.

At Yellesvaram in Andhra, along with the aureus of Septimius Severus, a unique pseudo-Roman red ware jar with a black band painted at the junction of the neck and the body has been found. The site has also yielded terracotta and stone figurines of nude goddesses probably of Graeco-Roman origin.

PLATE 14. TERRACOTTA HEAD OF APOLLO(?),
KODUMANAL (TAMILNADU)

Yet another pseudo-Roman object, discovered in Vadnagar (Gujarat), is an intaglio in clay depicting a woman with a flower in her hand. It was found along with red polished ware and a clay seal with an inscription palaeographically assigned to the second-third centuries AD. Terracotta plaques depicting Roman figures have also been reported from Adam in Maharashtra.

Among the other terracotta objects in India are the seals with Roman(?) legends recovered from Rajbadidanga. One of the seals bears the inscription 'OABORRA', probably a personal name; this seal was discovered along with other inscribed indigenous seals belonging to the fifth-sixth centuries AD. and later. Another terracotta seal from the same site bears the name 'HORAE'.

Terracotta objects, mainly human figurines revealing Graeco-Roman influence, are more common in north-west, north and east India than in the south. The political ties between the Greeks and the Mauryans resulted in Greek terracotta art directly inspiring and influencing the terracottas of the Mauryans and their immediate successors in north India.[27] Moreover, north India was, for centuries, exposed to the Gandhara school which itself was the fusion of several styles including the Hellenistic. Even the technique of casting terracottas in double mould, which was probably introduced in India by the foreigners, was more popular in north India than in the south during this period. Unlike north India, in the south, terracottas depicting foreign features are all confined to a limited number of trade-centres such as Dhulikatta, Arikamedu and Kodumanal.

## JEWELLERY

Jewels exhibiting non-Indian motifs have been recovered from sites in north-west, north, west and south India. These finds include finger rings, intaglios and cameos. The finger rings are the most numerous. While some of these jewels are part of Roman coin hoards, others have either been unearthed during the course of archaeological excavations or have been accidentally discovered from under the ground by farmers and treasure-diggers. The majority of the finds are of the first century AD.

Arikamedu has yielded two gems with carvings on them. One of them (carnelian?) is a surface find and portrays the head of Augustus in intaglio. The other intaglio is made of quartz and depicts the figure of Cupid and a bird, most probably an eagle. However, the exact circumstances of this find are not known. According to Wheeler, although this gem is of Graeco-Roman workmanship, the fact that the intaglio is untrimmed, indicates that it is an unfinished local product made by one of the Mediterranean craftsmen settled in Arikamedu.[28]

Arikamedu, specially the 'Northern Sector' of the site, seems to have been a thriving industrial centre during the period between the first century BC and the first century AD. Conch shell jewellery making, well known in Mantai (Sri Lanka) and several Tamilnadu sites including Alagankulam, was, in addition to the production of beads and intaglios, a major craft of the 'Northern Sector'. Fragments of unfinished bangles and crescent-shaped ear ornaments of conch shell have been recovered from the post-sigillata layers of this Sector. Another craft exclusive to this Sector was ivory carving. This is substantiated by the discovery of a few ivory pieces from the site. One of them, recovered from a pre-sigillata layer of the 'Northern Sector', is a long piece, elliptical in section and divided into zones with parallel lines incised on it. The other piece is a fragment of a handle(?) of planoconvex section, divided into zones by raised bands, the sides having two mortises and the intervening space decorated by rosettes. The precise stratigraphic position of this handle is not known. Both these pieces may be either semi-finished products or else 'waste-bits' discarded during the carving of large ivory products. The raw material for the ivory industry at Arikamedu appears to have reached there along with other merchandise from the Malabar area through the Palghat pass, because the breeding of elephants was almost unknown on the Coromandel coast at that time. It may be recalled that ivory was an item of export from India to Rome during the first century AD and a sizeable quantity of ivory exported may have been in the form of jewels such as bangles and finger rings, some of which may have been carved by the Mediterranean craftsmen residing at Arikamedu.

Further evidence in support of the fact that both local and the foreign artists of Arikamedu produced intaglios is furnished by the discovery of two unique rouletted potsherds, probably of the first century AD, from the site. One of the sherds depicts two figures—a lion standing majestically in an animated pose within an oval and also a standing lady. The other sherd depicts, within an oval the figure of a standing young lady holding a bronze(?) mirror in her hand. Potsherds engraved with such complex designs may have been used either as models to produce quartz intaglios or as moulds to cast signet rings. Significantly, the female figure on a gold signet ring, recently discovered at Karur,[29] is strikingly similar to the figure on the latter potsherd recovered from Arikamedu.

The signet ring from Karur is a unique find. Recovered from the dry bed of Amaravati river, the ring (weighing 15.6 gm.) has an oval face which measures 2.5 cm. in length and 1.5 cm. across. On the face, in intaglio, is the signet—a pair of *mithuna* figures—an amorous couple probably belonging to the Chera royal family (Plate 15). Both the figures are tall and slim, standing cross-legged. The damsel's left hand gently embraces the shoulders of her beloved while her right arm gracefully hangs downwards. She has long hair which has been tied at the back in a knot or bun, in a manner very common in the Tamil country to this day. Her supple face, slightly bent downwards, is expressive of her extreme bashfulness. Her prominent breasts and slender legs are clearly delineated. She is clad in a long, thin, loose, silk garment and is wearing large anklets and bangles. Her lover, standing to her left, affectionately touches her gently with his right arm while his left arm holds a half-bloomed flower. He is well groomed and clean-shaven. The sharp contours, the sense of proportion and symmetry of these figures undoubtedly reveal that this ring is one of the best specimens of south Indian art.

PLATE 15. *MITHUNA* FIGURE ON GOLD RING,
KARUR (TAMILNADU)

The art of engraving in intaglio is primarily that of the lapidary and not of the goldsmith. It is historically well known that several Roman traders specially came in search of the beryl found at Vaniyambadi and Padiyur as this gem is most suitable for engraving in intaglio. Thus, there can hardly be any doubt that the Karur ring was inspired by Roman lapidary art introduced in the Tamil country by foreign tradesmen. The fact that the lapidary was, in early historical Tamilakam, a highly respected and prosperous professional who could afford to bestow lavish gifts on others is evident from a Tamil-Brāhmī epigraph (third-fourth centuries AD) found at Arachalur in the Coimbatore region. The inscription was originally believed to record the gift of seven rock beds by a lapidary to the monks (Jain monks?). Another reading of the inscription which is flanked on either side by musical notes or notations arranged in straight lines, is that either the lapidary himself composed those musical notations or else assisted, probably in terms of funds, the scholar who composed the notations. The latter reading of the inscription indicates that the lapidary was himself a poet or one who patronized learned musicians. The term denoting the 'lapidary' used in this epigraph was originally read as '*maṇi-y-vaṇṇakan*' (lapidary dealing in gems) but has recently been interpreted as '*malai-y-vaṇṇakan*' (lapidary from the hills).[30] Incidentally, the term *vaṇṇakan* which frequently occurs in the Tamil Sangam literature mainly in the context of a lapidary who sometimes was either a poet or the son of a poet,[31] is a surname of a certain caste in the Coimbatore region even to this day. This caste name may have been derived from the name of the occupation, i.e. gem-cutting pursued by the people in ancient times.

Despite the fact that the technique of execution of the figures on the Karur ring is Graeco-Roman, the jewel is essentially Indian in its ethos and idiom and seems to have been influenced by the Amaravati school of Buddhist art. Initially, R. Nagaswamy and I. Mahadevan believed that the Karur intaglio, in form, flexion and treatment, has much in common with the 'middle phase' of Amaravati art and hence, they assigned the jewel to the first century AD. However, a recent re-examination of the find has convincingly revealed that the slim and elongated figures on the ring are more akin to a 'late phase' of the Amaravati school and hence, can safely be assigned to the second century AD.

At this juncture, it may be noted that the foreign artists visiting south India contributed to the evolution and refinement of the Amaravati school whose origin can be traced to the Mauryan period. The earliest sculptures of this school, somewhat crude and flat, are adorned with heavy garments and turbans. Following the influence of foreigners, the sculptures of the first two centuries AD are more supple and realistic. Roman warriors are rarely depicted in these sculptures.[32]

In addition to this ring, Karur has yielded several finds of coins and jewels mostly dated to the early centuries of the Christian era. Recently, the site has yielded ten gold finger rings depicting various Graeco-Roman motifs. These rings are unpublished and are in the possession of dealers. Among the other finds from the site are two inscribed rings—one in silver and the other in gold.[33] The silver ring is broken and its present weight is 740 mg. This ring carries the *nandi pāda* motif to the left of the Tamil-Brāhmī inscription which reads: '*Tittan*'. It may be noted that *Ahananūru* (122) mentions a Cōla chieftain named Tittan who ruled Uraiyur, not too far from Karur; it is likely that the descendants of this chieftain resided at Karur. Viewed in the context of the discovery of several Sangam Cōla coins from Karur, this ring proves that the town functioned as an industrial hub not only for the Cheras but also the Cōlas. As the inscription on the ring runs from left to right and the letters of the alphabet are in high relief, the ring could not have been a signet ring. The gold ring, weighing 3.72 gm., also bears a Tamil-Brāhmī inscription running, from right to left which reads, '*Ū pā an*', may be '*ūpācakan*', meaning 'devotee'; the legend is flanked by the crescent moon and the *triratna* motifs. The letters of the alphabet have been formed by incuse punches and therefore the ring may have been a signet ring. It may have belonged to a merchant of Karur who was a lay disciple of a Jain monk. Palaeographically, the gold ring may be assigned to the first century BC and the silver ring to the first century AD.

Another signet ring, recently discovered at Karur, bears the inscription '*Sātan Sātavēgi*' which was probably the name of a jeweller, a nobleman or a banker; the fish and taurine symbols below the legend may be the official insignia of a trade guild.

It is well known that signet rings were introduced in north India by the Indo-Greeks not earlier than the second century BC, although a finger ring with a small bezel has been reported from Harappa (2500 BC).[34] Similarly, the south would have learnt about signet rings from the Greek and Roman traders who frequented the peninsular coast from the first century BC onwards. These rings from Karur are among the earliest extant finger rings found in the Tamil country.

The discovery of ancient jewellery from the Chera capital of Karur indicates that the Chera rulers were fond of adorning themselves with various types of ornaments. A Tamil-Brāhmī inscription specifically refers to gold merchants residing at Karur. Even to this day, the town has shops selling gold ornaments and other expensive curios. Besides Karur, Kodumanal was also a major jewellery manufacturing centre which catered to the needs of the ruling elite of Karur. Recent excavations at Kodumanal have yielded, in stratified layers, enormous quantities of beads made of agate, lapis lazuli, garnet, carnelian, jasper, sapphire, amethyst quartz, coral, soapstone and even beryl.[35] The coral beads here are strikingly similar to the one excavated at Tiruvakkarai, not too far from Arikamedu.[36] The discovery of several semi-polished and undrilled beads as well as blocks and discarded chips of various semi-precious stones confirm the existence of a large bead industry in Kodumanal. Beryl, sapphire and quartz deposits are found in the vicinity of Kodumanal, coral was undoubtedly imported from Rome, lapis lazuli from Badakhshan in Northern Afghanistan and carnelian from Gujarat. The exchange of not only precious stones but also the techniques of bead-making between west and south India is further corroborated by the fact that several quartz beads unearthed during excavations at Mantai, a Sri Lankan port close to the Indian mainland, were found to be pierced with a double diamond bit, a technique hitherto recorded only in Gujarat.[37]

Among the other finds from Kodumanal, a standing copper tiger, inlaid from head to tail with alternating triangular pieces of carnelian and sapphire, is noteworthy. The site has also yielded copper and silver rings and 24-carat gold and silver spirals which were probably used as ear ornaments. It should, however, be noted that jewels revealing a synthesis of Indian and Graeco-Roman art are mainly confined to Karur and have not been found at Kodumanal. This indicates that while indigenous craftsmen worked at Kodumanal, foreign artisans worked in the Chera capital, probably under royal patronage.

Among the jewellery finds from the neighbourhood of Coimbatore, the one from Vellalur is a large and important one. The notable objects in the hoard, besides the Tiberian aurei, are two Roman gold finger rings. One of these rings depicts a dragon and the head of a Graeco-Roman soldier with a prominent headgear that can be observed only at a certain angle. The other ring is inlaid with a transparent violet coloured garnet or amethyst stone on which is engraved the figure of a standing nude Greek lady, dressing her hair. Interestingly, this female figure bears a resemblance to that on one of the rouletted potsherds of Arikamedu. The Vellalur hoard also includes two indigenous gold rings, one of which portrays a fish or some other imaginary denizen of the ocean and the other, a lion with a gaping mouth, a curved tail and a raised paw. Incidentally, the lion figure is similar to the one on a gold ring recently found at Karur; the Karur ring portrays a Greek or Roman warrior (Apollo?) mounted on the prancing lion whose mane, legs, paws and the partially uplifted and tufted tail are stylized. All the rings in the Vellalur hoard are believed to be either wedding-rings or those exchanged as a token of friendship.[38] A unique object in the hoard is an oval-shaped red carnelian intaglio with the figure of a grazing(?) horse, probably meant to be fitted on a ring. All the gold neck ornaments in the hoard are local products. Among them is a rectangular pendant measuring 3.3 x 2.8 cm. with the figure of a humped bull on one side and an elephant on the other; the borders of the pendant are profusely ornamented. The other pendants in the hoard include a pair of identical gold floral beads which would have once formed part of a single long chain; these two pendants are shaped like an intricately carved trident or an inverted *triratna*. Another object in the hoard is a small golden billhook with a handle measuring 3.6 cm.; this also appears to have been used as a pendant.

Another important piece of jewellery has been discovered from Kampelayam (Plate 16). The precise circumstances of the find remain a mystery. The exact location of the site is also unknown but it may be tentatively identified with a place called Kempupalayam, not too far from Coimbatore city.[39] This find is a unique circular Roman gold pendant 4 cm. in diameter and weighing 18.87 gms. The pendant has a horizontally placed cylindrical loop at the top, and it is made of two sheets of gold, beaten thin and cut in a circular shape of equal size and impressed in repousse with designs; a legend has been engraved in repousse on one of the sheets. The sheets, placed back to back, have been soldered together by two narrow strips (tubes?) of gold which run along the margins of the sheets. The solitary tiny hole near the edge of the pendant may have been meant for pouring molten lac to fill the interspace between the two sheets and to ensure that the repousse work did not get obliterated due to rough handling of the object. A series of around twenty tiny gold rings, two of which are missing to date, have been soldered at regular intervals, along the edge of the pendant. The gold beads, recovered along with the pendant, were probably meant to be grouped in the interstices between the rings and threaded through a gold wire or chain such that the pendant was laced with a chain of gold beads. Portions of this wire or chain have also been found along with the pendant.[40]

*Symbols of Trade*

PLATE 16. ROMAN GOLD PENDANT,
KAMPELAYAM (TAMILNADU): OBVERSE AND REVERSE

The figure on the obverse of the pendant is in high relief and represents a boldly modelled female bust whose facial features appear to be those of a Greek or Roman matron. The veil covering the head is similar to that on the royal ladies portrayed on Greek and Roman coins till the beginning of the third century AD. The reverse of the pendant appears to be blank but a close examination reveals a tall and narrow flagon on the left and a long cornucopia on the right; both these devices are in very low relief and are not clearly visible because of excessive crinkling of the reverse sheet. It may be noted that both the reverse devices have frequently been depicted on Roman coins.

The reverse of the pendant bears a legend running in a circle along the periphery. Since the jewel has been badly damaged, it is not clear whether some of the minute lines near the legend are part of the legend or mere crinkles. T.G. Aravamuthan has suggested that the legend, appears to be in Brāhmī.[41] Later, he himself has admitted that some of the letters in the legend are 'foreign' to Brāhmī and he has dismissed the inscription as undecipherable. A recent re-examination of the jewel has revealed that the legend is undoubtedly in the Roman alphabet but it is too worn out to be deciphered correctly. Roman letters such as 'C' and 'I' are, however, visible.

The only other piece of ancient jewellery which can be compared with the Kempupalayam pendant is from Karivalamvandanallur in the Tirunelveli region. The Karivalamvandanallur pendant, discovered in a hoard of six Roman aurei, comprises two circular gold discs welded together; the obverse of the pendant portrays the head of Ptolemy(?) of Egypt while the reverse depicts a cornucopia, a jar and a partly effaced legend along the margin. This pendant seems to have been laced, along the edges, with beads threaded through a chain as evidenced by the occurrence of fragments of a chain and a few beads along with the pendant. The Karivalamvandanallur hoard has also yielded other pieces of jewellery including two finger rings; however, details about these are not available.[42]

Among the jewellery finds from western India, mention may be made of a Roman cameo portraying a beautiful female head recovered from Karvan (Gujarat).

Taxila has yielded a few carved gems, and two of these are reported to be imports from the Mediterranean region. One of them, depicting the winged Cupid and a bird, is almost identical to the Arikamedu gem depicting the same theme.

The clay bullae modelled on the imperial Roman coins found in India, were also, as indicated earlier, often used as jewels.

With the decline of Indo-Roman trade, jewels portraying a synthesis of Graeco-Roman and Indian motifs and techniques also went out of fashion in India.

## NOTES

1.  For details about the site, see H.D. Sankalia and M.G. Dikshit, *Excavations at Brahmapuri (Kolhapur) 1945-46,* Poona, 1952. Also see R.S. Sharma, *Urban Decay in India (c.300-c.1000),* New Delhi, 1987, pp. 79-80.

2.  K. Khandalavala, 'Brahmapuri: A Consideration of the Metal Objects found in the Kundangar Hoard', *Lalit Kala,* vol. 7, 1960, pp. 29-75; R.M. Cimino and F. Scialpi, *India and Italy (Exhibition Organised in Collaboration with the Archaeological Survey of India and the Indian Council for Cultural Relations),* Rome, 1974, p. 41.

3.  Richard Daniel De Puma, 'The Roman Bronzes from Kolhapur', in *Rome and India: The Ancient Sea Trade,* ed. V. Begley and Richard Daniel De Puma, Madison, 1991, pp. 82-112.

4.  Sharma, *Urban Decay in India,* pp 79-80.

5.  Khandalavala, 'Brahmapuri', pp. 29-75; Cimino and Scialpi, *India and Italy,* p. 39.

6.  De Puma, 'The Roman Bronzes from Kolhapur', pp. 82-112.

7.  Khandalavala 'Brahmapuri', pp 29-75; Cimino and Scialpi, *India and Italy,* p. 39.

8.  De Puma, 'The Roman Bronzes from Kolhapur', pp. 82-112.

9.  P.J.Turner, *Roman Coins from India,* London, 1989, p. 24.

10.  Although such a view has not been explicitly stated, none of the scholars writing on the subject have ever regarded the Roman bronzes in India as commodities of regular trade.

11.  For details regarding these references, see the chap. on *Coins* in this volume.

12.  R. Champakalakshmi, 'Sangam Literature as a Source of Evidence on India's Trade with the Western World: Problems of Methodology and Interpretation', paper presented at the international seminar on *India and the Roman World Between the 1st and 4th Centuries A.D.,* Madras, 1990.

13.  S.B. Deo, 'Roman Trade: Recent Archaeological Discoveries in Western India', in *Rome and India: The Ancient Sea Trade,* ed., V. Begley and Richard Daniel De Puma, Madison, 1991, pp. 39-45.

14.  De Puma, 'The Roman Bronzes from Kolhapur', pp. 82-112.

15.  For details about the glass industry in ancient India, see M.G. Dikshit, *History of Indian Glass,* Bombay, 1969.

16.  R.E.M.Wheeler, 'Roman Contact with India, Pakistan and Afghanistan', in *Aspects of Archaeology in Britain and Beyond: Essays Presented to O.G.S. Crawford,* ed. W.F. Grimes, London, 1951, pp. 345-81.

17. E. Marianne Stern, 'Early Roman Export Glass in India', in *Rome and India: The Ancient Sea Trade*, ed. V. Begley and Richard Daniel De Puma, Madison, 1991, pp. 113-24.

18. Jean-Francois Salles, 'The Periplus of the Erythraean Sea and the Arab-Persian Gulf', paper presented at the international seminar on *India and the Roman World Between the 1st and 4th Centuries A.D.*, Madras, 1990.

19. Stern, 'Early Roman Export Glass in India', pp. 113-24.

20. In 1995-6, I made a comparative study of glass and semi-precious stone beads from Ridiyagama (Sri Lanka) and those recovered from various sites in Tamilnadu. O. Bopearachchi helped with the descriptions and colour photographs of many finds from Sri Lanka. Also see O.Bopearachchi, 'Archaeological Evidence on Changing Patterns of International Trade Relations of Ancient Sri Lanka', in *Origin, Evolution and Circulation of Foreign Coins in the Indian Ocean*, ed. O. Bopearachchi and D.P.M.Weerakkody, New Delhi, 1998, pp. 133-78; Kishor K.Basa, 'Early Glass Beads in India', *South Asian Studies*, 8, 1992, pp. 91-104; Peter Francis Jr., *Bead Emporium: A Guide to the Beads from Arikamedu in the Pondicherry Museum*, Pondicherry, 1987, pp. 8-11.

21. Stern, 'Early Roman Export Glass in India', pp. 113-24.

22. John Carswell, 'The Port of Mantai, Sri Lanka', in *Rome and India: The Ancient Sea Trade*, ed. V. Begley and Richard Daniel De Puma, Madison, 1991, pp. 197-203.

23. M.A. Dorai Rangaswamy, *The Surnames of the Cankam Age, Literary and Tribal*, Madras, 1968, pp. 195-6.

24. Champakalakshmi, 'Sangam Literature'.

25. K.V. Raman, 'Roman Contacts with Tamilnadu (South-eastern India): Recent Findings', paper presented at the international seminar on *India and the Roman World between the 1st and 4th Centuries A.D.*, Madras, 1990.

26. Cimino and Scialpi, *India and Italy*, pp. 20-1. Also see M.N. Deshpande, 'Classical Influence on Indian Terracotta Art', in *Le Rayonnement des civilisations grecque et romaine sur les cultures périphériques*, Paris, 1965, pp. 603-10.

27. F.R. Allchin et al., *The Archaeology of Early Historic South Asia: The Emergence of Cities and States*, Cambridge, 1995, pp. 272-3, 321, 324. Information on the terracotta art of ancient India is provided in a number of publications. See S.J.Mangalam, 'Satavahana Terracottas from Paithan', in *Satavahana Seminar Souvenir*, ed. P. Sitapati and V.V. Krishna Sastry, Hyderabad, 1981, p. 6; T.N. Ramachandran, 'Tāmraliptī (Tamluk)', *Artibus Asiae*, vol. XIV, 1951, pp. 226-39. Terracotta finds from many sites all over India are briefly mentioned in K.S. Ramachandran, *Radiocarbon Dates of Archaeological Sites in India*, Hyderabad, 1975.

28. R.E.M.Wheeler, A.Ghosh and Krishna Deva, 'Arikamedu: An Indo-Roman Trading-Station on the East Coast of India', *AI*, vol. 2, 1946, pp. 17-124.

29. I am grateful to I. Mahadevan for information about the ring and a colour photograph of the jewel. The ring was, until recently, in the hands of a private

collector (who prefers to remain anonymous) but is rumoured to have been smuggled out of India.

30. Opinion of I. Mahadevan. I discussed the topic with him on many occasions in 1991, 1992 and 1993, mainly in 1992 when he visited me in Madras.

31. See Rangaswamy, *The Surnames of the Cankam Age*, p. 80.

32. For details about the history and art of Amaravati, see O.C. Gangoly, *Andhra Sculptures,* Hyderabad, 1973, pp. 39-66; Robert Knox, *Amaravati: Buddhist Sculpture from the Great Stupa,* London, 1992; H. Sarkar and S.P. Nainar, *Amaravati,* New Delhi, 1972.

33. These two rings are in the possession of A. Sitaraman, Tanjavur. I am grateful to him for permitting me to study and photograph the jewels.

34. H.D. Sankalia, 'The Ur (Original) Rāmāyaṇa or Archaeology and the Rāmāyaṇa', in *Aspects of Indian History and Archaeology,* ed. S.P. Gupta and K. S. Ramachandran, Delhi, 1977, pp. 202-8.

35. Kodumanal has been subjected to a series of archaeological excavations, mainly by the Department of Epigraphy and Archaeology of the Tamil University, Tanjavur. I am grateful to Y. Subbarayalu and K. Rajan of the University for allowing me to examine the excavated objects in 1991, 1996, 1997, 1998 and 2000. In 1997 and 1998, I studied the objects along with O. Bopearachchi.

36. Tiruvakkarai was excavated in 1985 by the Department of Ancient History and Archaeology of the University of Madras. As a postgraduate student of the Department, I was involved in the process. For details about the site, see S. Suresh, 'Recent Archaeological Discoveries and Studies in Tamilnadu', *Quarterly Bulletin of the School of Historical and Cultural Studies, Calcutta,* vol. I, nos. 3 and 4, 1994-5, pp. 11-16.

37. Carswell, 'The Port of Mantai, Sri Lanka', pp. 197-203.

38. N. Devasahayam, 'Roman Jewellery from Vellalore Site during the Sangam Period', *Lalit Kala,* vol. 21, 1985, p. 53.

39. I am grateful to R.Champakalakshmi for this identification.

40. The pendant is in the Government Museum, Madras (Accession no. RB 209). The beads and the chain or wire could not be traced despite repeated visits to the Museum between 1989 and 1992.

41. T.G. Aravamuthan, 'Catalogue of the Roman and Byzantine Coins in the Madras Government Museum', unpublished, 1942, p. 16.

42. The coins in the hoard are in the Government Museum, Madras (Accession no. 324.141, 324.143, 324.144, 324.145, 324.148 and 324.154). The pendant and other jewels in the hoard are also believed to be in the museum but are to date not traceable.

# 5

# Epilogue

THE PRESENT study highlights the importance of archaeology for understanding the nature of Indo-Mediterranean contacts in ancient times. Literary accounts, both Graeco-Roman and Tamil, supplement the information culled from the artifactual remains.

There is lack of unanimity amongst scholars about the exact date of origin of this maritime trade. The evidence obtained from recent excavations at Arikamedu, Alagankulam and a few other sites in southeastern India, although quantitatively meagre, clearly indicate that the trade began long before the reign of Augustus (27 BC-AD 14), probably in the second century BC or even earlier. It has now been accepted that the nature of the monsoon winds sweeping across the Indian Ocean, upon which depended navigation, was known to Arab and Indian seafarers prior to its 'discovery' by the Greek sailor Hippalos, but the precise date of this 'discovery' is not clear. Probably, this 'discovery' was not a one-time event but was made in successive stages. In any case, it may be recalled that the Roman conquest of Egypt around 31 BC provided Romans not only the wealth and other resources of Africa but also the lucrative India trade which had been efficiently organized by the powerful Ptolemies, the Greek ruling family of Egypt, after the death of Alexander the great. Thus, it is clear that the imperial Romans under Augustus and his successors did not 'initiate' the trade but had merely 'inherited' it.

The distribution pattern of Roman antiquities, specially coins, in the Indian subcontinent, provides a valuable clue to the routes adopted by the traders while traversing from one region to the other. Initially, the Romans frequented the ports on the west coast of India because the circumnavigation of Cape Comorin was considered too hazardous. This is confirmed by the fact that all Roman Republican coins (first century BC) are confined to the Laccadives, Kerala and the sites near the Palghat pass. Such finds are unknown in coastal Tamilnadu and Andhra. The absence of Roman pottery in Kerala can be explained by the fact that majority of the Roman objects including ceramics reached India during the first century AD—the period when trade was more brisk along the Coromandel coast; the zenith of Kerala's contact with the Western world was probably in the late first century BC. Thus, it is not surprising that the *Ahananūrū* and the *Puranānūrū*, the earliest Tamil poems, describe trade activities at Muziris, while the Sangam works of a slightly later period, such as the *Pattinappālai*, refer to the Coromandel ports, specially Kaveripumpattinam, in considerable detail. Similarly, while the *Periplus* (first century AD) provides only limited information on the east coast of India, Claudius Ptolemy's *Geography* (AD150) contains copious references to the Coromandel ports.

It is well known that the Julio-Claudian coin finds are concentrated in the Coimbatore region, close to the Palghat pass which was a vital 'corridor' linking the Malabar and the Coromandel coasts. Hoards containing aurei of the second century AD have often been recovered from Andhra indicating that the ports of the region were very busy during that period. On the other hand, late Roman and Byzantine coins of the late fourth and fifth centuries AD are mostly confined to coastal Tamilnadu, Madurai, Karur and Sri Lanka, indicating another major shift in the regions connected with the trade. Roman coins are extremely rare in regions to the east of India and Sri Lanka. The few poorly recorded finds of such coins from regions around the Gulf of Siam (Gulf of Thailand) and China may not have reached there because of trade but were mere curios brought by diplomatic embassies or pilgrims.

Significant changes are discernible not only in the trade routes but also in the principal commodities of trade between the initial (first century BC-first century AD) and the later (fourth-fifth centuries AD) phases of the trade. In the initial period, the main items of export from India were luxury goods such as ivory, silks, pearls and precious stones, and the volume of trade, both in luxury and non-luxury items, was very large, thus necessitating the use of the Roman gold and silver issues in the high value transactions involved in the trade. By the third-fourth centuries AD, the volume of trade had considerably declined and the main area of Roman activity during this period was restricted to the Madurai-Karur region of Tamilnadu and Sri Lanka. Moreover, the main exports from India, at that time, were confined to articles of everyday use such as cotton fabrics and pepper, thus warranting the use of low value Roman copper issues in the transactions between the Indian and the Mediterranean merchants. While late Roman and Byzantine copper issues are not known outside the main areas of trade of this late period, a few late gold issues have been found in the Andhra-Karnataka-Kerala region. The solidi finds in some of these sites would have reached there from Madurai during the course of inland trade. However, it is clear that the people in all the regions outside Madurai-Karur were not willing to accept the late Roman copper issues but insisted on payment in gold.

Thus, although trade began, due to geographical reasons, along the west coast, bulk of the Indo-Roman commerce seems to have been carried on through the Coromandel ports. Many factors contributed to the growth of the Coromandel ports. The most important factor is that the famous Silk Route linking China with Rome, by land, became inoperative during the first century BC because of the hostile attitude of the Parthians in Central Asia and the Chinese were compelled to divert their goods to the Coromandel ports for onward transmission to Rome. By then, the ports of south-eastern India had become important 'transit depots' in the trade between China, South-East Asia, Sri Lanka and Rome. The Silk Route across the land was, to a large extent, replaced by the 'maritime silk route'.

The origin of trade coincided with the emergence, for the first time ever in south India, of a series of 'states' or 'kingdoms' each with its own distinct administrative and judicial systems. One of the direct consequences of the trade was the emergence of scores of urban centres[1] throughout south India, mainly in the Tamilnadu–Andhra region. These trade centres, which developed mainly due to royal patronage, fall under one or more of the following categories:

1. Capital cities such as Madurai, the capital of the Pāndyas, Uraiyur, the capital of the Cōlas and Karur, the capital of the Cheras. The location of Karur was, until recently, intensely debated by scholars. It has now been established beyond doubt that the modern town of Karur, on the banks of the river Amaravati in Tamilnadu, was the Chera capital. The town and its environs have, in recent years, yielded rock inscriptions and coins related to the Sangam Cheras. Significantly, all the capitals were commercially important. Karur was a jewellery-manufacturing centre. Madurai was famous for its cotton fabrics but there is no clear evidence that these were exported to Rome, particularly during the early period, because Roman coins of the first century AD number far less than those of the later centuries in the area. However, the 'Argaritic' muslin

produced at Uraiyur was in great demand in the Roman markets. Archaeological excavations at Uraiyur have revealed a dyeing vat similar to the ones reported from Arikamedu and Vasava-samudram.

2. Chief ports such as Muziris (Chera port), Kaveripumpattinam and Bandarpattinam (Cōla ports), Korkai and Alagankulam (Pāṇḍya ports) and Virai or Arikamedu which was used by traders from different kingdoms and chiefdoms including the Malaiyamāns who flourished in the area.

3. Sites rich in mineral resources: The most important among such sites is Kodumanal, a thriving craft centre where jewels, iron and steel implements and textiles were produced. Terracotta spindle whorls and a piece of cloth have been recovered from the stratified layers at the site. This cloth fragment is believed to be the oldest of such finds in south India.

4. Towns which lay on important trade routes: An example of such a town is Tirukoilur, on the right bank of the river Pennaiyar. The site, not too far from Arikamedu, was the capital of the Malaiyamān chieftains. The place abounds in the quadrangular copper coins issued by this ruling family.

Among the other 'trade route' centres are Nagarjunakonda, Amaravati and Kondapur (Andhra). It may be noted that many of the towns and cities in Andhra developed solely on account of their strategic location on the routes linking the ports of south-eastern India with Western Deccan (Maharashtra region). Several of these Andhra sites, located on the banks of major rivers, also served as 'inland ports'.

Yet another 'trade route' site is Sannati (Karnataka) which has also revealed edicts of the Mauryan emperor Asoka (third century BC).

All these urban centres frequently interacted with one another, both for regional commerce as well as transcontinental trade.

The precise 'role' or 'function' of the Roman coins in the towns and cities of early historical India has, for long, been a matter of considerable academic debate. The available evidence indicates that these coins did circulate as 'money' in parts of south India, specially the Tamil country, and also in Sri Lanka. The value of the foreign coins in relation to the indigenous issues is indeterminable. The *kāṇam* mentioned in the early Tamil poems as well as the terms *dināra* and *suvarṇa* appearing in epigraphs and Sanskrit literature may refer to the Roman aureus. The Roman denarii were rarely counterstruck by the Sangam Chera rulers for use in their territory. Imitations of Roman coins were produced in certain regions of India, whenever there was a shortage of the genuine foreign currency.

As the Roman coins, through the process of trade, reached almost all parts of the then known world, these coins acquired the status of a 'multinational' currency. In this respect, these coins may be compared to the present day US dollars which are accepted as valid legal tender in several commercial establishments in Singapore and Europe.

The ugly slash marks and the tiny countermarks including dots, curves and stars, are two peculiar features of the Roman coins in India. Several theories have been propounded that the slashes were intended to cancel out the issuing authority but none of these theories are convincing because of the extremely limited occurrence of the phenomenon. As far as the countermarks are concerned, most of them are undoubtedly ownership marks, meant to distinguish the coins of one owner from those of the other, specially on occasions when the coins of different individuals/agencies were deposited with a common banking institution or a moneylender.

The use of Roman coins and their metallic and clay imitations as jewellery was not as common as is generally believed. A small percentage of the coins were pierced or looped to be used as pendants of necklaces. The practice of using coins as jewels was not confined to the Roman coins alone; some of the Sātavāhana and Kushan coins were also converted into jewellery. The use of the Roman aurei as jewellery was mainly confined to the Andhra-Tamilnadu region presumably because in the north, the Kushan gold issues, based on the Roman weight standard, were available for use as jewellery whereas indigenous gold coins were not known in ancient south India.

Since the time of Wheeler, Indian archaeologists (including me) had assumed that rouletted pottery, mainly concentrated in eastern and south-eastern India, and the red polished ware, common in sites in Gujarat, are imports from the Mediterranean world. Recent studies of specimens of both these pottery types have, however, conclusively proved that they are indigenous products.

The amphorae recovered from select sites in west and south India exhibit variations in size, shape and surface treatment. Apart from wine, a variety of other items such as olive oil, honey, garum (a fish sauce) and fruits were brought to India in the amphorae. Imitations of the amphorae have been recovered mainly from a series of sites along the east coast of India.

It should be remembered that Indians would have learnt the technique and the external decorative features of Roman pottery not only from Rome and Africa, but also from the Hellenistic settlements thriving in the Persian Gulf region.

Some of the Roman objects, including the sigillata recovered in the subcontinent in extremely limited quantities, reached the country not as trade commodities, but either as 'personal belongings' of foreign traders or as 'gifts' for mercantile families, royal households and religious establishments. Interestingly, certain types of foreign objects such as bronze artifacts were carried to India both as 'trade items' and 'gift items' on different occasions.

The Buddhist *vihāras* were established along the major trade routes, specially in the Deccan region. The monks themselves participated in the trade on behalf of their patron-merchants. Hence, the presence of foreign objects such as amphorae sherds within the premises of ancient monasteries is not surprising. The use of foreign objects including bronze artifacts was also known in the *vihāras* of western India. In Tamilakam, however, archaeology has not shed much light on the precise 'link' between the Buddhist institutions and Roman trade.

There were a few colonies of Roman merchants in India. Ter, Arikamedu, Kaveripumpattinam, Madurai and Alagankulam appear to have housed such settlements.

Large-scale excavations at some of the principal trade sites, specially the port towns of Tamilnadu and Kerala, enhance one's knowledge about the trade. There is an urgent need to intensify efforts in this direction because many of the sites are rapidly deteriorating due to a host of factors such as erosion caused by the sea and rivers, agricultural operations and unauthorized digging and collection of antiquities, specially coins, by local treasure hunters. Also, in recent decades, towns such as Karur have seen intense construction activity and are no longer available for major archaeological operations. Even Karaikadu which was, till a few years ago, a little known isolated, undisturbed site, has been thoroughly spoilt due to the construction of a series of commercial establishments and offices almost atop the ancient settlement.

In conclusion, it should be reiterated that the Indo-Roman contacts were not confined to mere commercial ties. They extended to the exchange of diplomatic embassies and cultural interaction. The focus here, however, has been on an intensive study of Roman coins and other antiquities in India and their significance in trade, specially maritime trade. Regarding cultural interaction, while efforts have been made to highlight the results of such interaction in the case of jewellery, bronze antiquities, etc., it has not been dealt with extensively as such a study would include the art and monumental remains of the early historical period.

## NOTE

1. Detailed descriptions of some of these urban centres can be found in F.R. Allchin et al., *The Archaeology of Early Historic South Asia: The Emergence of Cities and States,* Cambridge, 1995; Aloka Parasher, 'Social Structure and Economy of Settlements in the Central Deccan (200 BC-AD 200)', in *The City in Indian History,* ed. Indu Banga, New Delhi, 1991, pp. 19-46; R. Champakalakshmi, *Trade, Ideology and Urbanization: South India 300 B.C. to A.D. 1300,* New Delhi, 1996 mainly chaps. 1, 2, 3; S. Suresh, 'Defence Architecture in the Early Tamil Country', *Proceedings of the Indian History Congress—Forty-ninth Session,1988,* Delhi, 1989, pp. 657-61; idem, 'Review of: F.R. Allchin et al.: *The Archaeology of Early Historic South Asia: The Emergence of Cities and States',* *The Book Review,* vol. XX, no. 5, 1996, p. 13.

# List of Roman Coin Finds in India

| Serial no. | Year of Find | Site | Context of Find | No. of Coins and Issuers | Metal | Associated Coins |
|---|---|---|---|---|---|---|
| (a) | (b) | (c) | (d) | (e) | (f) | (g) |
| | | | TAMILNADU | | | |
| 1. | Pre-1828 + | Alamporai or Alampara | S | 3+; Issuer(s): ? | AV (2+), AE (1+) | |
| 2. | 1936 | Akhilandapuram | H | 30; Augustus:2, Tiberius:3, Rest:? | AR | |
| 3. | 1984? | Annamalai | S | Total:? Tiberius:? | AR | |
| 4. | 1989-91 | Alagankulam | E | 4+; Theodosius I:1, Valentinian II:2+, Arcadius:1, Unidentified:1+ | AE | |
| 5. | 1990s | Bandarpattinam | S | 4; Arcadius:2, Honorius:2 | AE | PMC, medieval Cōla coins (?) |
| 6. | 1827 | Bishopsdown (Udhagamandalam) | S | 1; Claudius:1 | AV | |
| 7. | 1946 | Budinatham | H | 1398; Augustus: 369, Tiberius: 1029 | AR | |
| 8. | 1808 | Chavadipalaiyam | Mega-lithic grave | 1; Augustus:1 | AR | PMC (AR) |
| 9. | 1817 | Coimbatore Area | Mega-lithic grave? | 1; Augustus:1 | AR | |

S · Stray finds
E   Excavations
H   Hoards

| Serial no. | Year of Find | Site | Context of Find | No. of Coins and Issuers | Metal | Associated Coins |
|---|---|---|---|---|---|---|
| (a) | (b) | (c) | (d) | (e) | (f) | (g) |
| 10. | 1912 | Coimbatore area | S | 2; Tiberius:2 | AR | |
| 11. | 1974 | Coimbatore area | H | 73; Augustus, Tiberius:72, Gaius:1 | AR | |
| 12. | Nineteenth century | Cuddalore | S | Total:? Valentinian:?, Eudocia:? | AE | Die-struck coins (AE); Perforated Chinese coins |
| 13. | ? | Dharapuram | H(?) | ? | ? | |
| 14. | 1916 | Kalikanayak-anpalaiyam | S | 1; Justin I (?):1 | AV | |
| 15. | 1856 | Kaliyampattur | H | 63; Tiberius:6, Gaius:1, Claudius:18, Nero:17, Domitian:5, Nerva:2, Rest:? | AV | |
| 16. | 1909 | Kallakinar | H(?) | 2; Republican period:2 | AR | Other coins (AV, AR) (?) |
| 17. | 1801 | Kangayam or Kongeyam | H(?) | 10+; Augustus:?, Tiberius:? | AR | |
| 18. | 1932 | Karivalamva-ndanallur | H | 6; Nero:2, Vespasian:1, Domitian:2, Hadrian:1 | AV | |
| 19a. | 1806 | Karur | S | 5; Augustus:1, Tiberus:1, Claudius:3 | AV | |
| 19b. | 1856 | Karur | H | 100s; Augustus:? | AR | |
| 19c. | 1878 | Karur | H | About 500; Augustus:27, Tiberus:90, Rest:? | AR | |
| 19d. | 1904 | Karur | S | 1; Marcus Aurelius:1 | AV | |

| Serial no. | Year of Find | Site | Context of Find | No. of Coins and Issuers | Metal | Associated Coins |
|---|---|---|---|---|---|---|
| *(a)* | *(b)* | *(c)* | *(d)* | *(e)* | *(f)* | *(g)* |
| 19e. | 1980s (?) | Karur | E | 1; Augustus:1 | AR | PMC (?) (AR) |
| 19f. | 1990 | Karur | S | 1; Claudius:1 | AV | Mākkōtai Chera coins (?) (AR) |
| 19g. | 1992 | Karur | S | 2; Antoninus Pius (imitation?): 2 | AV | |
| 19h. | 1988-2000 | Karur | S | 1000s (genuine and imitation coins: unidentified but mostly of Constantine II and later) | AE | ? |
| 20. | 1913 | Kathanganni | H | 233; Augustus: 49, Tiberius:184 | AR | |
| 21. | 1887-90 | Kilakarai | S | 3+; Unidentified- AE:2, Bronze:1+ | AE, Bronze | |
| 22. | ? | Kodumanal | S | 2; Augustus:1, Tiberus:1 | AR | |
| 23. | 1987 | Koneripatti | H | 35; Augustus:6, Tiberius:29 | AR | |
| 24. | Pre-1930 | Korkai | S | ? | ? | |
| 25. | 1992 | Krishnagiri | S | 1; Republican period:1 | AR | |
| 26. | 1934(?) | Kulattupalaiyam | S | 1; TheodosiusI(?):1 | AV | |
| 27a. | Pre-1888 | Madurai | S | 1; Domitian:1 | AV | |
| 27b. | Pre-1888 | Madurai | S | 1; Leo III:1 | AV | |
| 27c. | Pre-1888 | Madurai area | S(?) | 100s; Honorius:?, Arcadius:?, Anastasius:? | AE | |
| 27d. | ? | Madurai area | S | 2; Theodosius II:1, Constantine II:1 | AV | |
| 27e. | 1917 | Madurai hills | H | 11; Claudius:5, Nero:3, Domiti-an:1, Rest:? | AV | |
| 27f. | 1950s | Madurai | S | 1+; Unidentified late Roman imitat-ions:? | AE | |

| Serial no. | Year of Find | Site | Context of Find | No. of Coins and Issuers | Metal | Associated Coins |
|---|---|---|---|---|---|---|
| *(a)* | *(b)* | *(c)* | *(d)* | *(e)* | *(f)* | *(g)* |
| 28. | ? | Mahabalipuram | S | Total:?; Theodosius I:?Valentinian:?, Eudocia:? | AE | |
| 29. | ? | Malaiyadiputhur | S | 4; Theodosius II:1, Anastasius I:1, Theodosius II imitation:2 | AV | |
| 30. | 1929 | Mambalam (Madras city) | H | 1; Augustus:1 | AR | 770 PMC (AR) |
| 31. | 1998 | Nathampatti | H | 9; Theodosius II:5, Leo I:4 | AV | |
| 32. | 1995-7 | Navalai | S | 1; Tiberius:1 | AR | |
| 33. | 1803 | Pennar | H | 1; Augustus:1 | AR | PMC (AR) |
| 34. | ? | Perur | S | 3; Constantine I: 1, Constantine II: 1,Theodosius (I or II?):1 | AE | |
| 35. | 1800 | Pollachi | H(?) | 6+; Augustus:?, Tiberius:? | AR | |
| 36. | 1990s | Pollachi | H | ? | ? | |
| 37. | 1898 | Pudukkottai | H | 501; Augustus:42, Tiberius:168, Gaius: 14, Claudius:156, Nero: 116, Vespasian:3, Rest:? | AV | |
| 38. | 1883(?) | Saidapet (Madras city) | S(?) | 1; Unidentified:1 | AE | |
| 39. | 1992 | Soriyapattu | H | 193+; Tiberius:3, Claudius:5, Nero:18, Vespasian:20, Titus:15, Domitian:7, Trajan:9, Hadrian:42, | AV | |

| Serial no. | Year of Find | Site | Context of Find | No. of Coins and Issuers | Metal | Associated Coins |
|---|---|---|---|---|---|---|
| (a) | (b) | (c) | (d) | (e) | (f) | (g) |
| | | | | Antoninus Pius:63, Marcus Aurelius:4, Septimius Severus:4, Caracalla:2, Unidentified imitations:?, Rest:? | | |
| 40. | ? | Sulur | S | 1+; Tiberius:1, Rest:? | AR | |
| 41. | ? | Tanjavur | S | 1; Diocletian:1 | AE | |
| 42. | ? | Tiruchirappalli | S(?) | 6; Issuers:? | AE | |
| 43. | ? | Tirukoilur | S | 3+; Issuers:? (fourth century AD) | AE | |
| 44. | ? | Tirumangalam | S | 1; Zeno:1 | AE or AV? | |
| 45. | ? | Tirunelveli | ? | 17; Issuers:? | AE | |
| 46. | 1990 | Tiruppur | S ✳ | 1; Republican period:1 | AR | |
| 47. | 1918 | Tondamanathan | H | 6; Augustus:1, Tiberius:3, Claudius:1, Nero:1 | AV | 27 PMC (AR) |
| 48. | ? | Udumalpet | S | 5; Augustus:2, Tiberius:3 | AR | |
| 49. | 1995-6 | Uthamapuram | H | 10; Augustus:?, Rest:? | AR | |
| 50. | 1961-2 | Vellaiyaniruppu (Kaveripattinam) | S | 1; Augustus(?):1 | AE | |
| 51a. | 1841 | Vellalur | H | 522; Augustus:135 Tiberius:378, Gaius:3, Claudius:5, Nero:1 | AR | |
| 51b. | 1891 | Vellalur | H | 547; Augustus:189 Tiberius:329, Gaius:8, Claudius:18, Nero:3 | AR | |

| Serial no. | Year of Find | Site | Context of Find | No. of Coins and Issuers | Metal | Associated Coins |
|---|---|---|---|---|---|---|
| (a) | (b) | (c) | (d) | (e) | (f) | (g) |
| 51c. | 1931 | Vellalur | H | 121(+23 unstruck blanks)Augustus:118, Rest:? | AR | |
| 51d. | 1939 | Vellalur | H | Total:?; Tiberius:? | AV | |
| 51e. | 1990s | Vellalur | H | ? | ? | |
| 51f. | 1990s | Vellalur | H | ? | ? | |
| 52a. | ? | Vellanthavalam | S | 1; Augustus:1 | AR | |
| 52b. | 1990s | Vellanthavalam | H | ? | ? | |

INDIAN ISLANDS

| Serial no. | Year of Find | Site | Context of Find | No. of Coins and Issuers | Metal | Associated Coins |
|---|---|---|---|---|---|---|
| 53. | 1949 | Kadmat Island, Lakśadvipa | H(?) | 15; Vespasian:5, Antoninus Pius:9, Commodus:1 | AV | |
| 54. | 1978-9, 1984 | Lakśadvipa | H(?) | 712; Republican period:266, Augustus:269 Tiberius:18, Gaius (with Agrippina):1, Claudius:1, Hadrian:1, Rest:? | AR | |

PONDICHERRY

| Serial no. | Year of Find | Site | Context of Find | No. of Coins and Issuers | Metal | Associated Coins |
|---|---|---|---|---|---|---|
| 55a. | Pre-1987 | Arikamedu | S(?) | 3; Tiberius:2, Imitation Tiberius:1 | AR | |
| 55b. | ? | Arikamedu | S | 1; Constantine I: 1 | AE | |

ANDHRA PRADESH

| Serial no. | Year of Find | Site | Context of Find | No. of Coins and Issuers | Metal | Associated Coins |
|---|---|---|---|---|---|---|
| 56a. | 1973- | Alluru | S | 2; Issuer(s):? | AV | |
| 56b. | 1974-5(?) | Alluru | S(?) | 1; Claudius:1 | AV | |
| 57. | 1959 | Akkanpalle | H | 1531; Augustus:698, Imitation Augustus:24, Tiberius:740, | AR | |

| Serial no. | Year of Find | Site | Context of Find | No. of Coins and Issuers | Metal | Associated Coins |
|---|---|---|---|---|---|---|
| *(a)* | *(b)* | *(c)* | *(d)* | *(e)* | *(f)* | *(g)* |
| 58. | Pre-1832 | Amaravati | S(?) | Imitation Tiberius:31, Gaius:2 Claudius:11, Nero:1, Unidentified:24 ? | AE(?) | |
| 59. | 1838 | Atirala | S | 1; Trajan:1 | AV | 'Old Hindu coins'(?) |
| 60. | 1982-6 | Bavikonda | E | 3; Augustus:?, Tiberius:? | AR | 1 Sātavāhana coin (lead) |
| 61. | Nineteenth century | Bezwada | S | 2+; Tiberius:2, Rest:? | AR | |
| 62. | 1943 | Bhagavanpavam | S | 2; Unidentified imitations:2 | AV | |
| 63. | 1983 | Darmavaripalem | H | 26; Tiberius:1, Nero:1, Imitation Nero:1, Domitian:1 Imitation Hadrian:2, Imitation Antoninus Pius:17 Imitation Commodus:1, Unidentified imitations:2 | AV | |
| 64. | 1975 | Dhulikatta | E | 1; Imitation Augustus:1 | AR | Sātavāhana coins (AR, lead and potin), Unidentified coins (AR) |
| 65a. | Pre-1945 | Ghantasala | H | ? | | |
| 65b. | 1945-55 | Ghantasala | S | 2; Issuer(s):? | | Sātavāhana coins (?) |
| 66. | 1933 | Gootiparti (Gaiparti) | S(?) | 3; Claudius:1, Trajan:1, Imitation Antoninus Pius:1 | AV | |

| Serial no. | Year of Find | Site | Context of Find | No. of Coins and Issuers | Metal | Associated Coins |
|---|---|---|---|---|---|---|
| (a) | (b) | (c) | (d) | (e) | (f) | (g) |
| 67. | 1990 | Gopalapuram | H | 2; Imitation Septimius Severus:2 | AV | |
| 68. | 1928 | Gumada | H | 23; Imitation Commodus:3, Septimius Severus:1, Imitation Septimius Severus:13, Imitation Geta:1, Imitation Constantine I:2, Rest 3:lost | AV | |
| 69. | ? | Guntur area | S | 3; Nero:1, Hadrian:1, Antoninus Pius:1 | AV | |
| 70. | 1980s | Hyderabad(?) | S(?) | Total:?; Gallienus:1, Diocletian:1, Constantine I:1, Constantius II:2, Rest:? | Bronze (?) | |
| 71. | ? | Kalingapatnam | E | ? | | |
| 72. | 1940 | Kondapur | E | 2; Imitation Tiberius:2 | Lead (1of the lead coins is plated with gold) | 1824 Sātavāhana coins (lead and potin), 10 PMC (AR) |
| 73. | 1915 | Kotapad | S | 4; Augustus:3, Tiberius:1 | AR | |
| 74. | Pre-1900 | Krishna district | S | 1; Imitation Antoninus Pius (Faustina type):1 | AV | |

| Serial no. | Year of Find | Site | Context of Find | No. of Coins and Issuers | Metal | Associated Coins |
|---|---|---|---|---|---|---|
| (a) | (b) | (c) | (d) | (e) | (f) | (g) |
| 75. | 1978-9 | Kudavelli | E | 2; Constantius II:1, Anastasius:1 | AV | Sātavāhana coins:1 Unidentified coins:1 |
| 76. | 1953 | Lingarajupalem (Lingarajapuram?) | S | 2; Imitation Augustus:1, Imitation Tiberius:1 | AR | 'Various Indian Antiquities' |
| 77. | 1914 | Mallayapalem | S | 4; Nero:1, Trajan:2, Antoninus Pius:1 | AV | |
| 78. | 1983 | Nagavarappupadu | H | 58; Augustus:6, Imitation Augustus:2, Tiberius:21, Claudius:24, Imitation Claudius:1, Nero:3, Unidentified coin:1 | AV | |
| 79a. | 1936 | Nagarjunakonda | S | 1; Hadrian:1 | AV | Sātavāhana coins |
| 79b. | 1956 | Nagarjunakonda | E | 2; Tiberius:1, Antoninus Pius:1 | AV | Ikśvāku coins (lead), Sātavāhana coins (AE) |
| 79c. | ? | Nagarjunakonda | E(?) | 2; Unidentified Imitations:2 | Copper coated (?) with gold | |
| 80. | 1933 | Nandyal | H | 161; Augustus:2, Tiberius:17, Claudius:8, Nero: 20, Domitian:1 Nerva:1, Trajan:2, Antoninus Pius:2, Rest:? | AV | |

| Serial no. | Year of Find | Site | Context of Find | No. of Coins and Issuers | Metal | Associated Coins |
|---|---|---|---|---|---|---|
| (a) | (b) | (c) | (d) | (e) | (f) | (g) |
| 81. | 1952 | Nasthullapur | H | 39; Augustus:12, Imitation Augustus:1, Tiberius:25, Imitation Tiberius:1 | AR | 8 PMC (AR) |
| 82a. | 1786 | Nellore | H (below temple) | About 40; Trajan:3, Hadrian:4, Antoninus Pius:1, Gordian:1, Rest:? | AV | |
| 82b. | Nineteenth century | Nellore | S | Valentinian:? Eudocia:? | AE | Die-struck coins (AE), perforated Chinese coins |
| 83a. | Pre-1904 | Ongole | ? | ? | AV | |
| 83b. | 1904 | Ongole | S | 2; Nero:1, Hadrian:1 | AV | |
| 84. | 1976 | Peddakodam-agundla | H | 3; Nero:1, Hadrian:1, Antoninus Pius:1 | AV | |
| 85. | 1968-9 | Peddabankur | E | 9; Augustus:?, Imitation Augustus:? Tiberius:? Imitation Tiberius:? | Genuine coins:AR, imitatons: lead | Sātavāhana coins |
| 86. | 1899 | Salihundam | H | 11; Tiberius:11 | AR | |
| 87. | 1903 | Tangulur (or Tangutur) | S | Few; Hadrian:? | AV | |
| 88. | 1980s | Totlakonda | E | 5; Tiberius:5 | AR | Sātavāhana coins |
| 89. | ? | Tirupati | S(?) | ? | AV(?) | |
| 90. | 1940s | Upparipeta | S | 2; Imitations:2 | AV | |
| 91. | 1980-4(?) | Veerapuram | E | 1;Imitation Tiberius:1 | Lead coated with silver | Sātavāhana/ Mahārathi coins (?) |

| Serial no. | Year of Find | Site | Context of Find | No. of Coins and Issuers | Metal | Associated Coins |
|---|---|---|---|---|---|---|
| (a) | (b) | (c) | (d) | (e) | (f) | (g) |
| 92. | 1951 | Veeravasaramu | H | 15; Tiberius:1, Unidentified imitations:14 | AV | |
| 93. | Pre-1888 | Vidyadurrapuram | S | 1; Tiberius:1 | AR | |
| 94. | 1889 | Vinukonda | H | 15; Tiberius:2, Vespasian:1, Domitian:1, Hadrian:2, Antoninus Pius:6, Marcus Aurelius:1; Commodus:1; Caracalla:1 | AV | |
| 95. | 1964 | Weepangandla | H | 3; Imitation ConstantineI:1, Seventh Century Byzantine imitations:2 | AV | 17 PMC (AR) |
| 96. | 1961-2 | Yellesvaram | E | 1; Septimius Severus:1 | AV | Sātavāhana coins |
| | | | KERALA | | | |
| 97. | ? | Allepey | H | Total:?; (Issuers: up to Nero), Tiberius:1+, Rest:? | AR | |
| 98. | 1945 | Eyyal | H ✻ | 83; Republican Period:5(AR), Augustus:47 (AR), Tiberius:6 (AR),8 (AV), Claudius:6 (AR),2 (AV), Nero:3 (AR),1 (AV), Trajan:1 (AV)Rest:? (AR) | AR:71, AV:12 | 34 PMC (AR) |
| 99. | ? | Idamakuduru | S | 1; Claudius:1 | AV or AR? | |
| 100. | Nineteenth century | Kilalur (Kizhoor) | S or H | ? | AV | |
| 101a. | 1847 | Kottayam | H | 1000s; Augustus: | AV | |

| Serial no. | Year of Find | Site | Context of Find | No. of Coins and Issuers | Metal | Associated Coins |
|---|---|---|---|---|---|---|
| *(a)* | *(b)* | *(c)* | *(d)* | *(e)* | *(f)* | *(g)* |
| | | | | 9+, Tiberius:28+ (majority of the hoard:Tiberius), Gaius: 3+, Claudius:17+, Nero: 16+ Caracalla:1+, Antoninus Pius:? | (Few coins: AR?) | |
| 101b. | ? | Kottayam | S | 1;Theodosius (I or II):1 | AV | |
| 101c. | ? | Kottayam | S | 1; Nero:1 | AV | |
| 102. | 1974 | Kumbalam | H | 9; Hadrian:1, Antoninus Pius:4, Marcus Aurelius:4 | AV | |
| 103. | 1963-4 | Mankada | S | 1; Nero:1 | AV | |
| •104. | 1992 | Nedumkandam | H | 50+; Republican period:8, Augustus:11, Rest:? | AR | |
| 105. | ? | Nirapam | S | ? | ? | |
| 106. | 1998(?) | Parur | H | 1000+, issuer(s)? | AV | |
| 107. | After 1944 | Poonjar | S(?) | 7+: Augustus:1 (AV),1 (AR), Claudius:2 (AV), Nero:1(AV), Antoninus Pius:2 (AV), Rest:? | AV:6+, AR:1+ | |
| 108. | ? | Puthankavu | H | 50+; (All postdate Theodosius I), Theodosius II: 1+, Rest:? | AV | |
| 109. | 1983 | Valuvally | H | 314+; Augustus:?, Nero:6+,Vespasian: 7+, Domitian:2+, Nerva:2+, Trajan:27+, Hadrian:96+ Antoninus Pius :172, | AV | |

| Serial no. | Year of Find | Site | Context of Find | No. of Coins and Issuers | Metal | Associated Coins |
|---|---|---|---|---|---|---|
| *(a)* | *(b)* | *(c)* | *(d)* | *(e)* | *(f)* | *(g)* |
| | | | | Imitation Antoninus Pius:2, Marcus Aurelius:? | | |

### KARNATAKA

| Serial no. | Year of Find | Site | Context of Find | No. of Coins and Issuers | Metal | Associated Coins |
|---|---|---|---|---|---|---|
| 110. | 1977 | Akkialur | H | 46; Septimius Severus:2, Caracalla:1, Late Roman / Byzantine rulers from Theodosius II to Justin I (some of these coins: imitations): 43 | AV | |
| 111a. | 1961 | Bangalore city(?) | S | 1; Hadrian:1 | Bronze | |
| 111b. | 1980s | Bangalore city | H | ? | AV | |
| 112. | 1980s | Belgaum area | H | Around 30; Tiberius: Around 30. | AR | |
| 113a. | 1909 | Chandravalli | E or S | 1; Augustus:1 | AR | 2 Sātavāhana coins—1 of lead and 1 of potin |
| 113b. | Pre-1929 | Chandravalli | S | Many Issuers:? | AR | |
| 113c. | 1929 | Chandravalli | E | 2+(?); Tiberius: 2+(?) | AR | |
| 113d. | 1947 | Chandravalli | E | 6(?); Augustus:1+, Tiberius:4+, Unidentified coins:1 | AR | Sātavāhana coin (potin) |
| 114. | ? | Gulbarga area | S | 2; Issuer(s):? | ? | |
| 115. | 1981-2 | Gulbarga area | H | 39; Byzantine rulers:39 | AV, | |
| 116. | 1965 | HAL Airport, Bangalore | H | 256; Augustus:29, Tiberius:227 | AR | |
| 117. | 1922 | Katryal | H | 48; Byzantine rulers:48 | AV | |

| Serial no. | Year of Find | Site | Context of Find | No. of Coins and Issuers | Metal | Associated Coins |
|---|---|---|---|---|---|---|
| *(a)* | *(b)* | *(c)* | *(d)* | *(e)* | *(f)* | *(g)* |
| 118. | ? | Mangalore area | S | 2; Augustus:1, Tiberius:1 | AR | |
| 119. | 1980s (?) | Mangalore area | H | Total:?; Septimius Severus:?, Antoninus Pius:? | AV | |
| 120. | 1882 | Mysore | S | 1; Commodus:1 | AV | |
| 121. | Early 1990s (?) | Nosagere | H | 3; Imitation Septimius Severus:3 | AV | |
| 122a. | 1976-7 | Vadagaon Madhavapur | E | 1; Unidentified coin:1 | AR | Sātavāhana (potin) and Kshatrapa coins |
| 122b. | ? | Vadagaon Madhavapur | S or E? | 1; Issuer:? | AE | |
| 123. | 1891 | Yeshwantpur | H | 163; Augustus: 4+, Tiberius:1+, Gaius: 1+, Claudius: 4+, Rest:? | AR | |

## WESTERN INDIA

## GUJARAT(G), MAHARASHTRA(M) AND GOA

| | | | | | | |
|---|---|---|---|---|---|---|
| 124. | 1970 | Adam (M) | H | 11; Augustus:1, Tiberius:10 | AV | |
| 125. | ? | Baroda area (G) | S | Total:?; Republican period:?:(AR); Nero:?, Vespasian:?, Domitian:?, Commodus:?, Septimius Severus:?: (AR, AE, Bronze); Byzantine Rulers:?: (AV) | AV AR AE Bronze | |
| 126. | Pre-1888 | Bombay area (M) | S | 2; Gallienus:1, Other coin:? | AR or Bronze? | |
| 127. | ? | Bombay area (M) | S | 2; Republican period:2 | AR | |

| Serial no. | Year of Find | Site | Context of Find | No. of Coins and Issuers | Metal | Associated Coins |
|---|---|---|---|---|---|---|
| (a) | (b) | (c) | (d) | (e) | (f) | (g) |
| 128. | 1840 | Dharpul (M) | H | 18; Antoninus Pius:?, Marcus Aurelius:1+, Lucius Verus: 1+, Commodus:?, Septimius Severus:5+, Caracalla:?, Geta:? | AV | |
| 129. | 1989 | Junagadh (G) | S | 1; Marcus Aurelius:1 | AV | |
| 130. | 1984 | Goa | H(?) | 1; Septimius Severus:1 | AV | 12 other coins |
| 131. | ? | Kalawad Shitala (G) | H | 64; Gallienus:?, Tetricus:?, Constantine I (?):?, Rest:? | Bronze | |
| 132. | 1982 | Kaprivani (M) | S | 2; Septimius Severus:2 | AV | |
| 133. | ? | Mandhal (M) | S | 6; Augustus:?, Tiberius:? | AV | |
| 134. | Pre-1890 | Nagdhara(G) | S | 1; Marcus Aurelius:1 | AV | |
| 135. | 1954-5 | Nevasa (M) | E | 1; Imitation Tiberius:1 | Lead | Sātavāhana coins |
| 136. | 1911 | Sampewada (M) | S | 2: Commodus:1; Unidentified imitation:1 | AV | |
| 137. | Eighteenth century | Surat (G) | S | ? | AE | Greek coins(?) |
| 138. | 1929-30 | Tadali (M) | S | 2; Issuer(s):? | AV | |
| 139. | ? | Uppavahr (M) | S | 2+(?) Septimius Severus:1, Imitation Septimius Severus/ Caracalla:1 | AV | |
| 140. | 1890 | Waghoda (M) | S | 1; Septimius Severus:1 | AV | |

| Serial no. | Year of Find | Site | Context of Find | No. of Coins and Issuers | Metal | Associated Coins |
|---|---|---|---|---|---|---|
| (a) | (b) | (c) | (d) | (e) | (f) | (g) |

EASTERN, NORTHERN AND NORTH-WESTERN REGIONS OF THE
INDIAN SUBCONTINENT: ORISSA (O), BIHAR, UTTAR PRADESH (UP),
MADHYA PRADESH (MP), PAKISTAN (P) AND AFGHANISTAN (A)

| | | | | | | |
|---|---|---|---|---|---|---|
| 141a. | 1879 | Ahin Posh (A) | Stupa Deposit | 3; Domitian:1, Trajan:1, Hadrian:1 | AV | 17 Kushan coins (AV) |
| 141b. | 1889 | Ahin Posh (A) | S | 5; Byzantine Rulers:5 | AV | |
| 142. | ? | Ajaigadh (MP) | S | 1; Republican period:1 | AR | |
| 143. | Nineteenth century | Allahabad (UP) | S | 2+; Diocletian:1, Rest:? | AE, Bronze | |
| 144. | 1860s or 1870s | Bamanghati (O) | H | Total:?, Constantine I:?, Gordian:? Rest:? | AV | |
| 145a. | Pre-1908 | Bilaspur(MP) | S | 1; Septimius Severus:1 | AV | |
| 145b. | 1911 | Bilaspur (MP) | S | 3; Hadrian:1, Commodus:1. Septimius Severus:1 | AV | |
| 146. | Nineteenth century | Bindachal or Brindachal (UP) | S | 1+(?): Diocletian (?):1, Rest:? | AE | |
| 147. | 1942 | Chakherbedha (MP) | S | 2; Commodus:1, Imitation Marcus Aurelius or Commodus:1 | AV | |
| 148. | ? | Charikar (A) | ? | ? | AE | |
| 149. | Nineteenth century | Chunar (UP) | S | 2+(?); Carinus:? Numerianus:? | AE | |
| 150. | ? | Ganjam (O) | S | 1; Tiberius:1 | AR | |
| 151. | Nineteenth century | Hadda (A) | Stupa Deposit | 5; Byzantine rulers (Theodosius, Marcian, Leo):5 | AV | 13 Late Kushan coins (AV:2AE:11);702 Sassanian coins |

| Serial no. | Year of Find | Site | Context of Find | No. of Coins and Issuers | Metal | Associated Coins |
|---|---|---|---|---|---|---|
| (a) | (b) | (c) | (d) | (e) | (f) | (g) |
| 152. | ? | Jabalpur (MP) | S | 2+; Augustus:1, Vespasian:1, Rest:? | AR | |
| 153. | Nineteenth century | Kanouj (UP) | S | Total:? Diocletian:? | AE | |
| 154. | Nineteenth century | Kabul Valley (A) | *Stupa* Deposit | Total:? Augustus:?, Leo:?, Anastasius:?, Justin:?Phocas:? | AV | |
| 155. | ? | Kohat (P) | H | 69+; Republican period:?, Rest:? | AR,AE | Indo-Greek coins (?) |
| 156. | Nineteenth century | Lahore (P) | H(?) | ? | ? | |
| 157a. | 1830 | Manikyala (P) | *Stupa* Deposit | 7; Republican period:7 | AR | 4 Kushan (AV) and 8 Indo Scythian (AE) coins |
| 157b. | 1886 | Manikyala (P) | S | 5; Antoninus Pius:5 | AV | |
| 158. | Pre-1951 | Mathura (UP) | S | 1; Caracalla:1 | AV | |
| 159. | 1973 | Memadakhedi (MP) | S | 1;Septimius Severus:1 | AV | |
| 160. | Nineteenth century | Mirzapur (UP) | S | 2+(?); Diocletian:? (AE), Carinus:? (Brass?) | AE, Brass | |
| 161. | 1898 | Pakli (P) | H | 24+; Republican period:8, Augustus:12, Tiberius:3, Hadrian:1 | AR | |
| 162. | Nineteenth century | Patna, Bihar | S | 5+; Nero:2, third century issues (?):3 | AE | |
| 163. | ? | Raipur (MP) | ? | ? | AE | |
| 164. | ? | Rajghat (UP) | S | 2; Diocletian:2 | AE | |
| 165. | Nineteenth century | Rewah (MP) | S | 2; Imitation Claudius:1 Imitation Commodus:1 | AV | |

| Serial no. | Year of Find | Site | Context of Find | No. of Coins and Issuers | Metal | Associated Coins |
|---|---|---|---|---|---|---|
| (a) | (b) | (c) | (d) | (e) | (f) | (g) |
| 166. | ? | Sar-i-pul (A) | ? | ? | AE | |
| 167. | ? | Shevaki(A) | *Stupa* Deposit | 1; Trajan:1 | AV | 2 Kushan coins (AV) |
| 168. | 1934 | Taxila (P) | E | 1; Tiberius:1 | AR | ? |
| 169. | ? | UP | S | 2; Republican period:1, Augustus:1 | AR | |

## NOTES AND CLARIFICATIONS

1. The nineteenth century finds from Coimbatore and Madurai regions (Tamilnadu) are very confusing. Often, any discovery from the districts of Coimbatore and Madurai are simply labelled 'Coimbatore find' and 'Madurai find' respectively. The available records embody only a fraction of the very large number of finds from these two places.

2. Roman issues continue to be recovered in very large numbers from the Coimbatore, Madurai and Karur regions (Tamilnadu). The finds from Coimbatore area are generally Julio-Claudian issues. The finds from Karur are usually late Roman coppers and their imitations, and occasionally, Julio-Claudian issues. The Madurai finds are invariably late Roman coppers and their imitations. Most of these finds are in the possession of local private collectors or are available in the antique markets abroad. Unfortunately, the new discoveries neither attract academic attention nor reach the local museums.

3. It is not clear whether Kohat (Pakistan) yielded one or two hoards. Some scholars believe that the site has yielded two hoards, both containing the Republican denarii and later issues.

4. It has very recently been reported that Roman coins have been found in Lingsugur and Sannati in Karnataka. But no details about these finds are known.

# List of Rouletted Ware Finds in India

| Serial no. | Site | Context of Find: E or S |
|:---:|:---:|:---:|
| (a) | (b) | (c) |
| | TAMILNADU–PONDICHERRY | |
| 1. | Arikamedu | E, S |
| 2. | Appukallu | E |
| 3. | Alagankulam | E, S |
| 4. | Kanchipuram | E |
| 5. | Karaikadu | E, S |
| 6. | Karur | E, S |
| 7. | Kaveripattinam | E, S |
| 8. | Kodumanal | E, S |
| 9. | Korkai | E, S |
| 10. | Kilaiyur | S |
| 11. | Kudikadu | E(?), S |
| 12. | Maligaimedu | E |
| 13. | Manapattu | S |
| 14. | Manigramam | S |
| 15. | Nallur | E |
| 16. | Nattamedu | E, S |
| 17. | Neidavasal | S |
| 18. | Nerumbur | S |
| 19. | Sendamangalam | E |
| 20. | Sengamedu | S |
| 21. | Sulur | S |
| 22. | Tirukoilur | E |
| 23. | Tiruvamattur | E |
| 24. | Uraiyur | E, S |
| 25. | Vanagiri | E, S |
| 26. | Vasavasamudram | E |
| 27. | Vellaiyaniruppu | S |
| 28. | Vellalur | S |
| | ANDHRA PRADESH | |
| 29. | Allur | S |
| 30. | Amaravati | E, S |
| 31. | Annangi Hill | S |
| 32. | Chagatur | S |
| 33. | Chandavaram | E |

| Serial no. | Site | Context of Find: E or S |
|:---:|:---:|:---:|
| (a) | (b) | (c) |
| 34. | Chebrolu | S |
| 35. | Chejerla | S |
| 36. | Chintamani Dibba | S |
| 37. | Dantavarapukota | S |
| 38. | Daranikota | E |
| 39. | Duvvuru | S |
| 40. | Gandavaram | S |
| 41. | Ghantasala | E |
| 42. | Jambuladinne | S |
| 43. | Kalingapatnam | E, S |
| 44. | Kambaduru | S |
| 45. | Karpakala | S |
| 46. | Kesarapalle | E, S |
| 47. | Kondapur | E |
| 48. | Kotamitta | S |
| 49. | Kotesvaralayam | S |
| 50. | Kothapatnam | E, S |
| 51. | Kudavelli | S |
| 52. | Medarametla | S |
| 53. | Mittapalli | S |
| 54. | Mukhalingam | E, S |
| 55. | Mylavaram | S |
| 56. | Nagarlapet | S |
| 57. | Narasapatnam | S |
| 58. | Neredubandaguddu | S |
| 59. | Nilugondla | S |
| 60. | Pagidigutta | E |
| 61. | Paritala | S |
| 62. | Pithapuram | S |
| 63. | Ramatheertham | S |
| 64. | Salihundam | E |
| 65. | Sasanakota | S |
| 66. | Satanikota | E |
| 67. | Siddhirajalingapuram | S |
| 68. | Simhapur(Singupuram) | S |
| 69. | Tippaipalli | S |
| 70. | Vaddamanu | E |
| 71. | Vaikuntapuram | S |
| 72. | Vamulapadu | S |
| 73. | Veerapuram | E |
| 74. | Vyaparladevipadu | S |

ORISSA

| | | |
|:---:|:---:|:---:|
| 75. | Manikpatna | S |
| 76. | Sisupalgarh | E, S |

| Serial no. | Site | Context of Find: E or S |
|:---:|:---:|:---:|
| (a) | (b) | (c) |
| | WEST BENGAL | |
| 77. | Atghara | S |
| 78. | Bachri | S |
| 79. | Baral (Boral) | S |
| 80. | Berachampa | S |
| 81. | Chandraketugarh | E, S |
| 82. | Deulpota | S |
| 83. | Hadipur | E |
| 84. | Hariharpur | S |
| 85. | Harinarayanpur | S |
| 86. | Mahinagar | S |
| 87. | Mangalkot | E |
| 88. | Saptagram | S |
| 89. | Tamluk | E, S |
| | UTTAR PRADESH | |
| 90. | Ayodhya | E |
| 91. | Rajghat | E |
| | MAHARASHTRA | |
| 92. | Adam | S |
| 93. | Arni | E |
| 94. | Nashik | E |
| 95. | Nevasa | E |
| 96. | Junnar | S |
| 97. | Paithan | S |
| 98. | Ter | E |
| | KARNATAKA | |
| 99. | Banavasi | E, S |
| 100. | Brahmagiri | E |
| 101. | Chandravalli | E |
| 102. | Maski | E |
| 103. | Roja | S |
| 104. | Sannati | S |
| 105. | TNarsipur | E |

## NOTES AND CLARIFICATIONS

1. IAR 1961-2 (pp. 26-7) states that several coastal sites in Tanjavur district (Tamilnadu) have yielded rouletted ware. But the report is too brief and not clear. The sites have not been exhaustively listed and hence, the information is not beyond doubt. Site-names such as Kilaiyur, Manigramam, Neidavasal and Vanagiri have, however, been mentioned in the report and have been included in the present listing.

2. Karaikadu, Kudikadu and Nattamedu are neighbouring coastal sites in South Arcot district, Tamilnadu.

3. K.V. Raman (1991) has stated that rouletted ware and probably, amphora finds were recovered during the trial excavations conducted in the 1960s within the premises of the Santhome Church, Mylapore (Madras city) by the Church authorities. Unfortunately, no record, published or otherwise, about these finds is available. According to the local scholars, information about these finds may not be true.

4. In recent years, archaeologists have unearthed rouletted ware in many little known sites in Bengal region. Since precise details about most of these finds are not available, they have not been listed here. For the names of some of these sites, see Vishwas D. Gogte (1997).

# List of Amphora Finds in India

| Serial no. | Site | Context of Find: E or S |
|:---:|:---:|:---:|
| (a) | (b) | (c) |
| | **TAMILNADU–PONDICHERRY** | |
| 1. | Alagankulam | E |
| 2. | Arikamedu | E, S |
| 3. | Karaikadu | E, S |
| 4. | Karur | E |
| 5. | Nattamedu | E |
| 6. | Tirukoilur | E |
| 7. | Vasavasamudram | S |
| 8. | Vellalur | S |
| 9. | Vijayamangalam | S |
| | **ANDHRA PRADESH** | |
| 10. | Daranikota | E |
| 11. | Kondapur | E |
| 12. | Nagarjunakonda | E |
| | **ORISSA** | |
| 13. | Manikpatna | S(?) |
| | **KARNATAKA** | |
| 14. | Chandravalli | E, S |
| | **GUJARAT** | |
| 15. | Ajabpura | S |
| 16. | Amreli | E |
| 17. | Devnimori | E |
| 18. | Dhatva | S |
| 19. | Dwaraka | E |
| 20. | Junagadh | S |
| 21. | Maspur | S |
| 22. | Modhera | S(?) |
| 23. | Nagara | E |
| 24. | Prabhas Patan | E |

| Serial no. | Site | Context of Find: E or S |
|---|---|---|
| (a) | (b) | (c) |
| 25. | Sathod | S |
| 26. | Shamalaji | E(?) |
| 27. | Shrimala (Binnamala) | S(?) |
| 28. | Triveni | S |
| 29. | Vallabhi | E,S |

### MAHARASHTRA

| | | |
|---|---|---|
| 30. | Akota | S(?) |
| 31. | Bhokardan | E |
| 32. | Brahmapuri | E |
| 33. | Junnar | S |
| 34. | Nevasa | E |
| 35. | Paithan | E |
| 36. | Paunar | E |
| 37. | Rajbandar | S |
| 38. | Ter | E |

### MADHYA PRADESH (MP), UTTAR PRADESH (UP) AND PAKISTAN (P)

| | | |
|---|---|---|
| 39. | Mathura (UP) | E |
| 40. | Taxila (P) | E |
| 41. | Ujjain (MP) | E |

# Bibliography

Allchin, F.R. et al., *The Archaeology of Early Historic South Asia: The Emergence of Cities and States,* Cambridge, 1995.

Altekar, A.S., 'A Unique Kushano-Roman Gold Coin of King Dharmadamadhara(?)', *JNSI,* vol. XII, 1950, pp. 1-4.

Arasu, P., 'Ancient Ceramic Industry from Kanchipuram Excavations', unpublished M.Phil. dissertation, University of Madras, Madras, 1979.

Aravamuthan, T.G., 'Catalogue of the Roman and Byzantine Coins in the Madras Government Museum', unpublished, 1942.

Ardika, I.W., P.S. Bellwood, R.A. Eggleton and D.J. Ellis, 'A Single Source for South Asian Export-Quality Rouletted Ware?', *Man and Environment,* vol. XVIII, no. 1, 1993, pp. 101-9.

Basa, Kishor K., 'Early Glass Beads in India', *South Asian Studies,* vol. 8, 1992, pp. 91-104.

Begley, V., 'Arikamedu Reconsidered', *AJA,* vol. 87, 1983, pp. 461-81.

———, 'Rouletting and Chattering, Decoration on Ancient and Present-day Pottery in India', *Expedition,* vol. 28, no. 1, 1986, pp. 47-54.

———, 'Rouletted Ware at Arikamedu: A New Approach', *AJA,* vol. 92, 1988, pp. 427-40.

———, 'Ceramic Evidence for Pre-*Periplus* Trade on the Indian Coasts', in *Rome and India: The Ancient Sea Trade,* ed. V. Begley and Richard Daniel De Puma, Madison, 1991, pp. 157-96.

Begley, V. et al., *The Ancient Port of Arikamedu—New Excavations and Researches, 1989-1992 I,* Pondicherry, 1996.

Behera, K.S., 'On a Kushana Gold Coin from Orissa', *JNSI,* vol. XXXVII, 1975, pp. 76-82.

Berghaus, P., 'An Indian Imitation of an Augustan Denarius', in *Praci-Prabha, Perspectives in Indology—Essays in Honour of Prof. B.N. Mukherjee,* ed. D.C. Bhattacharyya and Devendra Handa, New Delhi, 1989, pp. 101-5.

———, 'Roman Coins from India and their Imitations', in *Coinage, Trade and Economy (3rd International Colloquium, January 8th-11th, 1991),* ed. A.K. Jha, Nashik, 1991, pp. 108-21.

———, 'Three Denarii of Tiberius from Arikamedu', in *Indian Numismatics, History, Art and Culture—Essays in Honour of Dr. P.L.Gupta, I,* ed. D.W. MacDowall, Savita Sharma and Sanjay Garg, Delhi, 1992, pp. 95-8.

————, 'Roman Aurei from Kumbalam, Ernakulam District, Kerala', *SSIC*, vol. III, 1993, pp. 29-42.

Bolin, S., *State and Currency in the Roman Empire to 300 AD*, Stockholm, 1958.

Bopearachchi, O., 'Some Observations on Roman Coins found in Recent Excavations at Sigiriya', *Ancient Ceylon*, vol. 7, 1990, pp. 20-37.

————, 'Review of: R. Krishnamurthy: *Late Roman Copper Coins from South India— Karur and Madurai*', *Oriental Numismatic Society Newsletter*, vol. 141, 1994, pp. 3-4.

————, 'Archaeological Evidence on Changing Patterns of International Trade Relations of Ancient Sri Lanka', in *Origin, Evolution and Circulation of Foreign Coins in the Indian Ocean*, ed. O. Bopearachchi and D.P.M. Weerakkody, New Delhi, 1998, pp.133-78.

Bouzek, Jan, Jiří Břeň and Petr Charvát, 'The Chronology of the Local Pottery and Other Finds and Features Uncovered in the SW Sector of the Abhayagiri Vihara (Anuradhapura, Sri Lanka)', *Archeologické Yozhledy*, vol. XXXVIII, 1986, pp. 241-62.

Burnett, A., 'Roman Coins from India and Sri Lanka', in *Origin, Evolution and Circulation of Foreign Coins in the Indian Ocean*, ed. O. Bopearachchi and D.P.M. Weerakkody, New Delhi, 1998, pp. 179-89.

Caldwell, R., *A Description of Roman Imperial Aurei found Near Calicut*, Trivandrum, 1851.

Carswell, John, 'The Port of Mantai, Sri Lanka', in *Rome and India: The Ancient Sea Trade*, ed. V. Begley and Richard Daniel De Puma, Madison, 1991, pp. 197-203.

Casson, L., *Ships and Seamanship in the Ancient World*, Princeton, 1986.

————, 'P. Vindob G 40822 and the Shipping of Goods from India', *Bulletin of the American Society of Papyrologists*, vol. 23, 1986, pp. 73-9.

————, 'Ancient Naval Technology and the Route to India', in *Rome and India: The Ancient Sea Trade*, ed. V. Begley and Richard Daniel De Puma, Madison, 1991, pp. 8-11.

————, 'New Light on Maritime Loans : P.Vindob G.40822', in *Trade in Early India*, ed. Ranabir Chakravarti, New Delhi, 2001, pp. 228-43.

Champakalakshmi, R., 'Sangam Literature as a Source of Evidence on India's Trade with the Western World: Problems of Methodology and Interpretation', paper presented at the international seminar on *India and the Roman World between the 1st and 4th Centuries A.D.*, Madras, 1990.

————, *Trade, Ideology and Urbanization: South India 300 B.C. to A.D. 1300*, New Delhi, 1996.

Chattopadhyaya, B.D., *Coins and Currency Systems in South India c. AD 225-1300*, New Delhi, 1977.

Chumble, P.D., 'A Rare Roman Coin' *IIRNS Newsline*, 3, 1994, p. 7.

Cimino, R.M. and F. Scialpi, *India and Italy (Exhibition Organized in Collaboration with the Archaeological Survey of India and the Indian Council for Cultural Relations)*, Rome, 1974.

Codrington, H.W., *Ceylon Coins and Currency, Memoirs of the Colombo Museum,* series A, no. 3, Colombo, 1924.

Comfort, H., 'Terra Sigillata at Arikamedu', in *Rome and India: The Ancient Sea Trade,* ed. V. Begley and Richard Daniel De Puma, Madison, 1991, pp. 134-50.

Deo, S.B., 'Roman Trade: Recent Archaeological Discoveries in Western India', in *Rome and India: The Ancient Sea Trade,* ed. V.Begley and Richard Daniel De Puma, Madison, 1991, pp. 39-45.

Deraniyagala, S.U., 'The Citadel of Anuradhapura 1969: Excavations in the Gedige Area', *Ancient Ceylon,* vol. 2, 1972, pp. 48-169.

Deshpande, M.N., 'Classical Influence on Indian Terracotta Art', in *Le Rayonnement des civilisations grecque et romaine sur les cultures périphériques,* Paris, 1965, pp. 603-10.

———, 'Roman Pottery in India', in *Potteries in Ancient India,* ed. B.P. Sinha, Patna, 1969, pp. 275-84.

Devaraj, D.V., 'A Roman Terracotta Pendant from Sannati in Karnataka', *SSIC,* vol. VII, 1997, pp. 45-8.

Devasahayam, N., 'Roman Jewellery from Vellalore Site during the Sangam Period', *Lalit Kala,* 21, 1985, p. 53.

De Puma, Richard Daniel, 'The Roman Bronzes from Kolhapur', in *Rome and India: The Ancient Sea Trade,* ed. V. Begley and Richard Daniel De Puma, Madison, 1991, pp. 82-112.

de Romanis, Federico and A. Tchernia, eds., *Crossings—Early Mediterranean Contacts with India,* New Delhi, 1997.

Dikshit, M.G., *History of Indian Glass,* Bombay, 1969.

Dorai Rangaswamy, M.A., *The Surnames of the Cankam Age, Literary and Tribal,* Madras, 1968.

Francis, Peter, Jr., *Bead Emporium: A Guide to the Beads from Arikamedu in the Pondicherry Museum,* Pondicherry, 1987.

Gangoly, O.C., *Andhra Sculptures,* Hyderabad, 1973.

Garnsey, Peter and Richard Saller, *The Roman Empire—Economy, Society and Culture* London, 1987.

Ghosh, A., ed., *Ajanta Murals,* New Delhi, 1967.

Ghosh, N.C. and K. Ismail, 'Two Foreign Gold Coins from Excavation at Kudavelli, District Mahabubnagar, Andhra Pradesh', *JNSI,* vol. XLII, 1980, pp. 11-17.

Ghosh, N.C., *Excavations at Satanikota 1977-80,* New Delhi, 1986.

Gobl, R., 'The Roman-Kushanian Medallion in the British Museum', *JNSI,* vol. XXXVIII, no. 1, 1976, pp. 21-6.

Gogte, Vishwas D., 'The Chandraketugarh-Tamluk Region of Bengal: Source of the Early Historic Rouletted Ware from India and Southeast Asia', *Man and Environment,* vol. XXII, no. 1, 1997, pp. 69-85.

Gokhale, Sobhana, 'Junnar in Trade during Satavahana Period', in *Coinage, Trade and Economy (3rd International Colloquium, January 8th-11th, 1991),* ed. A.K. Jha, Nashik, 1991, pp. 55-7.

Gopal, R., 'A Greek Copper Coin from Hassan', *SSIC,* vol. III, 1993, pp. 51-2.

Grace,V.R., *Amphoras and the Ancient Wine Trade,* Princeton, 1979.

Gupta, Chandrashekhar, 'Foreign Denominations of Early Indian Coins', in *Foreign Elements in Indian Indigenous Coins,* ed. A.M. Shastri, Varanasi, 1982, pp. 109-23.

Gupta, P.L., *Roman Coins from Andhra Pradesh,* Hyderabad, 1965.

————, 'Kushana-Murunda Rule in Eastern India— Numismatic Evidence', *JNSI,* vol. XXXVI, 1974, pp. 25-53.

————, 'British Museum Romano-Kushana Medallion: Its Nature and Importance', *JNSI,* vol. XXXVIII, no. 2, 1976. pp. 73-81.

————, 'Coins in Rome's India Trade', in *Coinage, Trade and Economy (3rd International Colloquium, January 8th-11th, 1991),* ed. A.K. Jha, Nashik, 1991, pp. 122-37.

Gurumurthy, S., *Ceramic Traditions in South India (Down to 300 A.D.),* Madras, 1981.

Harrauer, H. and P.J. Sijpesteijn 'Ein neues Dokument Zu Roms Indienhandel: P. Vindob. G 40822', *Anzeiger der Akademie der Wissenschaften, Wien, Philologisch-historische Klasse,* vol. 122, 1985, pp. 124-55.

Hill, G.F., 'Roman Aurei from Pudukota, South India', *NC* (3rd series), vol. XVIII, 1898, pp. 304-20.

————, 'Untitled Note', *NC* (3rd series), vol. XIX, 1899, p. 82.

Hill, P.V., 'A Puzzling Aureus of Septimius Severus from India', *Spink Numismatic Circular,* vol. XCII, 1984, p. 259.

————, 'Second Thoughts on the Severan Aureus from India', *Spink Numismatic Circular,* vol. XCII, 1984, p. 323.

Jayasurya, R., 'The Trading Community in Early Tamil Society up to 900 A.D.', unpublished M.Phil. dissertation, University of Madras, Madras, 1980.

Joshi, M.C. and A.K. Sinha, 'Discovery of an Amphora-Handle from Mathura', in *Indian Archaeological Heritage—Shri K.V. Soundara Rajan Festschrift I,* ed. C. Margabandhu, K.S. Ramachandran, A.P. Sagar and D.K. Sinha, Delhi, 1991, pp. 255-9.

Khandalavala, K., 'Brahmapuri: A Consideration of the Metal Objects found in the Kundangar Hoard', *Lalit Kala,* vol. 7, 1960, pp. 29-75.

Knox, Robert, *Amaravati: Buddhist Sculpture from the Great Stupa,* London, 1992.

Krishnamurthy, R., 'Seleucid Coins from Karur', *SSIC,* vol. III, 1993, pp. 19-28.

————, 'Coins from Phoenicia found at Karur, Tamilnadu', *SSIC,* vol. IV, 1994, pp. 19-27.

————, *Late Roman Copper Coins from South India: Karur and Madurai,* Madras, 1994.

————, 'Coins from Greek Islands, Rhodes and Crete found at Karur, Tamilnadu', *SSIC,* vol. V, 1995, pp. 29-36.

————, 'A Roman Coin Die from Karur, Tamilnadu', *SSIC,* vol.VI, 1996, pp. 43-8.

Krishnan, K.G., 'Some Aspects of South Indian Coinage', *SSIC,* vol. II, 1992, pp. 9-18.

Krishna Sastry, V.V., *Roman Gold Coins—Recent Discoveries in Andhra Pradesh,* Hyderabad, 1992.

Kulkarni, P.P., 'Early Roman Coins in India', *JNSI ,* vol. XLVI, 1984, pp. 37-8.

Lal, B.B., 'Śiśupālgarh 1948: An Early Historical Fort in Eastern India', *AI,* vol. 5, 1949, pp. 62-102.

Longhurst, A.H., 'Rock-Cut Tomb Near Calicut', *Archaeological Survey of India Annual Report (1911-12),* pp. 159-60.

MacDowall, D.W., 'Trade on the Maritime Silk Route—The Evidence of Roman Coins found in India', paper presented at the international seminar on *India and the Roman World between the 1st and 4th Centuries A.D.,* Madras, 1990.

———, 'Indian Imports of Roman Silver Coins', in *Coinage, Trade and Economy (3rd International Colloquium, January 8th –11th, 1991),* ed. A.K. Jha, Nashik, 1991, pp. 145-63.

———, 'The Evidence of the Gazetteer of Roman Artefacts in India', in *Tradition and Archaeology—Early Maritime Contacts in the Indian Ocean,* ed. H.P. Ray and Jean-Francois Salles, New Delhi, 1996, pp. 79-95.

MacDowall, D.W. and N.G. Wilson, 'The References to the Kuṣāṇas in the Periplus and Further Numismatic Evidence for its Date', *NC* (7th series), vol. X, 1970, pp. 221-40.

Mangalam, S.J., 'Satavahana Terracottas from Paithan', in *Satavahana Seminar Souvenir,* ed. P. Sitapati and V.V. Krishna Sastry, Hyderabad, 1981, p. 6.

Marianne Stern, E., 'Early Roman Export Glass in India', in *Rome and India: The Ancient Sea Trade,* ed. V. Begley and Richard Daniel De Puma, Madison, 1991, pp. 113-24.

Marshall, J., *Taxila,* vols. I, II, III, Cambridge, 1951.

Mattingly, H., *Coins of the Roman Empire in the British Museum, Volume I: Augustus to Vitellius,* London, 1965.

Mehta, R.N., 'Urban Centres of Western India and the Western World', in *India and the West (Proceedings of a Seminar Dedicated to the Memory of Hermann Goetz),* ed. Joachim Deppert, New Delhi, 1983, pp. 139-48.

Meile, P., 'Les yavanas dans l'Inde tamoule', *Journal asiatique,* vol. 232, 1940-1, pp. 85-123.

Mukherjee, B.N., *The Indian Gold: An Introduction to the Cabinet of the Gold Coins in the Indian Museum,* Calcutta, 1990.

———, *Indian Museum Bulletin XXV—Kharoshtī and Kharoshtī-Brāhmī Inscriptions in West Bengal (India),* Calcutta, 1990.

Nag, Arun K., 'Identification and Origin of the Sprinkler', in *Śri Dineśaćandrika Studies in Indology,* ed. B.N. Mukherjee, D.R. Das, S.S. Biswas and S.P. Singh, Delhi, 1983, pp. 389-95.

Nagaswamy, R., 'Alagankulam: An Indo-Roman Trading Port', in *Indian*

*Archaeological Heritage—Shri K.V. Soundara Rajan Festschrift I,* ed. C. Margabandhu, K.S. Ramachandran, A.P. Sagar and D.K. Sinha, Delhi, 1991, pp. 247-54.

————, *Roman Karur—A Peep into Tamils' Past,* Madras, 1995.

Nagaswamy, R. and A. Abdul Majeed, *Vasavasamudram (A Report on the Excavation conducted by the Tamilnadu State Department of Archaeology),* Madras, 1978.

Narasimha Murthy, A.V., 'A Roman Coin Mould from Banavasi', *JNSI,* vol. XLVI, 1984, pp. 45-6.

Narasimha Murthy, A.V. and D.V. Devaraj, 'A Roman Coin Mould from Talkad Excavations', *SSIC,* vol. V, 1995, pp. 59-62.

Orton, Nancy Pinto, 'Red Polished Ware in Gujarat: A Catalogue of Twelve Sites', in *Rome and India: The Ancient Sea Trade,* ed. V. Begley and Richard Daniel De Puma, Madison, 1991, pp. 46-81.

Parabrahma Sastry, P.V., 'Some Aspects of South Indian Numismatics', *SSIC,* vol. III, 1993, pp. 9-18.

Parasher, Aloka, 'Kondapur: A Forgotten City (Reflections on the Early History of Telangana)', *Indian History Congress—Proceedings of the Forty-eighth Session,* Delhi, 1988, pp. 82-90.

————, 'Social Structure and Economy of Settlements in the Central Deccan (200 BC-AD 200)', in *The City in Indian History,* ed. Indu Banga, New Delhi, 1991, pp. 19-46.

Pillay, K.K., *South India and Sri Lanka (Sir William Meyer Lectures, 1958-59— University of Madras),* Madras, 1975.

Radhakrishnan, P.V., 'Korkai and its Environs', unpublished M.Phil. dissertation, University of Madras, Madras, 1987.

————, 'A Punch-marked Die from Karur', *SSIC,* vol. IV, 1994, pp. 51-6.

Rajan, K., 'Stratigraphical Position of Russet-Coated Painted Ware', in *Indian Archaeological Heritage—Shri K.V. Soundara Rajan Festschrift I,* ed. C. Margabandhu, K.S. Ramachandran, A.P. Sagar and D.K. Sinha, Delhi, 1991, pp. 241-6.

Ramachandran, K.S., *Radiocarbon Dates of Archaeological Sites in India,* Hyderabad, 1975.

Ramachandran, T.N., 'Tāmraliptī (Tamluk)', *Artibus Asiae,* vol. XIV, 1951, pp. 226-39.

Ramadass, S., 'Sirupānārruppadai—A Historical Study', unpublished M.Phil. dissertation, University of Madras, Madras, 1984.

Ramamurthy, V., *History of Kongu,* Madras, 1986.

Raman, K.V., 'Archaeological Excavations in Kanchipuram', *Tamil Civilization,* vol. V, nos. 1 and 2, 1987, pp. 61-72.

————, 'Roman Contacts with Tamilnadu (South-eastern India): Recent Findings', paper presented at the international seminar on *India and the Roman World between the 1st and 4th Centuries A.D.,* Madras, 1990.

———, 'Further Evidence of Roman Trade from Coastal Sites in Tamilnadu', in *Rome and India: The Ancient Sea Trade*, ed. V. Begley and Richard Daniel De Puma, Madison, 1991, pp. 125-33.

———, 'Roman Coins from Tamilnadu', *SSIC*, vol. II, 1992, pp. 19-34.

Rao, S.R., *Excavations at Amreli, A Kshatrapa-Gupta Town*, Baroda, 1966.

Raschke, M.G., 'New Studies in Roman Commerce with the East', *Aufstieg und Niedergang der Römischen Welt*, vol. 2.9.2, 1978, pp. 604-1378.

Ray, H.P., 'The Yavana Presence in Ancient India', *Journal of the Economic and Social History of the Orient*, 31, 1988, pp. 311-25.

———, 'The Yavana Presence in India', in *Athens, Aden, Arikamedu—Essays on the Interrelations between India, Arabia and the Eastern Mediterranean*, ed. Marie-Francoise Boussac and Jean-Francois Salles, New Delhi, 1995, pp. 75-95.

———, 'A Resurvey of "Roman" Contacts with the East', in *Athens, Aden, Arikamedu—Essays on the Interrelations between India, Arabia and the Eastern Mediterranean*, ed. Marie-Francoise Boussac and Jean-Francois Salles, New Delhi, 1995, pp. 97-114.

Rodewald, C., *Money in the Age of Tiberius*, Manchester, 1976.

Salles, Jean-Francois, 'The Periplus of the Erythraean Sea and the Arab-Persian Gulf', paper presented at the international seminar on *India and the Roman World between the 1st and 4th Centuries A.D.*, Madras, 1990.

Sankalia, H.D., 'The Ur (Original) Rāmāyaṇa or Archaeology and the Rāmāyaṇa', in *Aspects of Indian History and Archaeology*, ed. S.P. Gupta and K.S. Ramachandran, Delhi, 1977, pp. 202-8.

Sankalia, H.D. and M.G. Dikshit, *Excavations at Brahmapuri (Kolhapur) 1945-46*, Poona, 1952.

Sankalia, H.D., B. Subbarao and S.B. Deo, *The Excavations at Maheshwar and Navdatoli, 1952-1953*, Poona, 1958.

Santhakumar, R., 'Roman Coins in Tamilnadu', unpublished M.Phil. dissertation, University of Madras, Madras, 1985.

Sarkar, H. and B.N. Misra, *Nagarjunakonda*, New Delhi, 1980.

Sarkar, H. and S.P. Nainar, *Amaravati*, New Delhi, 1972.

Sarma, I.K., *Religion in Art and Historical Archaeology of South India: Contacts and Correlations*, Madras, 1987.

———, 'Historical Archaeology of Tamilnadu and Kerala', *Tamil Civilization*, vol. V, nos. 1 and 2, 1987, pp. 48-60.

———, 'Roman Coins from Andhra Pradesh: Their Contexts, Chronology and Cultural Significance', *SSIC*, vol. II, 1992, pp. 35-50.

———, 'A Critical Study of the Numismatic Evidences from Nagarjunakonda Excavations', *SSIC*, vol. IV, 1994, pp. 63-78.

Sastri, T.V.G., M. Kasturi Bai and M. Veerender, *Vaddamanu Excavations (1981-85)*, Hyderabad, 1992.

Sathyamurthy, T., *Catalogue of Roman Gold Coins (In the Collections of Department of Archaeology, Kerala)*, Thiruvananthapuram, 1992.

————, 'Angamali Hoard of Silver Punch-marked Coins', *SSIC*, vol. IV, 1994, pp. 45-50.

————, 'Numismatic Finds from Bandar Pattanam in Tamilnadu', *SSIC*, vol. VII, 1997, pp. 49-55.

Seneviratne, S., 'The Ecology and Archaeology of the Seruwila Copper-Magnetite Prospect, North East Sri Lanka', in *From Sumer to Meluhha: Contributions to the Archaeology of South and South West Asia in Memory of George F. Dales, Jr. (Wisconsin Archaeological Reports 3)*, ed. Jonathan Mark Kenoyer, Madison, 1994, pp. 261-80.

————, 'The Ecology and Archaeology of the Seruwila Copper-Magnetite Prospect, North East Sri Lanka', *The Sri Lanka Journal of the Humanities*, vol. XXI, nos. 1 and 2, 1995, pp. 114-45.

Sengupta, Gautam, 'Archaeology of Coastal Bengal', in *Tradition and Archaeology —Early Maritime Contacts in the Indian Ocean*, ed. H.P. Ray and Jean-Francois Salles, New Delhi, 1996, pp. 115-28.

Sewell, R., 'Roman Coins found in India', *JRAS*, 1904, pp. 591-637.

Shanmugam, P., 'Some Aspects of Monetary System of the Pallavas', *SSIC*, vol. III, 1993, pp. 101-8.

————, 'Two Coins of Tamil Origin from Thailand', *SSIC*, vol. IV, 1994, pp. 95-100.

Sharma, R.S., *Urban Decay in India (c.300-c.1000)*, New Delhi, 1987.

Shastri, A.M., 'Imperial Roman Coins in Early Deccanese Inscriptions', *SSIC*, vol. II, 1992, pp. 77-87.

————, 'Kondapur: A Satavahana Silver Coins Mint', *SSIC*, vol. III, 1993, pp. 81-5.

————, 'Three Satavahana Mint-Towns', *SSIC*, vol. IV, 1994, pp. 57-62.

————, 'Junnar: A Mint-Town of the Satavahanas', *SSIC*, vol. V, 1995, pp. 51-6.

Sidebotham, S.E., 'Ports of the Red Sea and the Arabia-India Trade', in *Rome and India: The Ancient Sea Trade*, ed. V. Begley and Richard Daniel De Puma, Madison, 1991, pp. 12-38.

Silva, R. and J. Bouzek, 'Mantai—A Second Arikamedu', *Antiquity*, 1985, pp. 46-47.

Slane, K.W., 'Observations on Mediterranean Amphoras and Tablewares found in India', in *Rome and India: The Ancient Sea Trade*, ed. V. Begley and Richard Daniel De Puma, Madison, 1991, pp. 204-15.

Srinivasan, K.R., 'Archaeology of Tamilnadu and Kerala—Accomplishments and Prospects', *Tamil Civilization*, vol. V, nos. 1 and 2, 1987, pp. 10-29.

Srivastava, B., 'Economic Significance of Roman Coins found in India', *JNSI*, vol. XXVI, 1964, pp. 222-7.

Subbarao, B., *Baroda Through the Ages*, Baroda, 1953.

Subrahmanyam, R., *A Catalogue of the Ikshvaku Coins in the Andhra Pradesh Government Museum*, Hyderabad, 1979.

Sumathi, R., 'Trade and its Impact on the Early Tamils—The Cōḷa Experience', unpublished M.Phil. dissertation, Jawaharlal Nehru University, New Delhi, 1984.

Suresh, S., 'Defence Architecture in the Early Tamil Country', *Proceedings of the Indian History Congress—Forty-ninth Session, 1988*, Delhi, 1989, pp. 657-61.

————, 'Roman Vestiges in Kanchipuram', in *Kanchi—A Heritage of Art and Religion*, ed. Nanditha Krishna, Madras, 1992a, pp. 56-61.

————, *Roman Antiquities in Tamilnadu*, Madras, 1992b.

————, 'Early Roman Finds in Madras City', in *Aspects of Madras—A Historical Perspective*, ed. G.J. Sudhakar, Madras, 1993, pp. 13-16.

————, 'Recent Archaeological Discoveries and Studies in Tamilnadu', *Quarterly Bulletin of the School of Historical and Cultural Studies, Calcutta*, vol. I, nos. 3 and 4, 1994-5, pp. 11-16.

————, 'Review of: F.R. Allchin et al.: *The Archaeology of Early Historic South Asia: The Emergence of Cities and States', The Book Review*, vol. XX, no. 5, 1996, p. 13.

————, 'Countermarks of Buddhist Symbols on the Roman Coins found in Andhra Deśa', paper presented at the international seminar on *Contribution of Andhra Deśa to Buddhism*, Hyderabad, 1997.

————, 'Countermarks of Buddhist Symbols on the Roman Coins found in Andhra Deśa (Synopsis of the Paper)', *Contribution of Andhra Deśa to Buddhism—Souvenir*, Hyderabad, 1997, pp. 51-2.

————, 'Religion and Trade: Spread of Jainism in Ancient Andhradeśa and Tamiḷakam', paper presented at the national seminar on *Jainism (Art, Architecture, Literature and Philosophy)*, Hyderabad, 1999.

————, 'Religion and Trade: Spread of Jainism in Ancient Andhradeśa and Tamiḷakam (Synopsis of Paper)', *National Seminar on Jainism (Art, Architecture, Literature and Philosophy)—Souvenir*, Hyderabad, 1999, pp. 42-3.

————, 'Roman Coins found in India: A Study of the Countermarks', paper presented at the international seminar on *Trade and Economy of Ancient Sri Lanka, India and South-East Asia: Archaeological and Literary Evidence*, Colombo, 1999.

————, 'Roman Denarii Hoard From Koneripatti, Tamilnadu', in *Kaveri-Studies in Epigraphy, Archaeology and History (Prof. Y. Subbarayalu Felicitation Volume)*, ed. S. Rajagopal, Madras, 2001, pp. 267-72.

Tchernia, André, 'Le Dromadaire Des Peticii Et Le Commerce Oriental', *Mélanges De L'École Française De Rome-Antiquité*, vol. 104, no. 1, 1992, pp. 293-301.

Theobald, W., 'Note on Mr. G.F. Hill's Theory Regarding the Defacement of Roman Aurei from Pudukota', *NC* (3rd series), vol. XIX, 1899, p. 81.

Thurston, E., *Madras Government Museum, Coins-Catalogue No. 2: Roman, Indo-Portuguese and Ceylon*, Madras, 1894.

Turner, P.J., *Roman Coins from India*, London, 1989.

Usha, I., 'Trade and Mercantile Community during the Sangam Period', unpublished M.Phil. dissertation, University of Madras, Madras, 1985.

Victor Rajamanickam, G. and Y. Subbarayalu, eds., *History of Traditional Navigation*, Tanjavur, 1988.

Walburg, R., 'Late Roman Copper Coins from Southern India', in *Coinage, Trade and Economy (3rd International Colloquium, January 8th-11th, 1991)*, ed. A.K. Jha, Nashik, 1991, pp. 164-7.

Walker, M.J. and S. Santoso, 'Romano-Indian Rouletted Pottery in Indonesia', *Asian Perspectives*, vol. 20, no. 2, 1977, pp. 228-35.

Warmington, E.H., *The Commerce between the Roman Empire and India*, Cambridge, 1928 (rpt. 1974).

Wheeler, R.E.M., 'Roman Contact with India, Pakistan and Afghanistan', in *Aspects of Archaeology in Britain and Beyond: Essays Presented to O.G.S. Crawford*, ed. W.F. Grimes, London, 1951, pp. 345-81.

Wheeler, R.E.M., A. Ghosh and Krishna Deva, 'Arikamedu: An Indo-Roman Trading-Station on the East Coast of India', *AI*, vol. 2, 1946, pp. 17-124.

————, *Rome Beyond the Imperial Frontiers*, London, 1954.

Whitcomb, D.S. and J.H. Johnson, eds., *Quseir al-Qadim 1978 Preliminary Report*, Princeton, 1979.

Whitehouse, D. and A. Williamson, 'Sassanian Maritime Trade', *Iran*, vol. 11, 1973, pp. 29-49.

Will, E.L., 'The Mediterranean Shipping Amphoras from Arikamedu', in *Rome and India: The Ancient Sea Trade*, ed. V. Begley and Richard Daniel De Puma, Madison, 1991, pp. 151-6.

Xinru Liu, *Ancient India and Ancient China: Trade and Religious Exchanges, A.D. 1-600*, New Delhi, 1988.

Yazdani, G., 'Excavations at Kondapur: An Andhra Town, c. 200 B.C.- 200 A.D.', *Annals of the Bhandarkar Oriental Research Institute*, vol. 22, 1941, pp.171-85.

————, *Ajanta I*, Delhi, 1983.

Zvelebil, K., 'The Yavanas in Old Tamil Literature', in *Charisteria Orientalia*, Prague, 1956, pp. 401-9.

————, *The Smile of Murugan*, Leiden, 1973.

# Index